WORKING FOR THE MOUSE

AND OTHER PLAYS

BY

TREVOR ALLEN

EXIT
PRESS
SAN FRANCISCO

Working for the Mouse and other Plays
by Trevor Allen

Published by EXIT PRESS

Book Design by Richard Livingston and C White
and
Cover Art by Cheshire Isaacs

Please direct performance inquiries to the author at
trevor@blackboxtheatre.com

ISBN: 978-1-941704-02-8

EXIT PRESS
156 Eddy Street
San Francisco, CA 94102-2708
mail@theexit.org

First Edition: 2016

DEDICATION

This collection of my plays is dedicated to my wife, Karen, without whom none of these plays would exist and with whom I am thankful to exist.

Thanks:

To the Shirley's: Howard, Antoinette, Susan, Andrea, Erin and Michael, my first audience.

To the McKevitt Family and all of the audience members who came to see these shows over the years.

To Rob Melrose, Kent Nicholson and Paul Walsh for their kind words about my work.

To Cheshire Isaacs for the book design and the *Working for the Mouse* ice cream cone logo.

To the directors, casts and crews of the world premieres of each of these plays, thank you for bringing them to life.

To the many small theatre companies that have had a hand in shaping these plays and to the incubators of new plays, much love and appreciation.

This fistful-of-plays collection was made possible by EXIT Press. Many thanks to Richard and Christina and to the EXIT Theater for all they do.

THE REVIEWS ARE IN...

WORKING FOR THE MOUSE

"Very funny... Mouse is an uplifting comic tale well told... Comparisons with David Sedaris' hilarious Santaland Diaries are obvious."
—*San Francisco Chronicle*

"Amusing, skillful, and contagiously warmhearted... You may not believe your ears (or Pluto's) on this unofficial guided tour behind the scenes... C is for 'See it real soon.'"
—*San Francisco Bay Guardian*

"Fascinating... Infectious... He's got more than a magic bag full of fun anecdotes, and the charisma of Peter Pan to pull off telling them."
—*San Francisco Examiner*

"Vivid... Touching... If you've ever had a job that looked like a dream from the outside and a fevered hallucination from the inside, you'll want to see "Working for the Mouse"... Allen shares his Disneyland experience with warmth, style, and tremendous humor."
—*East Bay Express*

THE CREATURE

"Allen strips away almost two centuries of stage and one of film melodrama to get to the heart of Shelley's 1818 novel. He mixes and matches its three narrators' stories to bring out the thematic parallels between the hubris of Frankenstein's attempt to create life and Captain Walton's polar expedition, and their contrast with the Creature's simple need for love. It's Allen, though, who's skillfully reassembled the body parts to build this monster."
—*San Francisco Chronicle*

LOLITA ROADTRIP

"'Once upon a time there was a little girl who loved to tell stories,' says (the) determined but fragile graduate student in Trevor Allen's "Lolita Roadtrip." The little girl isn't the only one. Stories–true, false and in between–intersect, overlap and jostle each other to telling effect in the world premiere."
    —*San Francisco Chronicle*

"Congratulations to San Jose native Trevor Allen, whose play, "Lolita Roadtrip," had its world premiere Saturday night at San Jose Stage Company. The packed house for opening night responded with a standing ovation for the show, a multi-layered drama that uses "Lolita" author Vladimir Nabokov's 1941 journey from New York to Stanford University as a springboard for a modern tale that echoes his famous novel."
    —*San Jose Mercury News (Pizarro)*

"Mystery, history and the puzzle of the subconscious intertwine in Trevor Allen's beguiling new play. The playwright best known for "The Creature" and "Tenders in the Fog" riffs on Nabokovian themes in this captivating piece in its world premiere... Allen writes such vivid monologues that each of his characters instantly seduce the imagination, although we only here snatches of their tales. One speaks and then another cuts off the reverie, so that we hear each story in counterpoint to the one that came before, like a chaotic musical composition...The playwright beautifully captures the vertigo of burning with love in a chilly universe."
    —*San Jose Mercury News (D'Souza)*

TENDERS IN THE FOG

"The skill of the telling is in Allen's arrangements of the word music in his spoken ballad. …ambitious and intriguing… mesmerizing… Allen capably increases the tension as the story reaches its climax, with a light tip of his hat to Orson Welles' version of War of the Worlds."
    —*San Francisco Chronicle*

"Not since the heyday of Adrienne Barbeau horror flicks has fog had this much stage presence…"
    —*San Jose Mercury News*

CHAIN REACTIONS

"The audience is in on something in the making here, as writer-director Trevor Allen concocts a suite of beguiling monologues, quartets and one duet for a company of four absorbing voices."
    —*San Francisco Chronicle*

CONTENTS

INTRODUCTION

In his *Speculations* about theater and writing and thinking, playwright Mac Wellman (that damnable scribbler), disparages what he calls "Geezer Theater"—the theater of the Already Known—and "the geezerly obsession with managing what is new, under the auspices of the Already Known." Instead, Wellman writes, it is the Strange that keeps us in the theatrical present and Charm that draws us in.

Trevor Allen is no fan of Geezer Theater (though he is a fan of Mac Wellman). His stories are strange and have the power to charm. They unravel in bursts, not lines, scattering across the space and time of the stage in surprising and always charming configurations, drawing attention to the act of telling as much as to what is told. "What scatters, occupies." Wellman writes. And elsewhere: "The jumble may be jumbled but the story remains in some senses tellable even if such a telling appeals not to the better class of theatre geezer."

These are cubist tales of refracting perspectives; fragments woven into arias and duets and fugues that capture the poetry of speech and the metaphysics of the commonplace. They are strange tales at times, but familiar; and they push us to ask our own questions and question our own answers. They are tales of what the Physicist in *Chain Reactions* calls "complementary realities" in which words fail and also succeed as "the chaos dissolves into order." There is hope in Trevor's interrogation of the chaos and obsessions out of which we construct our lives for (as the creative writing teacher Professor Keith says to his student in the same play) "what's ugly and dumb today…could be Picasso tomorrow."

Trevor has a talent for fracturing what is known or remembered vaguely (Mary Shelley's tale of Frankenstein in *The Creature*, Nabakov's Lolita complex in *Lolita Roadtrip*, Disney's Magic Kingdom in *Working for the Mouse*, memories of banshees and selkies and merrows in *Tenders in the Fog*, or Leó Szilárd convincing Albert Einstein to sign a letter in 1939 that resulted in the Manhattan Project in *Chain Reactions*) to reveal unsuspected truths. His chosen form is the fugue, which is not only a musical form but also a dissociative disorder resulting in a breakdown of identity and flight from one's usual environment. Contrapuntual movement, after all, need not always be harmonic. Order, beauty, and even meaning may reside elsewhere, as these tales suggest. Knowing this pushes these plays out of the geezerly and into the 21st century.

Sometimes Trevor favors stories that speak to their audiences directly (as the Shanachie does in *Tenders in the Fog*). Sometimes he favors stories that speak to their audience obliquely as the eight figures in *Chain Reactions* do, weaving a tale of disaster and hope out of the fragments of mundane utterances. But always he favors stories that speak. Words may fail, but they are the stuff of discoveries and memories and moments of recognition, linking teller to tale and maker to what he has made. Whether Einstein or Frankenstein, the creator here is as inextricably linked to his creature as the playwright is to his play: "bound together by chains," as the Creature says. There is an obsession in these plays with the act of telling and it is this that demands these plays be performed. They gain power when embodied by actors. They deserve an audience of listeners. These tales long to be performed (and each has been performed and deserves to be performed again), because, like the Irish Shanachie, they bear witness to a wisdom that is ancient if forgotten in the day-to-day cacophony of speech, and that can only be made present in the telling.

To a certain extent each of these plays is a tale of compulsion and obsession, as if the stories themselves (like Frankenstein's creature) proclaim: "I have pursued my creator to utter ruin—." *Lolita Roadtrip* is obsessed with the fading memory of youth in the shape of an under-aged boy. *Working for the Mouse* is obsessed with the promise of eternal youth in the figure of Peter Pan. *Chain Reaction* is obsessed with ordering patterns in the face of apparent chaos. *Tenders in the Fog* is obsessed with the fateful sea and the curses carried on the tides. And *The Creature* is obsessed with the need to tell one's story and create life by harnessing the power of words. "I made a discovery of great importance," Frankenstein's Creature says in *The Creature*: "I found these creatures possessed a method of communicating their experiences and feelings to each other by articulate sounds. I saw that the…words…they spoke sometimes produced laughter or sadness. This was a godlike art." Each of these plays tells a tale that unravels or unfolds as it proceeds, making strange again what seemed once to have been known and playing on our eyes and our ears with alluring charm.

"Cacophony is home to me," Trevor once said in an interview. "I have become accustomed to having a chorus of voices in my head." Here those voices coalesce into five strange tales to charm the stage.

Paul Walsh
Professor of Dramaturgy and Dramatic Criticism
Yale School of Drama

TREVOR ALLEN'S PLAYS

When I was a "wee" one studying music and beginning a singing career which somehow morphed into a directing career, I was taught a song which helped me define the nature of a fugue. It went like this: "A fugue is an odd sort of form/it jumps it skips/it's far from the norm." It's a catchy little lyric written to a J.S.Bach tune which perfectly describes the work of Trevor Allen.

Perhaps it's that early training, but I have always been attracted to writers whose work has an innate musicality to it. This is why Trevor's work has always been of particular interest to me. It's not just that he writes what he describes as "fugues," but his plays can really mostly be understood best as a kind of musical composition.

More seriously, Merriam Webster defines a fugue as "a musical composition in which one or two themes are repeated or imitated by successively entering voices and contrapuntally developed in a continuous interweaving of the voice parts." When we look at the plays in this anthology, even the ones that don't immediately strike us as following this structure, we find that Trevor unfailingly gives us a look at a multiplicity of voices repeating and imitating each other until their themes begin to transform into one larger one.

In *Tenders in the Fog*, one of the pieces more directly attached to the fugue form, Trevor tells the same story through the interior monologues of four different characters, three generations of fisherman and a Selkie found off the coast of Northern California. And of course the Selkie transforms into a Shanachie, and serves as a guide, telling the audience the story and delivering up a "moral" for good measure. While our doomed fisherman complete repetitive tasks, and relive their own failures and generational conflict over and over, we get to listen to all three perspectives, drawing our own conclusions and letting our sympathies slide between grandfather, father, and son. Life is complex. And short. And unpredictable. And we often can't see ourselves clearly because the fog can get really thick. By flowing through the current on this ever drifting boat, the reward we receive is getting a chance to cut through the fog, literally, and see the bigger picture of how our lives gain some meaning by the addition of small details.

In *The Creature*, we get not so much a fugue as radio for the stage. What's remarkable about this piece is its point of view. Mary Shelley wrote *Frankenstein* from Victor Frankenstein's point of view. But *The Creature* flips that script and uses Shelley's own text to reverse our sympathies and understand that maybe Frankenstein was the monster, not the Creature who wanted nothing more than to be human. The play never lets us forget Shelley's original by keeping Frankenstein as a sometimes narrator, but really allows the

Creature's voice to be paramount. Again, by juxtaposing the two voices side by side, contrapuntally, we see a bigger picture and eventually have to ask if we aren't our own worst enemies as well as our own best friends when we can fully admit to our own humanity.

Even in a solo play such as *Working for the Mouse*, there's a multiplicity of voices ringing out. The Mad Hatter, Alice, Peter Pan, Gary, Tammi, and of course the young Trevor himself. These voices weave a tapestry of life off-stage at the "happiest place on earth." The story, as many of Trevor's stories are, is non-linear, moving back and forth through the major incidents of his time as an employee. And while we laugh at the many indiscrete actions of the actors inside the suits, we also get a story of a young man who doesn't want to grow up, but eventually learns that he must. It's touching but not at all sentimental, in part because we see the ramifications for those who choose to stay behind and continue as perpetual adolescents. Life backstage may be fun for a while, but it starts to become a little seedy the longer you stay.

I've had the good fortune to work on all three of these plays directly with Trevor. Building them together, watching and listening as he carefully places each voice side by side, overlapping, and orchestrating them for maximum impact. In each instance, the visuals were left for me to work with, deciding how best to let these stories be heard and helping to tell them by creating a visual world to support that telling. A rotating ship, changing its perspective and relationship to the audience as the story unfolds. A radio play. And a bench in front of a brick wall. That's how we chose to do this. But the options are really endless. The text tells the tale, but Trevor is interested in how others will choose to show it to us.

This isn't kitchen sink drama after all. It's a complex world, with complex problems, and a multiplicity of personalities and characters to fill it. These plays are interested in how these voices and disparate personalities interact. So it's only fitting that a world filled with a multiplicity of performers and directors and designers and producers should all get their crack at telling these stories. I hope you have as much fun making them sing as I did.

Kent Nicholson
Director, Playwrights Horizons, New York

ACTING AND TREVOR ALLEN

Last year I was at the Golden Mask Festival in Russia and was on the metro next to the wonderful theater scholar Maria Shevtova talking with her about the art of acting. She said to me, "Rob, the older I get, the more I think that to be a great actor, you first need to be a great listener." I would add a caveat to this rule: "To be a great actor in one of Trevor Allen's plays, you need to be a phenomenal listener!"

I directed the premieres of *The Creature* and *Chain Reactions* and have had the pleasure of seeing the other plays in this volume in performance. Trevor has a remarkable ear and a tremendous sense of music in his writing. In a conventional play, an actor needs to listen to his or her partner and respond in a way as if hearing the line for the very first time. In a Trevor Allen "fugue" the actor needs to listen to ALL the other actors while speaking simultaneously about things that may or may not have anything to do with what he or she is saying. I've seen actors start the process thinking, "Well, I'm just going to focus on my track and not worry about what the other actors are saying. Since my character doesn't hear these other characters then I as actor don't need to listen to the other actors." Guess what? That doesn't work. Like good *a cappella* singing or playing in an orchestra, the actor in a Trevor Allen play must be completely committed to his or her part and at the same time must be listening carefully to what everyone else is doing. I've had an actor throw their script across the room saying, "This is impossible!" It is very difficult, but not impossible, and when the actors get it right, the results are extraordinary! Talk about dramatic compression. The audience gets wave after wave of a variety of experiences all at the same time and in a way that is musical and beautiful. All of these plays make for a very rich experience in the theater and I encourage all theater artists to give them a whirl and bring their best selves to them.

The Creature

I think *The Creature* is Trevor's masterpiece. It is simultaneously the most faithful adaptation of Mary Shelley's *Frankenstein* and the most experimental. It is the most faithful because it uses much of Shelley's own words and captures all the best moments from the novel and gets right to the most important themes in the novel: the act of creation, man vs. god, loneliness, the impossibility of human relationships, prejudice, jealously, the nightmares of parenthood, the way humans learn and our relationship to literature. I think when most people read Shelley's novel they are surprised to find how sophisticated and complex it is after seeing numerous "monster movie" adaptations. Trevor's play is the only adaptation

I know of that really privileges Shelley's themes and words over a kind of horror-film experience. Because of the way Trevor fugues different sections of the novel, the audience gets the experience of many characters at once and gets a highly compressed and refined distillation of the novel. At the same time, the audience is clued into numerous parallels and mirrorings that a reader only discovers in the novel after multiple readings. It is a terrific play, and my hope is that with this publication, it can become a Halloween staple at theaters in the same way that *Christmas Carol* is for Christmas.

Chain Reactions

I had the great pleasure of developing *Chain Reactions* in Cutting Ball's *Risk is This: Experimental New Plays Festival* and then directing it at C.A.F.E. in San Francisco. It combines the two things I like best about Trevor: a willingness to tackle big ideas and a desire to show the simple, intimate moments that make us human. What I admire most about it, however, is how Trevor makes the form of his play match the content. Since the play is about physics, the atomic bomb, and how we are all connected— the structure of the play is like a science experiment with isolated scenes and monologues first studied in isolation and then allowed to interact with the others to see what results. The results are very exciting and reveal yet another layer to the work. As the scenes and monologues fugue with the others, new sentences reveal themselves through the combinations. So in the same way the characters are unaware of the tremendous effect their actions have on each other, they are also unaware of the meanings that are created when their lines are mixed with the other characters' lines onstage. It is a lovely play with a lot more going on than meets the eye.

Working for the Mouse, Tenders in the Fog, and Lolita Roadtrip

While I did not work on these plays, I saw all of them in the theater and am a big fan. I love the humor of *Working for the Mouse*, the complexity of *Lolita Roadtrip*, and the mystery of *Tenders in the Fog*.

All five plays in this volume are tremendously different but they all share Trevor's innovations in structure, his willingness to tackle big issues, and his wonderful sense of humanity. Trevor has been prolific here in the Bay Area and I hope that this book helps his good work spread far and wide.

Rob Melrose
Artistic Director, The Cutting Ball Theater
San Francisco

PREFACE

Working for the Mouse

What can I say in print that I haven't already said onstage except… fair use, parody, satire and stories from my own life are mine but any resemblance to persons living or dead is strictly coincidental. All names have been changed to protect the author's assets etc. Yes, in the late 80's, I did portray certain costumed characters at the "Happiest Place on Earth" including The Mad Hatter. It was during four years of my life that I was also completing a B.A. degree in Theatre at U.C.L.A. Working for the Mouse came out of my memories of the best/worst of those pixie dust laden times. The script is for a solo show… and seems odd to have all the characters names delineated. I have done it many times, over many years in many theatres in the San Francisco Bay Area, Silicon Valley and Hollywood and even once at the Center Camp at the Burning Man Festival. I owe each director a debt of gratitude for helping me find the magic in the story each time I performed it. Now that I see it in print. I wonder what a full cast version would be like? A huge musical production? Now that the production rights are available, who knows? Be careful what you wish upon a star for…

Program note from the World Premiere:

> A wise man once said, "Parents, if you love your children, do not take them backstage at Disneyland." And who should know better than Robin Williams? Now, just in case you were wondering, you are not in for an evening of all-out Mouse-bashing. Sorry, but I'm afraid I'm a bit like a lapsed "believer" in that department, the kind that still says "bless you" when somebody sneezes. This is just the story of a kid who didn't want to grow up, but did anyway… while working in Anaheim. The kid just happened to be me, the time was many years ago and the place was "The Happiest Place on Earth." Ever since I took a solo performance workshop with Charlie Varon in '96 and he convinced me to do a short piece about my time as a "Casual Seasonal Pageant Helper" at the Magic Kingdom and Character! got "best of" the San Francisco Fringe Festival that year, people have been asking me for more details about the time I spent in costume, covered in pixie dust. It has since evolved into this full-length play and a book in progress. For more mouse tales, go to workingforthemouse.com.

Lolita Roadtrip

Program note from the World Premiere:

The idea for the play that became *Lolita Roadtrip* came from a butterfly, *Cyllópsis Pertepída Dorothéa*. It all started in 2008. My world had just been turned upside down. I had very suddenly lost the nonprofit theatre job that I had held for eight years due to an unforeseen and dramatic downsizing. Overnight I had become one of the nation's growing number of unemployed. But I had three things going for me: a new play commission from PlayGround, for which I am truly grateful, a month long playwriting residency at the Djerassi Resident Artist Program, which was a life changing experience and a thoughtful, loving wife who pointed out that I was officially a fulltime playwright, for the first time in my life.

That winter, while in residence up in the Santa Cruz Mountains overlooking the sea and contemplating a play based on *Lolita* and its author, Vladimir Nabokov, I had an epiphany. I realized that I didn't want to attempt an adaptation of the book, because it had been done but also because I was currently working on *The Creature*, my own adaptation of *Frankenstein* for three actors and so I wanted to attempt something completely new. I read an article about Nabokov and his passion for butterfly collecting and I was struck by an item concerning a trip he and his family had made out to California in 1941. They had been driven all the way from New York to Palo Alto by a woman who he had met in the public library.

The moment the light bulb went on was when I read about Nabokov and the butterfly. He named a certain specimen that he collected while at the Grand Canyon after this woman. I began to write *Nabokov's American Blues, a roadtrip*. I know, a catchy working title, right? My initial impulse was to write a play about that original trip, but the truth of that journey was far less dramatic than it was psychologically interesting. So, I filed it away. But that butterfly kept appearing in my dreams. There were also many butterflies fluttering around the fields during my long walks in the hills during my playwriting residency. I kept coming back to that central image.

Then I re-read *Lolita*. I had read it while in high school, but frankly, I didn't get it then. After all, I was the same age as the character of Danny in my play and I had a very similar negative reaction to the novel. Having read it a second time as an adult I comprehended the significance of the work, while still reserving some ethical questions about the story. It was brilliant, comic and tragic. I felt strongly that I really wanted to deal with the same material but from a different perspective. Putting the gun in the hands of Lolita came to mind. But then the idea of an older woman and a younger man suggested itself. But where? I just began writing late one night and then, as if planned all along, Julia and Danny's roadtrip began. I set out after that illusive butterfly and after a few years, several drafts and a couple of staged readings with some remarkable directors and actors, *Lolita Roadtrip* finally found a home at the San Jose Stage Company.

I couldn't ask for a more talented director, cast or a more supportive crew. Appropriate to the subject material, the rehearsal process was both thrilling and terrifying. Seeing this story come to life during the rehearsal process with costumes, lights and a road has reminded me why I write for such a collaborative art form. Theatre is magic! Creating something out of nothing. I especially want to thank the staff of the Stage Company for their courage and ongoing commitment to bringing new stories to the theatre.

People have asked me, "You've written a play for four storytellers, but whose story is it really?" When pressed, I tell them politely that it's Julia's story. But in a way, it's also my story, because it's something that I created and pieced together slowly and patiently over a number of years. It's a fiction, loosely based on the many stories that I've heard from the men and women in my life. I slowly stitched it all together like my Great Grandmother's Tennessee quilt that I recently inherited after the death of my ol' Great Aunt Emma. It's a patchwork of stories all woven together and as Emma would say, "Honey, it was mine but now it's yours. I hope it keeps you warm."

The Creature

Program note from the World Premiere:
I grew up watching the old black and white Frankenstein films with my father on late night TV shows like "Creature Features." It wasn't the horror or Sci Fi elements that captivated me most, it was the sad story of that unnamed monster. But it wasn't until I read Mary Shelley's novel for a comparative literature course at UCLA that I actually fell in love with the original story. It was much deeper, more complex and heartbreaking than the one that I thought I knew.

Early on, I realized that I empathized with the humanity of the outcast monster as much as with his maker, and with this in mind, I sought to adapt it for the stage. This has been a long journey, one which has relied on the assistance of many fellow creatures and perhaps bordered on dramaturgical madness. The script evolved greatly along the way, beginning with a three hour version and culminating, many years later, in a three person play that was produced by my wife, Karen McKevitt, and my own theatre company, BlackBoxTheatre.com, in 2009, and now in this version collected in print.

Originally, Mary Shelley created a trio of first-person narrators who each related their own versions of these incredible events: the Captain, Frankenstein and the Creature himself, an abandoned child, forced to make his own way in the world without friends or family. Following her lead, I remixed, intercut and reordered much of the original text for dramatic purposes, augmenting it occasionally with additional material of my own for clarity and to tell the Creature's tale. But above all, it has been important for me to remain faithful to the spirit of the original work, while interweaving the three parallel storylines and bringing them to their inevitable conclusion.

The story of Frankenstein is simultaneously a meditation on the loss of innocence, an outsider's despair, the nature of evil, and the importance of personal responsibility, as well as being a timely cautionary tale warning of the horrible, unintended consequences of well-intentioned science such as biological and genetic engineering. However, the thing that struck me most is that this is ultimately a story about a father and his son. This play began its life several Halloweens ago as a radio play that I recorded as a live audio podcast in San Francisco by Black Box Theatre Company at the Magic Theatre. I always felt that the words formed a kind of music. This text is meant to be spoken aloud by candle light.

Tenders in the Fog

Program note from the World Premiere:
The idea for the piece originally came out of a Black Box Theatre Company scene night held a few years ago at the Exit Theatre. It was just a ten-minute play about three generations of fishermen on a boat. When I received PlayGround's playwriting fellowship in 2003, I was asked to pitch three ideas for full-length scripts, one of which the company would choose to commission. I submitted ideas for *Zoo Logic*, a piece about the four years I spent working at the San Francisco Zoo, and *The Eagle And The Child*, named after a famous pub and based on the summer I spent studying theatre in Oxford. The third and most unlikely piece was just called *Tenders* and was about three generations of lobster (yes, lobster) fishermen lost off the coast of New England. It was meant to be very experimental in form—fugue-like, even. To my utter astonishment, PlayGround chose this one, and I started writing the script, working with Paul Walsh, then the Dramaturg at ACT and my mentor on the project.

Being a Bay Area boy, I quickly realized that I wanted to set the play in San Francisco, so I changed coasts and made the fishermen Dungeness crabbers. I guess the fog came from the fact that my wife and I have lived out on the Great Highway in San Francisco's Sunset District for a decade, and during the summer, we go for months at a time without seeing the sun. The whole Irish/Celtic influence in the story came from my family background and the stories I read growing up (although truth be told, I am a bit of a mutt, parts English/Scottish/Irish/German and even Latino on my mother's side). But I knew early on that I wanted a mythical element to the tale and I loved the idea of mixing something very old (a traditional Shanachie) and something very new and postmodern (nonlinear, fugue-like dialogue) to create a series of stories within stories. After working on several of the key scenes at the Magic Theatre's Gym, I produced a first draft of the play.

The Playground reading directed by Robin Stanton went well, with two members of Stage Company's cast involved: Nick Sholley and Jessa Brie Berkner. But afterwards no company seemed interested in producing it. After a couple rejections and some rewrites, I had another staged reading at City Lights Theatre Company of San Jose. Kent Nicholson, who is helming Stage Company's production, also directed that reading.

This second draft was tighter, and the reading went exceptionally well. Before I even had the chance to start sending the script out, Stage Company Artistic Director Randall King contacted me to let me know he wanted to produce the world premiere. So I went back to doing rewrites.

I couldn't ask for a better cast or a more supportive crew. Appropriate to the subject material, the rehearsal process was both thrilling and terrifying. After ten years of writing plays, this was my first professional production and the fact that it was being produced in my "home town" made it all the more significant for me. Working with Kent again was such a wonderful experience that I would do it again in a heartbeat. I especially want to thank Randy, Cathy, Rick and the rest of the staff of the San Jose Stage Company for taking a risk on a local playwright and new work. I owe them a huge debt of gratitude for their courage and commitment to bringing new stories to the theatre.

The play's influences are traditional Irish tales of banshees, merrows and selkies, true stories of fishermen disappearing at sea and a short theatre piece called *PLAY* by Samuel Beckett in which a trio of voices are doomed to repeat their stories over and over again. But music also figured prominently in the formation of the piece, including the way the scenes are structured. The play is laid out like a piece of music, somewhere between a Bach fugue and a Phillip Glass string quartet. Beethoven's "Ghost" Piano Trio also figured heavily in the plot's outline. The themes are familiar yet timeless: love, loss, family and the idea that sometimes as much as we try to communicate our true feelings to each other, it seems no one is listening. But ultimately, this is really just an old ghost story set in a modern world. People have asked me, "But whose story is it?" I guess the only real answer to that is—it was the Shanachie's story, and now it's yours. I hope you enjoy it.

Chain Reactions

Program note from the World Premiere:
>   Everything is interconnected.

The original *Chain Reactions* script that was presented at the San Francisco Planetarium was essentially a glorified staged-reading of three separate short pieces done at music stands, the only off-book parts were the individual monologues. The short piece "Synchronicity" had staged reading and "A Chain Reaction" was based on a collaboration text and dance piece with Rebecca Salzer Dance Theatre. "The Mistaken Variations" in an early form was performed at PlayGround but I adapted and reordered the text for inclusion in the larger piece. It was my original intention to take these three separate short pieces and re-cut and re-write them into a single full-length piece for the Planetarium Show. But due to the nature of the performance space, the actors had to perform in near darkness with only a single spot light for their monologues. It proved to be too difficult given the Fringe's short format of under sixty minutes. The original idea of a cast of eleven proved impractical given our resources, besides scheduling would have been a nightmare. However, the piece was well received, sold out and was given Best of the Fringe that year. It went on to have a full cast production World Premiere in a wonderful converted church theatre in San Francisco. *Chain Reactions* is about interconnections at the subatomic level and at an everyday level. Chains of events and unintended consequences. Looking for answers to eternal questions and perhaps finding none. Each piece is made of much smaller pieces, they are all essentially monologues, but they have been intercut to create a resonance between characters as in music. Patterns emerge from the chaos. These patterns then create a kind of "narrative constellation." Put simply, it is an experiment in structure, a fractal, if you will, of narrative forms. Steve Winn said in the *San Francisco Chronicle* that it was about "Physics, fear and love…" I guess that's partly true, at least on the surface. But, the piece is meant to function as both a particle and as a wave. The monologues being the particles and when in motion like a wave, as dialogue. It sounded really good in a Planetarium and an old church. Here it is now in print. I hope you can still hear the music.

WORKING FOR THE MOUSE

BY

TREVOR ALLEN

Working for the Mouse

Ever wonder what really goes on at the Happiest Place on Earth? This solo show chronicling the life of a costumed character answers this and other burning questions like, "Is it hot in there?", "Where do you see out of?" and "What kind of underwear does Mickey wear under there?" Playwright and performer Trevor Allen spent a few years in Southern California playing Pluto, the White Rabbit, Mister Smee, the Mad Hatter and other characters on his quest for voice clearance and his dream of becoming Peter Pan. He recounts his tales of backstage debauchery, militant managers and his quirky coworkers in this unique coming of age tale that blows pixie dust in your eyes while offering a glimpse behind the ears of the Magic Kingdom.

Production Information

Best of San Francisco Fringe Festival: TEA Theatre Co. at EXIT Theatre (as *CHARACTER!*) , San Francisco September 1996

Director:	Kristine McIntyre
Cast:	All characters played by Trevor Allen

World Premiere of *Working for the Mouse*: Impact Theatre, Berkeley 2003

Artistic Director:	Melissa Hillman
Director:	Kent Nicholson
Cast:	All characters played by Trevor Allen

Working for the Mouse: Cease and Desist Tour, 2011

Producer:	Karen McKevitt
Director:	Nancy Carlin
Stage Manager:	Read Tuddenham
Cast:	All characters played by Trevor Allen

WORKING FOR THE MOUSE

CHARACTERS

TREVOR: A young version of the Narrator wearing a nametag.

NARRATOR: A magical storyteller. Robin Williams on speed.

JIMMY: A character supervisor. Short, chubby and by the book.

GARY: A "little person" Donald Duck's inner gruff sailor.

COMMANDMENT VOICE: Intoned as if in a very big church.

SCOTTY: A seven year-old, terminally ill, innocent boy.

PLUTO: Mickey's bitch, the happy yellow dog himself.

SCOTTY'S MOM: A mid-western homemaker, losing her son.

LORI: A friendly fellow "Zoo Crew" cast member.

CAPTAIN HOOK/JASON: A perpetually stoned surfer dude.

PETER PAN/DAVID: A cool guy. Jack Nicholson's bastard son.

PSYCHO MIKE: A character groupie extraordinaire.

RIDE OPERATOR: A button pusher on a pirate ship.

SNOT-NOSED KID: A child with a cold.

TEENAGER: A "too cool" for fantasyland kid.

BRAT: A loudmouthed magic-hating child.

MAD HATTER: A hatter who sounds a lot like Ed Wynn.

KID 1: A loud, eight year-old agnostic.

KID 2: Another even louder child.

KID 3: An amazingly loud child with a bad attitude.

TAMMY: A very kind and beautiful young woman.

ROOMMATE: A middle-aged surf bum.

LARS: A very tall, thick-necked, V-shaped guy.

ROOKIE: A pixie dust soaked, bright-eyed cast member.

ICE PRINCESS: An aging princess and head supervisor.

ZEKE: An amalgam of the worst tourists ever encountered.

BOSS: A warped, frustrated, small man in a cheap suit.

MICKEY'S VOICE: A certain rodent's disembodied voice.

INTRODUCTION

Setting: A bare black stage with a long bench. A small red sign up center reads "Disneyland employees only past this point." A man on stage alone. He is wearing white tennis shoes, blue shorts, knee pads and a white T-shirt with the words "Disneyland zoo crew" on it.

TREVOR (*on a phone*) Hello this is Casual Seasonal Pageant Helper, Trevor... five foot five... and a half, and I'm fully available!

NARRATOR (*to the audience*) It's five-thirty in the morning and I'm calling in my availability for today like I do everyday. You see, I grew up in the shadow of the Matterhorn, not the one in the Alps, the other one, in Anaheim. I climbed to the top of the Swiss Family Robinson's treehouse, all by myself, before I could ever climb a real tree. Pirate ships and castles and cartoon characters that came to life were all part of my childhood. Because, for a few days every year I lived at the Happiest Place on Earth and when I graduated from high school at the age of seventeen... I did the next best thing I could think of to running away and joining the circus. I moved to L.A. And I got a job at the "Magic Kingdom," as a "Casual Seasonal Pageant Helper." For those of you who don't speak "Disney-ese," I was a Character... And for a little while my dream of never having to grow up seemed like an attainable goal.

TREVOR (*back on the phone*) Uh... I'd prefer an in-park shift, please... if there's any available. I'll take anything.

NARRATOR Then I'd try to go back to sleep until they called me. But if the call came... it was usually a "Hotel Breakfast" shift. A SHIT shift. Only a couple of hours, so the money sucked, NOT that I was doing it for the money. But it meant that I was over at the Disneyland Hotel... at seven in the morning inside a restaurant... animating to kids who didn't want to be there. Because they just wanted to get to the park early and go on the rides and their parents, who just wanted them to eat their overpriced mouse-eared pancakes, while all they really wanted to do was go back to bed... or sit by the pool sipping Piña Coladas out of coconuts. But today was gonna be different...

FIRST DAY IN PARK STORY

NARRATOR It's seven a.m. I'm in the "Head Room." I've only been with the company a week and I'm getting ready for my shift.

JIMMY (*a short, chubby and annoying guy*) There's been a slight change in plans. You're not going to be going to the Hotel.

NARRATOR It's Jimmy... my "Lead" and he says—

JIMMY We've had an opening. You're going to be in the "Fab-Five" unit today. Now, I want you to get your costume together and get down to the Egg House Break Area. Since this is your first day in-park, I'll assign you a buddy. Ask for Gary, (*Smirks.*) he's going to be your buddy.

NARRATOR I'd never been "in-park" before. I went over and took my head off the shelf. It was light, only about 20 pounds. I grabbed my body off the rack and threw it over my shoulder. I picked up my paws and ran down the service road to the break area. When I got there I set my costume down on a bench and looked around. There were all these disembodied character parts scattered around, arms legs, tails everywhere. Then I saw the face characters. Peter Pan. And Alice in Wonderland. And the whole Snow White unit going out on set. I couldn't wait to get out there.

> *Flashback.*

Now I had spent three summers as a character at Great America during high school and I thought I had seen and done it all. So in my senior year I made the trip down south to audition for the parades department. But, I didn't make the cut. Partly because I had two left feet. Literally. After they taught us the basic dance routine, we were supposed to do it in partial costume but the paws I got were not only too big, they were BOTH left feet. I did my best… and I tried to explain… but the Dance-Captain was not amused. But… I got a lot of laughs… So they told me to come back for the "atmosphere-characters" auditions in a couple of weeks. They were all non-union… minimum wage. But I didn't care. I was floating on air. I was one step closer to my dream.

> *Back to present.*

I asked the nearest person without a head on if he was Gary. He just laughed and he pointed at a bench. Lying on it was… a pair of duck feet… and a duck's body wearing a sailor suit… topped off by a man's head and it's snoring. And he's like the shortest person I've ever seen. He wakes up and sees me staring at him—

GARY (*a "little person" with a heart of gold and a voice like a cement mixer*) What are you lookin' at? (*Beat.*) Your buddy? Who sez? (*Beat.*) Jimmy, huh? That fat little Nazi. Okay. Hey kid, have you ever done this before? Hotel Breakfast! Oh shit! (*Beat.*) Huckleberry Hound and Captain Caveman? Never heard of 'em. Where? Great America? What the fuck's so great about it? Look… park it rookie. Put your feet on. That one goes on your right. Your other right. I've got three rules of thumb for ya… One! Never let 'em get behind you. When you get out there… it's "back against the wall." Clear field of vision. So's you can see who's coming at ya. Two! Never stand in direct sunlight. That's death. I've seen guys get dehydrated in half an hour. It's not a pretty sight. Yeah, I don't care how much they beg you to get into better light. Stay in the shade. That's why God created flash photography. Three! Watch your ass. The suits are everywhere. Yeah, the Ice Princess only comes out of her air-conditioned office to check up on us. But "the Leads" are out to get you. Hell, one time Jimmy popped out from behind a bush and he sez "I saw what you were doin'." Bullshit! He didn't see nothin'. It wasn't even my stogie, somebody dropped it, I just picked it up. I was gonna put it out... eventually. Okay, let's get you zipped up. Bend down. I can't reach you. That's better. Hey, uh Captain. Huckleberry? You do know you got your freakin' head on backwards. (*Laughs.*)

NARRATOR I knew that. I was just checking the head gear. And I watched as he put his head on and I followed Donald Duck out "on stage."

THE FIRST SET AS PLUTO

NARRATOR Main Street USA. My first set. I stopped for a second to get my bearings. There was the Emporium, and the Gazebo and the train station. It wasn't that crowded so I did a little walkin' and wavin'. Just then the train pulled up and three hundred families got off, all with kids. And they're pourin' down the steps towards me going PLUTO! PLUTO! PLUTO! There's a lot of 'em and it was like they'd never seen a six foot yellow dog before.

> *Backs up.*

I found the perfect spot. Right between Bank of America and The Disney Story, behind an elm tree in the shade. They gathered around me. A sea of kids thirty deep. And it's sign an autograph, wave, take a picture, take a picture, take a picture. And after about fifteen minutes of this, I've calmed down enough to stop SMILING for the pictures. I look over at Donald and he's waving at me. So, I wave back. No. He's pointing at something. What's he—WHAM!

> *Doubles over as if he's been hit in the groin.*

In the back of my mind I hear Character Commandment #3.

COMMANDMENT VOICE Thou shalt not retaliate.

NARRATOR But, I looked around for the culprit. And I hear a laugh. So I grab for the laugh and it's a baseball cap. Well this kid's never gonna see this hat again. (*Pulls it off.*) It's goin' in the bushes, it's goin' in the trees. It's goin' on the train tracks. It's—the wrong kid. I look and he's bald. I don't mean a shaved head, I mean bald. He doesn't even have any eyebrows. He's lookin' up at me with these big blue eyes with dark circles under them like "why'd you take my hat?" Then I saw the shirt. A white

T-shirt a couple of sizes too big for him, three words on it, MAKE A WISH! And I start to put the hat back on his head. He laughs and says—

SCOTTY That's okay Pluto. You can wear my hat.

NARRATOR And I put the hat on Pluto's top knot and it fit perfectly. Then I did something that both Gary and Jimmy told me to never do. Gary because it was suicide and Jimmy because it wears out the knees of the costume. I got down on his level.

   Kneels down.

SCOTTY Hi Pluto, my name's Scotty. I'm gonna be seven in a month. Wanna see what I found?

PLUTO/TREVOR And I said... Well I couldn't say anything. I didn't have voice clearance. So I said—(*Pants like a dog.*)

NARRATOR I held out my paw and he put something into it. I couldn't feel it because in Pluto they make you wear these thick pads so that when people shake your hands they can't feel the human bone structure. It was kinda hard to make it out through the Plexiglas of Pluto's Pupil. It was just a rock.

SCOTTY It's a magic rock. I found it here, it's magic.

PLUTO/TREVOR And I gave him back his priceless piece of asphalt that he'd picked up in the parking lot. His mother came over and said—

SCOTTY'S MOM Pluto I saw the little boy that kicked you in the privates. Do you want me to get security?

PLUTO/TREVOR (*shrugs*) I went (*Mimes writing.*) and she fished a pen out of her purse. I took off the hat and signed, "To Scotty with love Pluto" and I made the "o" into a paw print like they showed me how to do. I put it on his head and he smiled and scratched me behind the ear. (*Stamps foot.*)

SCOTTY I'm going on the Peter Pan ride do you want to come?

NARRATOR In the back of mind I hear Character Commandment #7

COMMANDMENT VOICE Thou shalt not ride any attractions while in costume.

NARRATOR I looked up at his mother.

SCOTTY'S MOM No honey, he can't come with us he has to stay here with Mickey.

PLUTO/TREVOR So he gave me a big hug and whispered in my ear—

SCOTTY Good-bye Pluto. Don't forget my birthday!

NARRATOR I could barely hear him through the fiberglass. There aren't any ear holes. I nodded and I watched as Scotty and his mother and the Make A Wish Foundation volunteers disappeared down Main Street heading towards the castle and Fantasyland. I heard Donald give the signal to come in.

Stomps three times.

When suddenly I was accosted by twenty-seven Japanese businessmen all wearing suits and Nikons. I spent the next fifteen minutes of my break trying to get backstage. Big group picture.

Mimes trying to get off set and sucked into one last picture.

NARRATOR When I finally made it backstage I took my head off and collapsed onto a bench. I bummed a cigarette off a "Club 33" waitress, it's the only place you can get a drink in the park. She lit it for me.

Takes a drag.

I didn't even smoke. (*Coughs.*) Menthol?!?

Smiles weakly.

I look around and I'm thinkin'... I'm at the "Happiest Place on Earth???" And then I see the Seven Dwarfs heads... on posts. There's Sleepy, Sneezy, Dopey, Jimmy, Grumpy... Jimmy!!! My lead! And I realize... I've got Pluto's head in my lap!

JIMMY Do you know what you're doin'? You're smokin' in costume. Do you want me to give you a written on your first day?

NARRATOR Before I can answer, Gary, out of costume, steps out from behind the bench, and says—

GARY What smokin'? He was holdin' it for me. I had to take a leak. You got a problem with that, Jimmy?

JIMMY Well, don't let it happen again Mr. Oh, by the way, you two haven't seen the Peter Pan unit have you? They were last spotted on top of the Swiss Family Robinson's tree-house. Keep an eye out.

Exits.

GARY Hail Eisner!

GARY Nazi salutes JIMMY and then looks at TREVOR.

Menthol?!?

SANDY DUNCAN MUSIC CIRCUS STORY

NARRATOR Being Pluto was cool... But it wasn't what I really wanted to be. When I was five my Grandmother took me to see a production of Peter Pan at the Music Circus in Sacramento starring Sandy Duncan. Sandy! I thought Sandy was a boy's name, I mean I grew up watching Flipper. We were in the third row and since the theater was in the round when Peter flew overhead some of the glitter they were using for pixie dust landed on me and I swear I could feel myself levitating in my seat a fraction of an inch, if it had been a larger dose I would have flown right out of the theater. But it was only second-hand dust, still I saved what I could and put it in my pocket, for later use. After the show we went back stage, because I had to have Peter's autograph… imagine, the real life Peter Pan. I made my Grandma wait half an hour in front of that tent.

Finally this woman comes out and she's older than my mother and I ask "Where's Peter?" and she laughs and says "Silly, I'm Peter." Ever since that day I was convinced that Peter Pan should be played by a boy!

DISNEYLAND PAN

NARRATOR Later that year when I went down to Disneyland for the "annual family pilgrimage." I noticed for the first time that their Peter Pan WAS a guy. I remember watching him climb the rigging of the old Chicken of the Sea tuna pirate ship in Fantasyland. He was fighting with a couple of pirates when he dropped his dagger, so I ran over and handed it back to him. He said "Thanks a lot" and went on to defeat the pair of buccaneers. It wasn't until later that it dawned on me. He was an actor. That was his job. To be a boy that would never grow up and to play all day at Disneyland. I had found my career goal.

BULLSHIT / WELCOME TO MAUSCHWITZ

NARRATOR It's two weeks later and the guy I'm replacing still hasn't come back. Something about back injuries? So, I'm "Pluto A" five days a week. I'm even allowed to sit in on the card games with the "Veterans." They've sort of accepted me. We're playin' "Bullshit." It's three's to me.

TREVOR One three.

NARRATOR I just bought a birthday card for Scotty over at the Emporium using my employee discount. It's fours to Lori and I ask Lori, whose cousin works for the Make A Wish Foundation, for their address so I can send Scotty his card and she says—

LORI Oh, didn't you hear? They can't find a donor, they don't think he's going to— One four.

NARRATOR Then Jason says—

JASON Oh man, what a waste. They'd give him anything he wished for, and he came here. That's tragic. One five.

GARY Well, he's probably going to a better place. One six. (*Beat.*) Hey, sevens to you.

TREVOR Hmm? Oh, uh one seven. Yeah anywhere's better than here, huh?

GARY Bullshit!

TREVOR What, Oh… Take 'em. Look, I better go… I don't wanna be late…

NARRATOR I went over and I started to get back into costume. When Gary came over—

GARY Hey rookie. Look, I saw you the other day with that "chemo kid." Last rule of thumb. You never get emotionally attached. It'll rip your fuckin' heart out. That dog suit is like emotional armor, use it. They don't want to see you. They want Pluto. They want the Magic! And I got news for you kid there ain't any. And the sooner you learn that the sooner you'll fuckin' grow up. Welcome to Mauschwitz!

NARRATOR I stood there with Pluto's head in my hand. And I thought. But, I don't want to grow up, I want voice clearance, I want to be a face character, I want to be… Peter Pan.

BEGINNING FOURTH OF JULY

NARRATOR It's the fourth of July at four-thirty p.m. There are about a hundred thousand people in the park. And I'm about to be fired from the Happiest Place on Earth. This is not going to look good on my resume. I'm sitting at a desk, in a cubicle, on the top floor of the old America Sings building in Tomorrowland. You know, the rotating building that used to house an animatronic salute to those all-American folk songs, like "Pop goes the weasel." Well it used to rotate, until a cast member was crushed to death by it, then they made it into an office building and sent the robots over to Splash Mountain to sing zip-a-dee-doo-da. There's an "incident" report form in front of me and a miniature golf pencil, without an eraser. Jimmy's standing behind me and he's just told me to "write down what actually happened, in your own words." In the cube on my left is Jason "it seemed like a good idea at the time" Gardener. In the cube on my right is David "the ringleader" Jones.

THE PAN UNIT PART 1: THE HEAD ROOM

NARRATOR The day started out okay. I was in the Head Room getting my costume together. Mr. Smee, first mate of the pirate ship the Jolly Roger. I'd traded several shifts for this one. I'd agreed to do a Grad-Night Eeyore, a photo Friar Tuck and three Hotel Breakfast Pluto's just so I could get this gig. This costume was the best in my height range,

5'5" to 5'7". Great vision, light-weight, it was like wearing clothes and a mask. Standard issue white gloves, with five fingers for a change. But the real reason I wanted to be in Smee was because he was in the Pan unit! I wanted to spend a day with Peter, get his character down. The face character auditions were coming up and I knew that they were looking for a weekend Pan. (*Cross to chair.*) I was trying on my Smee feet when Jason came over to me in Captain Hook and said—

CAPT. HOOK/JASON Hey rookie, I hear you're in my unit today. Let me give you a little piece of advice... Stay out of my way.

NARRATOR And he went over to clean his head out with rubbing alcohol when Gary waddled over to me.

GARY So Dog boy, I see you're movin' up the food chain. A pirate, huh? Who died?

TREVOR Nobody, Donny's in Maui.

GARY Donny huh? I'd spray that head out real good if I was you. No tellin' where it's been.

TREVOR Hey Gar, do you think I could make it as a face character?

GARY Sure kid, you'd make a cute Snow White.

TREVOR I'm serious.

GARY What the fuck do you wanna be a face for?

TREVOR I don't know.

GARY What's wrong with Pluto? I'm tellin' ya. Ya got talent kid. I seen 'em come and go 'round here but you got somethin'. You wanna throw it all away and be one o' them? What, you don't like gettin' sweaty? Who do ya wanna be anyway... a chimney sweep?

TREVOR Peter Pan...

GARY You really wanna run around with a fairy wearin' green tights and a tunic? Let's be honest kid you don't have the legs for it.

TREVOR Tinkerbell's a pixie not a fairy. And I'm gonna try out for it.

GARY Fine but yer settin' yerself up for a fall kid. They don't let ya do face till ya been here a while.

TREVOR Look just because you're gonna be a duck for the rest of your life doesn't mean I have to be a dog—

GARY Fine. I gotta go. I got autographs to sign. Take care of yerself kid. (*To David.*) Well, well if it ain't the Jolly Green Giant. Looks like you got some competition pretty boy.

Exits.

PETER/DAVID What's got his feathers in a flap?

NARRATOR David was Peter Pan. He was a couple years older than me but he had that peaches and cream complexion that made him look perpetually prepubescent. He gave Jason a high five, well, a high hook. He looked at me and said to Jason—

PETER/DAVID Where's Donny?

CAPT. HOOK/JASON Vacation, can you believe it? They sent us that—

PETER/DAVID Is he cool?

CAPT. HOOK/JASON He better be, I mean, it's all set. Today's the day. We've only got one left. Just like Donny to wuss out.

PETER/DAVID (*to me*) Well welcome aboard. I'll get my shit together and we'll take off.

NARRATOR He waltzed on by me into face character country. There was a long makeup mirror on one wall. He sat down at an empty stool between Merlin and Mary Poppins who were busy putting on their wigs. He popped the one little zit on his face, hairpined his green hat to his head and buckled his knife and belt on. He bounded back over to Jason and me.

PETER/DAVID Well crew are you ready? Today's a good day to fly!

NARRATOR We practically ran down the service road to the backstage entrance of Tomorrowland. We checked our costumes out in the full-length mirror. I looked at my set schedule…

TREVOR Hey, guys aren't we're supposed to be over at Critter Country…

CAPT. HOOK/JASON Oh man!

PETER/DAVID Let me see that—set schedules? We don't need no stinking set schedules.

> *Tears it up.*

If we stuck to the schedule the suits would know where to find us.

TREVOR But, aren't they supposed to protect us—

CAPT. HOOK/JASON Aw, man! I told you he wasn't gonna work out.

NARRATOR And I watched as Jason put his head on and suddenly Captain Hook was scowling down at me like—

CAPT. HOOK'S VOICE Mr. Smee, you can either walk the plank… or we'll throw you overboard… UNDERSTAND !?!

TREVOR So, where are we going?

PETER/DAVID Trust me. Ready Cap'n? Ready crew. C'mon everybody here we go off to Eisnerland!

THE PAN UNIT PART 2: IN PARK TO "PIRATES"

NARRATOR I put on my head and as I started to turn the corner I saw one of the sweeper people appear out of nowhere and remove the pieces of torn schedule with a broom and dustpan. There was no going back. We were off. (*Running in place.*)

Our cover was that we were chasing Peter Pan, not that anyone got that. Peter was halfway to the Matterhorn before I caught up. Hook was brushing aside tourists with disdain. I was waving and shaking hands as fast as I could. I followed Peter to what I believed to be a break area. It turned out to be the exit of an attraction. Guests were shuffling past us in various degrees of wetness from merely damp to completely soaked. We arrived at a dock where people were being offloaded from boats. It turned out David knew the ride operator. Five minutes later I found myself in a boat, in the Pirates of the Caribbean ride, in full costume. David's reasoning was that it was in character for the three of us to be here. In keeping with that spirit he required that we all sing the pirate song, from Peter Pan—for effect.

> *Oh, a pirate's life is wonderful life, A rovin' over the sea—*
> *Give me a career as a buccaneer, The life of a pirate for me!!!*

TREVOR Guys… Shouldn't we duck or something?

NARRATOR They just laughed. As we floated past the Blue Bayou restaurant where guests dined on "faux-nouveaux" Cajun cuisine, someone came over to the railing and called to us.

PSYCHO MIKE Hey, Peter Pan say cheese!!!

NARRATOR Before I knew what was happening, Hook and Peter were standing up with me in between them posing for this person to take our picture. (*Click.*)

TREVOR Are you crazy! If anyone sees that picture we're dead!

CAPT. HOOK/JASON Calm down dude he's with us.

PETER/DAVID That's Psycho Mike: character groupie extraordinaire. We have an arrangement. Whenever we hit the rides he's our personal photographer. We've got a whole album, I'll have to show you sometime. We'll pick up the Polaroid later. Relax and enjoy the ride. Oh…

> *Oh, a pirates life is a wonderful life*
> *You'll find adventure and sport,*
> *But live every minute*
> *For all that is in it*

The life of a pirate is short.
Oh, the life of a pirate is short.

NARRATOR We disembarked and exited through a service door before the ride ended. They knew all the tricks. We picked up the Polaroid from Psycho Mike and took our break over at the Pit. A park map was produced with several areas marked with red X's. Peter took a red pen out of his scabbard and crossed off Pirates of the Caribbean with a flourish.

THE PAN UNIT PART 3: MINE CAR RIDE & BUSTED!

PETER/DAVID Well boys, there's nothin' left. We're goin' on a little treasure hunt.

CAPT. HOOK/JASON Cool! The mine car ride?

PETER/DAVID The abandoned mine car ride.

NARRATOR There were very few places that were off limits to cast members that were still on stage and in the public view. The mine car ride had been closed down years ago and turned into scenery. We suited up and headed out. There was a fence. There was a big fence, Tigger would have had trouble getting over this fence. We climbed it. On the other side were weeds, wilderness and wild growth. Unheard of in the immaculately manicured Magic Kingdom. Peter found the mine car tracks, they led into a tunnel. Captain Hook suggested that I go first. I stepped forward into total darkness. It smelled old and musty. I followed the tracks by feel around a bend, the guys were right behind me. (*Hums "Lollipop Lollipop."*) I always hum when I'm scared out of my skull. The tunnel opened out into broad daylight and there were the rivers of America and Tom Sawyer's Island. Peter took the lead. The three of us are shuffling down the tracks which led behind a waterfall.

TREVOR (*singing*) LOLLIPOP LOLLIPOP!!! (*Making a pop sound.*) Ba Da Um Bum Bum!

NARRATOR I'm no longer at Disneyland, I'm in Neverland. I'm one of the Lost Boys out on an adventure with Peter Pan. The roar of the waterfall is deafening overhead. For the first time since coming to work for the Mouse… I feel FREE!!! Just as we cleared the waterfall, the pirate ship *Columbia* sailed around the bend of Tom Sawyer's Island with about a hundred guests leaning over the railing staring at us, well at the waterfall, cameras in hand. I heard a voice—

RIDE OPERATOR ABOARD THE COLUMBIA Ahoy matey, what are you doin' under the waterfall???

NARRATOR The cameras were flashing, the camcorders were rolling. Instinctively, I started waving. Then I realize… (*Beat.*) I'm alone. Peter and Hook were gone. I turned and ran after my companions. I caught up with them halfway down the service road. They were both very quiet as we approached the break area. We still hadn't taken our heads off when Jimmy popped out from behind a dumpster with two security guards dressed as keystone cops. They sauntered up to us.

JIMMY Well boys, is there anything you feel you ought to be telling me?

CAPT. HOOK/JASON Uh… Happy Independence Day, Jimmy?

JIMMY (*twitch*) You wouldn't happen to know anything about some people under a waterfall would you?

JASON No.

DAVID No.

TREVOR Um… No.

JIMMY Fine, Keep your heads on and come with me.

NARRATOR They marched us in a line through the park up to America Sings. Then they separated us out. We didn't even have time to get our story straight.

THE END FOURTH OF JULY

JIMMY Now there's the right way and the wrong way, and then there's the Disney way. We've got rules for a reason. We know the three of you weren't where you were supposed to be. Now write down what actually happened in your own words.

NARRATOR Well, that's what really happened. What I wrote on the report was…

TREVOR I was just following Peter.

NARRATOR It was my first offense. I hoped they would go easy on me. They collected our forms.

JIMMY Well boys, you haven't given us much to go on. You're all suspended for three days pending an investigation. We'll call you and let you know if you get to keep your jobs.

NARRATOR They marched us down to the head room where they took our heads and our costumes and then down to the zoo crew locker room, and Jimmy stood over us as we cleaned out our lockers. David knew the routine. He'd been suspended three times and was prepared with a duffel bag for his personal belongings. Jason had been suspended a total of seven times and had taken to not leaving things in his locker for just this reason. I handed in my T-shirt, shorts and socks. They escorted us up to Harbor House the Employee Exit and took our nametags and I.D.'s. As I stood there in the employee parking lot and the monorail passed overhead. I felt sick.

CAPT. HOOK/JASON I got to hand it to you rookie. I thought you were gonna talk.

PETER/DAVID Don't worry about it, It's the busiest time of the year. What are they gonna do fire us? We're goin' back in the park, you wanna come? No? Suit yourself. Oh, here, you earned it.

NARRATOR He handed me the snapshot of the three of us in the boat with the simulated Bayou backdrop. Then David and Jason went back into the park to watch the fireworks.

WAITING FOR THE CALL

NARRATOR I went back to my shitty motel room in East Anaheim where I was living to wait for the phone call. That night as the "fantasy in the sky" fireworks were going on and the shockwaves were setting off car alarms… and annoying the crack-house pit bulls next door. I thought… "God I hope they don't fire me. I love Disneyland!"

Lying on the floor… I flashed back to the auditions. They were a grueling two-day marathon of improvisations and movement routines. I made every single cut that first day. But then I made a huge mistake, I ate at a dive burger joint near the park and got the worst food poisoning of my life. I spent the night on the bathroom floor with the roaches and when it came time to actually try on the costumes for the final cut, I had dry heaved every ounce of moisture out of my body. But I forced myself to get through it, with the occasional trip to the rest room. I didn't think I did very well. We were told that they would "call us."

After spending the eight-hour road trip home passed out in the back of the car, I finally got back to my parents' house. And the call came. I was in… apparently one of the panelists had been in the next stall and had overheard my "predicament." He said that if I was that determined to be a character then I was ready to "Work for the Mouse." So, I packed my bags and moved to Anaheim. To the Ha' Penny Inn on Harbor Boulevard. It was cheap, all I could afford really. It was one of the few places that would rent by the week. I think they actually rented by the hour, being right in the middle of the red light district. But I didn't care, I was a finally a "Disney Character"!

It's three days later and they still haven't called… And I haven't been outside once. Then the phone rings. (*Ringing sound.*)

TREVOR Hello, yes this is he… yes, I understand, but I promise I'll never do it again… what? Five five and a half…why? Hotel Breakfast Pluto six-thirty tomorrow morning? (*Beat.*) Of course I'll be there!

NARRATOR After all, the face character auditions were coming up. I had learned my lesson, have fun, but just don't get caught.

MY OWN PRIVATE HADES

NARRATOR For the rest of the summer, I was trying to make up for the waterfall incident. I accepted every shift they offered me—breakfasts, a.m.s, p.m.s, closing shifts… Getting off work at two in the morning. Doing back to back shifts—they called it "extending." I was doing twelve hours a day, in Pluto. I was Pluto, in my own private Hades.

SNOT-NOSED KID Are you a boy or a girl?

PLUTO (*does muscle pose.*)

TEENAGER Where do ya see out of???

PLUTO (*points to his eyes.*)

BRAT Where's Mickey?

PLUTO (*pointing towards the mouse as if a large compass needle.*)

NARRATOR We were all "Mickey Compasses." We always knew where that damned MOUSE was. But I longed for voice clearance. I began to have this recurring nightmare where I'm coming off set at the end of a closing shift. It's past midnight. I look around the break area, but everyone's gone home. They've forgotten about me. I can't get myself out of costume because the zipper's in the back. So, I go over to the full-length mirror and I try to reach around to undo the Velcro, but I can't get a grip on it. I look down at my hands and they look like real paws. I look in the mirror and I've turned into a big yellow dog. "Fuck" and my reflection says back at me, "woof." I had to get out of Pluto… but I had no seniority. So the only other costume in my height range that nobody else wanted to do was the White Rabbit.

TAMMY INTRO / THE WHITE RABBIT

NARRATOR Mister White Rabbit was one of the hottest "fur" costumes, lousy vision and feet the size of snowshoes. But whenever a shift opened up I'd put in a request to do it. Because it meant that I could be in the Alice unit. With Alice… Well, alright, with Tammy uh… Smith. Twenty-one, blue eyes and long blonde hair. She didn't even have to wear the wig. She just tied it up with a bow and put on her English accent. It was a devastating combination. Okay, I was smitten, I was seventeen. But she didn't know I existed. I was just another sweaty rookie in a bunny suit. I saw the way she flirted with the other face characters out on set. I really wanted to be Peter Pan now… but face character auditions were still a few weeks off. I was determined to get her to notice me… and I did. One set, while the Mad Hatter was off doing card tricks and the Tweedles were playing tag over by the tea cups, I got to sit next to Alice while she told a story to a group of kids under the Caterpillar's Mushroom. She was doing the one about playing croquette with the Queen, and I decided to act it out for the kids. Okay, I was showing off and it was going fine until… I tripped over a sprinkler and lost my head. Literally. It went up and up and up… right over a low fence and into a hedge. So I did the only thing I could think of… I jumped in after it. I mean, a full decapitation out on set is grounds for termination… especially if somebody captures it on videotape and it makes it onto America's Stupidest Home Videos. So I spent the rest of the set upside down in the bushes with my rabbit's feet sticking out, waving in the air until Dee and Dum finally came over and helped me out. Tammy was just laughing too hard to help. But… I had made an impression. Unfortunately, Jimmy saw the whole thing and pulled me out of the White Rabbit and stuck me back into Pluto. I couldn't even meet Tammy's eyes in the break area, she'd just start laughing. She'd never go out with me now.

FACE CHARACTER AUDITION

NARRATOR The day of face character auditions finally arrived. I was ready. I had watched the movie a hundred times, I even read the book, although it had almost nothing in common with the Disney version. I went over to the audition sheet and signed in under the Peter Pan column. They put me in a hall full of guys waiting to audition and they all looked like Peter Pan. But I knew I wanted it more. They called us into the conference room one at a time. A panel of leads and supervisors was seated along one wall. My turn.

TREVOR (*as PETER PAN*) C'mon everybody here we go off to Neverland!

NARRATOR They whispered among themselves. Jimmy came over to me.

JIMMY Thank you, but you're just too tan. You've got the voice down, but how would that look. A tan Pan? Malibu Pan? Stay out of the sun and re-audition next year. Next.

NARRATOR I was devastated. I couldn't go back to Pluto, I might go postal. It was true, I was very dark at the time, I was spending all my free time down by the pool. But to come right out and say it like that… Now I understood why some of the girls came out crying. They were told that they had the wrong color eyes for Alice or too many freckles for Snow White or that they needed to lose thirty pounds to be Cinderella. I went back over to the signup sheet. I put my name down in every category. The next group was going in…Chimney Sweeps.

TREVOR (*as a SWEEP*) Cheery O' Gov'na! Mahatma Gandhi, now there was a brilliant bloke. But he didn't eat much, so he was very frail and when he did he ate curries, consequently he had bad breath. So when he'd walk down the street people would say... there goes that super fragile mystic, vexed by halitosis. You could say it backwards which is "suoitodilapxecitsiligarfilacrepus" but that's going a bit too far wouldn't you say?

JIMMY Sorry, you're just not "Dick Van Dyke-y" enough! Okay, send in the Princes!

TREVOR (*as PRINCE*) Hello there. I'm Prince Charming, (*Smiles.*) I'm afraid I've lost someone... would you mind sticking your foot in this?

JIMMY You're too short! Merlins!

TREVOR (*as MERLIN*) Higatus figatus migatus mum prestadigatonium (*Pulls sword, stops.*) I say, this sword appears to be stuck... You there, lad, would you mind pulling it out?

JIMMY Too young! Petes!

TREVOR (*as PETE*) Hi, my name's Pete. Welcome to Passamaquoddy. Have you seen my Dragon???

JIMMY Too old!

NARRATOR I was desperate! They said, "Can you do a Mad Hatter voice?" I said, "what's that supposed to sound like?" They said, "Ed Wynn."

MAD HATTER (*mouths*) Ed Wynn? (*Beat, then as Ed Wynn.*) Well of course I can! Don't let's be silly, now Fred Gwyn, that's different! My goodness. Would anyone like some tea??? I'm celebrating my un-birthday today, don't cha know?

NARRATOR They cast me on the spot. They fitted me with a latex nose, buck teeth and a white wig. My costume was a huge hat, big shoes and a ridiculous yellow trench coat. But, at last! I had voice clearance!

THE ALICE UNIT

NARRATOR So the following week I was back in the Alice unit but this time as a face character. Tammy was the star you see, I was just an insane hat salesman with a thing for tea. The official character handbook describes him as "a befuddled little man who is extremely eccentric and completely crazy." Typecast again. But I got to say lines from the movie like: "I have an excellent idea, let's change the subject" and "Well, if you don't think you shouldn't talk" and "those are the things that upset me!" (*Beat.*) But that summer the Alice unit suffered from downsizing, we lost a couple of costumes, the Walrus was canned. The Queen of Hearts got axed because she looked too scary. They even got rid of the "Tweedles" Dee and Dum because guests had complained to management that they looked like "Mongoloid children." True story. People really said crap like that. So it was just Alice, the White Rabbit and me. It was my job to walk around with a beautiful girl in a blue dress, and a six-foot white rabbit. That part was cool. Tammy even started to flirt with me out on set. But the novelty of being the Mad Hatter wore off pretty quickly. It was like doing an eight-hour improv every day. In front of the toughest audience you can imagine. Eight-year-old agnostics.

KID 1 You're not real!

MAD HATTER I have an excellent idea, let's change the subject!

KID 2 I don't think that's your real nose.

MAD HATTER Well, if you don't think you shouldn't talk.

KID 3 Why IS a raven like a writing desk?

MAD HATTER Those are the things that upset me!

NARRATOR Being a face character wasn't all that I thought it would be. Oh, I enjoyed the fact that my character was crazy. It helped.

MAD HATTER "Why is a raven like a writing desk?" Hmmm let's see, well because… Poe wrote on both, ya see. Edgar Allen, Poe, The Raven… tough crowd. Well happy un-birthday… oh, it IS your birthday? Well then… UN-happy un-birthday… to you!

NARRATOR But my favorite part were the "story sets." Now we were supposed to stick to these pre-approved Disney fairy tales… but we tried to play around a bit…

MAD HATTER Now Fifer Pig played the fife and his house was made out of… straw, that's right and Fiddler Pig played the fiddle and his house was made out of… sticks, very good, and Practical Pig didn't play at all. (*Beat, looks around.*) That's because he was an accountant you see and his house was made out of aluminum siding! Well, it's wolf proof don't cha know. (*Laughs.*)

NARRATOR I loved how Tammy would laugh at all my stupid jokes. But Jimmy soon heard about our "story sets" and put stop to them. No sense of imagination.

THE LUAU PARTY

NARRATOR Things were looking up. I even lucked out in the housing department. I was crashing at a friend's brother's cousin's roommate's place on Newport Beach. But when the "party people" found out, they tried to convince me to have a "raver" there.

JASON Oh come on dude, it'd be so bitchin'! Sand, surf, sex!

DAVID You're one of us now… Time to LIVE a little.

JASON Yeah, lighten up—

TAMMY Hey guys, what's up? Are you pickin' on my Hatter again?

JASON Nah, Tam—we were just planning for the big luau at his beach house, this Sunday. You're comin' right?

TAMMY Oh, wouldn't miss it… I'll wear my grass skirt. Aloha boys.

NARRATOR So, I asked my surf-nazi roommates if it would be okay to throw a small get together. They said "sure…" as long as I invited Cinderella and Sleeping Beauty and the rest of the "royal hotties." I didn't have the heart to tell them that those two were only hot for each other. Now, I had heard about the "Jungle Boat" party that had gotten of hand… so I said—

TREVOR Now we're just gonna invite a few character people over, right… um right, Jason?

JASON Leave it to me… a buddy of mine over in production is makin' up all the flyers now.

DAVID We'll get the booze. You get the decorations.

NARRATOR Next thing I knew, everyone in the department was coming, and by the end of the day, there where flyers all over the back-park bearing the title "Sunday, Sunday, Sunday! Maui Madness and Beach Bonfire" over my address. Now it was a very small place on the strand. I mean really tiny. But I went and decorated it with Tiki torches… and waited for the party to start. I actually bought and barbecued a couple of steaks, just in case Tammy wasn't really a vegetarian. Even though all I ever saw her eat were carrots sticks and spring water. Well people came, and came and they kept on coming as they got off work. I recognized most of them from the park. But there were people there that I didn't know and they didn't look like they met Disney grooming standards, but they all had flyers. Everybody was dressed in pseudo-Polynesian attire. The drummers from the Tahitian Terrace hula show even came with their own drums. Most of the partygoers were from the Entertainment department, but I didn't know their names. I could only identify them from the characters they played. The place was packed. There were bodies everywhere! I just sat in a corner…

TREVOR Hey Gary, have you seen Tammy?

GARY The devil with the blue dress? Nah. Hey great soiree, kid… But you might want to check the hot-tub, it's overflowin'. Too many people in it.

TREVOR What? Yeah, okay. Hey, we don't have a "hot-tub…"

JASON Well you've got a bathtub and hot water… so I just added a little bubble bath and ALOHA! Hey, are we out of Blue Hawaiian mix?

NARRATOR It was insane! Over three hundred people actually showed up. Robin Hood and his Merry Men were smoking out… Out on the deck… Pinocchio was doing lines with Dumbo in the guest bathroom… and the Fantasyland Brass guys were running around covered in body paint and nothing else. I went to hide in my room… But there was some kind of orgy going on in there with most of the Seven Dwarves and the Three Little Pigs and just as my roommates got back from surfing… the doorbell rang. Hoping it was Tammy, I answered it, with a coconut filled with Kahlua… it was the Newport Police… Jackboots and all. They made the Samoan drummers put out the bonfire… and the party was officially over. (*Beat.*) The guy who was actually named on the lease didn't take kindly to a citation for under-aged drinking and disturbing the peace. After everybody had left. He said—

ROOMATE Man, you're no longer an asset… you're a liability.

NARRATOR And he told me to pack up and get out. I had nowhere to go… So, I went back to work to check out the housing board and sleep down in the locker room. (*Lays down on bench.*)

TAMMY'S PLACE

NARRATOR The next day, I was back in the Alice unit, when Tammy came up to me and said—

TAMMY Hey, I heard about what happened at the party… sounds wild… sorry I couldn't make it, but something came up.

TREVOR Oh, that's okay… No big deal.

TAMMY Did you really get kicked out?

TREVOR You heard? Yeah. I guess it's back to the Ha' Penny Inn until school starts next week.

TAMMY Look, you can stay with me until you find someplace.

NARRATOR Now that's what she actually said… What I heard was "You can LIVE with me." I had never "LIVED" with a woman before. All right, now I know the difference between when somebody says… "stay with me" and "live with me." But I spent the rest of the day skipping around on set and blowing Alice kisses, completely out of character of course. That night when I showed up on her doorstep, suitcases in hand, a very tall, thick-necked, "V-shaped" guy answered the door in his boxer shorts. I thought I had the wrong address. Until she poked her head around from behind Mr. Big. It turned out that THIS was the "something that had come up." Her boyfriend Lars was a Matterhorn Mountain Climber in the park and a fanatical body-builder. The first thing he asked me was...

LARS So, Mr. Mad Hat guy... vat do you lift? Eh?

TREVOR (*as the MAD HATTER*) Uh... Luggage? (*Smiles.*)

LARS Very funny guy!

NARRATOR And he punched me in the arm. Tammy guided me to "the guest bedroom" and they went back to what they were doing. The place was really nice, but it had very thin walls... I stayed for a very, very long week... until I found student housing up in L.A.

GANJA BROWNIES

NARRATOR Now there are no controlled substances allowed at the "Happiest Place on Earth." Oh sure, occasionally after a grad night you'd hear about a group of kids dropping acid and going on the Haunted Mansion and freaking out. And a lot of them would fill up those Davy Crockett water bottles with Everclear or take Ecstasy and the security guards would find them in the bushes over by Bear County by following the trail of discarded underwear. But I soon found out that a lot of employees would partake of certain "recreational substances."

    Beat.

Like the time Winnie the Pooh took acid and went on a little trip... Literally. He tripped at the top of the steps by the train station and rolled all the way down Main Street, laughing the whole way.

    Beat.

But I never did anything like that... (*Beat.*) really. Well all right, once... But it doesn't really count because it wasn't on purpose. It was a few months after the luau party and Tammy and I had become "friends." It was her birthday and she said that she had a surprise for us. Before we went out on the first set, she offered me a homemade brownie that Jason had brought in for her. He said he'd gotten the recipe from somebody named Chef Rah, something called Kick-'em-in the-head, fudge'n-hashbrownies. I didn't know he baked. They were good. The whole Alice unit had some. It wasn't until about fifteen minutes into the first set that I started to feel... really funky... I couldn't stop laughing. I went over to the rabbit...

MAD HATTER Do you feel funny... bunny? You don't think there was something in those brownies do ya?—

NARRATOR The girl inside just kept saying "Hash!" and giggling.

MAD HATTER Ssshhhhhh. Fine, don't talk in costume.

NARRATOR So I figured I'd go ask Alice. Tammy was standing by the wishing well, staring down into it and listening to "When you wish upon a star..."

MAD HATTER Hey Blue... What was in those brownies?

TAMMY/ALICE Hash, silly. Now make a wish...

MAD HATTER Oh, right hash... but... OH! Right... um...

NARRATOR She handed me a penny. Now, I believed in wishes, so I wished that we wouldn't get caught.

TAMMY/ALICE What did you wish for?

MAD HATTER I can't tell you or it might not come true...

TAMMY/ALICE Oh come on, isn't there something you really want?

NARRATOR Several things came to mind. I said—

MAD HATTER I really just want... to be Peter Pan...

TAMMY You'd make a cute Peter... Is that why you're working here?

TREVOR (*as himself*) I guess... I just don't want to grow up...

TAMMY (*as herself*) Neither do I. C'mon get the rabbit and follow me. This'll be fun.

MAD HATTER Where are we going?

TAMMY To Wonderland.

NARRATOR She took me and the White Rabbit by the hands... and we went on the Alice in Wonderland attraction. She said she had gotten the approval from the Ice Princess herself and I believed her. She had the seniority and it was a special occasion. I wasn't worried. Besides it was Jimmy's day off. But still... What if... and that was when the paranoia kicked in. Do yourself a favor kids... Don't do drugs at Disneyland. A mind is a terrible thing... when it's wasted!

We hopped onto the back of a purple caterpillar, I sat next to her and the rabbit was behind us. Tammy looked like a little kid going on the ride for the first time. But then we got into the dark ride with the black lights and psychedelic colors. I had forgotten how freaky the story is. Tulgey Wood was really bad and I kept expecting the Jabberwocky to jump out at us... and the part where the Queen flips out was really intense. The rabbit nearly wet herself. But when we got to the dream sequence with the caterpillar, the smoke rings and the Cheshire Cat, Tammy reached over and held my hand. I forgot about everything else. At the end... as the un-birthday cake exploded, she leaned over and kissed me. The ride through Wonderland seemed to last forever... but I looked at my watch and only a couple of minutes had passed. We exited and went backstage without an incident. The rest of the day was a blur. But every time she caught my eye after that, she gave me a little wink.

GOOFY GOLF

NARRATOR My one glorious "date" with Tammy was when she was between boyfriends and she invited me out. It started out perfectly innocent, with a round of Goofy Golf which I let her win and some frozen yogurt but then we went to her place... where she taught me how to drink tequila poppers and do body shots and then we ended up climbing into... a tree... A Weeping Willow tree in the park by her house that for some reason she called Winston. So there we were twenty feet off the ground, me ready to confess my undying love to her, or get violently sick whichever came first when she confided in me... that she just couldn't find Mr. Right and that all the guys she dated were complete assholes who were only after her for one thing and that she was so glad to have me to talk to... kind of like a little brother. It was at that moment that I leaned forward to kiss her... and fell out of the tree. The next morning I woke up on her couch... Alone. With a huge hangover... Late for work. She didn't have to work weekends, but I was scheduled in the parade.

THE PARADE & IMAGINARY BASEBALL GAME

NARRATOR That summer the atmosphere characters were doing the daytime parades. They taught us this lame little dance routine, but basically we were just supposed to walk and wave along the parade route. We were coming around the hub in front of the Castle when the float in front of us, a great big birthday cake, broke down. Now, instead of just walking around it and finishing the parade. We had to wait until it was fixed. The parade captains told us to just go up and down the sidewalks and wave at people. But after about fifteen minutes of this... I suggested that we do something else. I pulled an imaginary baseball out of my trench coat and showed it to the crowd.

MAD HATTER Anybody wanna play baseball??? We need a batter. Any volunteers???

NARRATOR Five minutes later and we had the field set up. Mickey, Donald and Goofy were on first, second and third. Pluto was catching. All the other characters where in the outfield. I was pitching, of course. Our first batter was Ian, a little round kid. The kind that would usually get picked last.

MAD HATTER Okay, keep your eye on the ball, Ian. Here we go.

(*Clonk.*) Wow what a hit! Hey Little John get it. It's by your foot, no, no your other foot.

NARRATOR The outfield scrambled as fifteen characters ran around looking for this imaginary ball. Ian ran to first.

MAD HATTER Okay Aiesha, here it comes. (*Clonk.*) Almost took my hat off… Hey Geppetto get it. Oh, I know you've got a bad back… there you go, Pinocchio—

NARRATOR Kids are lining up to bat. They're still fixing the axle on the birthday cake. The bases are loaded now. Peter's calling for a relief pitcher, everybody wants in the game. The pressure's on…

MAD HATTER We need a clean up batter…

NARRATOR And then I saw two blue eyes staring out from under this baseball cap with a paw print on it—

MAD HATTER How about you there… with the hat. You look like a heavy hitter. What say ma'am, can he come out and play.

SCOTTY Can I mom… please?

SCOTTY'S MOTHER Okay honey, you just be careful out there.

MAD HATTER Nice hat. Okay Scotty, keep your eye on the ball… What do ya mean you don't see it. (*Pause.*) That's because it's a magic ball, you have to believe in it. Here it comes. (*Clonk.*) Oh my goodness. Would you look at that? It's going, it's going, it's—

NARRATOR The whole crowd turned to see where this imaginary ball was going… when Jimmy stomped up to the mound.

JIMMY Game over Babe. Get these kids back on the sidewalk.

MAD HATTER But why? The kids love it.

JIMMY It's not safe.

NARRATOR The crowd started to boo Jimmy. Scotty was rounding third.

JIMMY Why can't you just march with the others?

NARRATOR I saw Scotty cross home plate and give Pluto a huge hug.

JIMMY End this, now.

MAD HATTER I'm sorry folks, but the game's been called on account of reality.

NARRATOR They got the float moving again and we finished the parade. I got a guest commendation from Scotty's mother for making his day, and a written reprimand from Jimmy for disrupting the parade.

THE BLACK AND WHITE BALL

NARRATOR I wanted to ask Tammy to the Character's End of the Year Black and White Ball. I figured she might go with me even as a friend because she and Lars had broken up. But I just kept chickening out. By the time I worked up the nerve to ask her, it was too late. She was going with Prince Charming, literally. Steve "toothpaste commercial smile" Bellini. So I went stag and sat at the rookie table until I was snatched up by the party people who had found out that it was my 18th birthday... so I got invited up to the suite they had at the Disneyland hotel and they taught me to play quarters... with peppermint schnapps. To this day I can't even look at a peppermint candy without gagging. Now, I don't remember too much, just blurry images of drunken dancing midgets, flashing lights and swimming. I woke up in the sand by the swimming pool wearing only a towel and my dress shoes which were wet and smelled like chlorine. Later, the story I got told was that a group of us rookies had been "initiated" by the "lifers" who made us stand in the fountain where they do the "dancing waters" show and sing (*He sings.*) "It's a small world after all—" in our underwear. But it didn't matter to me because I was no longer a rookie.

CHRISTMAS IN THE BREAK AREA

NARRATOR I went back to school in the fall, to study theatre at UCLA taking classes like Shakespearean acting taught by Robert Reed... Mr. Brady from The Brady Bunch... explains a lot doesn't it? But I kept my part-time status. When the holidays rolled around I had to be fully available. My first Christmas away from home was during a hurricane. Now it never snows at the Happiest Place on Earth... It hails.

The sound of jingle bells.

NARRATOR It's 9:45 p.m. Christmas eve in the break area, and there are all new faces, except Gary and Jason, who had been banned from playing Captain Hook after "falling" into a fountain in New Orleans Square and then going for a swim.

TREVOR Hey Jas. In Tigger huh? Must be warm in there?

JASON Yeah, hot fuckin' costume, dude.

GARY So, furry, what are you doin' this for?

JASON Brain damage, what's your excuse? Nah, I love this job man. It's like half an hour on half an hour off. Like for... uh, thirty minutes you're a rock star and then ya take off the suit and BANG you're nobody again. It's kind of addicting. Hey dude... didja hear about David? He was doin' Peter and he climbed up on top of the Carnation milk truck and jumped off... nah he didn't get hurt... he just picked himself up, dusted himself off and he says, "oops, no pixie dust!!!" It was classic. But Jimmy was over at Coke corner, hiding behind the piano. He saw the whole thing, man. Didn't even wait for him to get back stage, just fired his ass. (*Pause.*) I still like this gig, but it's gettin' too serious man. I mean no way a kid's gonna try and fly just because they saw Peter Pan do it. Duh!!! Kids aren't that stupid. Right? (*Beat.*) Oh shit, I'm gonna be late. Zip me up. (*Zips.*) Thanks, Merry X-MAS (*Tigger laugh.*) TTFNA!

TREVOR TTFNA? Ta Ta for now... uh..?

GARY Tell The Fuckers No Autographs!

TREVOR So, they're looking for a new Peter then huh?

GARY Maybe...

TREVOR Hey Gar, How's it goin?

GARY I'm tellin' ya it's all fuckin' changed kid. It just keeps gettin' worse. I mean, what would Walt say? You see this? Thirty years and what do I got to show for it? A pin on my name tag. Charactering used to mean something, we were part of the show. Now the suits just want warm bodies, they'll hire anything, no offense. They got sixteen year old girls in gummi bears droppin' dead from heat exhaustion, and they're wonderin' why? I'm wonderin' what the fuck is a gummi bear? They're getting' rid of anybody that's talkin' union. They just want disposable people, walking photo opportunities, autographing automatons, you know what I'm sayin'?

TREVOR So, why are you still here?

GARY Oh, they won't get rid of me. I'm grandfather claused. Yeah, I could leave, but then what? Back to the carney? Or the circus with the other freaks? Nope, I'm here till they carry me out in a box. (*Beat.*) Excuse me, kid... Hey you there, rookie! Yeah you... getting' into Goofy. Why're you doin this?

ROOKIE Well, I consider myself to be an American Kabuki artist.

GARY Bullshit, you're a fast food mime and Michael Eisner's wet dream. Oh don't cry. Go on, get out there and frolic! What about you? Mad as a Hatter, what's in this for you?

TREVOR It's fun. It's like I get paid to play.

GARY Yeah, well that's gonna change. Have you heard about "Toon Town?" It's a regular character concentration camp. They're gonna put us all in one place and throw away the key. I can see it now. Geppeto's Ghetto. I've seen the plans. A long hallway full of doors, and a Mickey Mouse behind every door. That's what they want, no unions, no freedom... just cheap mass produced entertainment. You don't want to be a lifer do ya kid? Get out now, while you still can.

TREVOR (*looking at name tag*) Hey Gary... Where's Tammy?

GARY Didn't ya hear? That's the trouble with you part-timers, you're never here. I heard that she got busted for joining the "Matterhorn-y Club".

TREVOR What?

GARY Yeah there's a break area at the top of the mountain where they push Tinkerbell off and it's filled with old sand bags. She got caught bonking Dick Tracy in the back of an old bobsled up there. They were both in partial costume at the time. Fired on the spot. I heard she moved back to Kansas or wherever she came from. Oh, sorry kid. Here.

> *Hands him a flask of something.*

TREVOR Oh... (*Takes it.*) thanks.

> *Drinks, coughs and hands it back.*

Merry Christmas Gary.

GARY Yeah. Merry Christmas. The king is long dead, long live the Magic Kingdom.

ENGLAND

NARRATOR I took a leave of absence that summer for a month to study acting in Oxford, England. But that's another show. (*Beat.*) When I got back, I was more serious than ever about my Character work. I'd been to the land of J.M. Barrie and Lewis Carroll. I'd read Stanislavski, my eyes had been opened. I was thinking... union wages. And I knew that I could be the best damn Peter Pan they had ever seen.

LAST SUMMER

NARRATOR When I got back there was a heat wave. One hundred and ten degrees in the shade. And just in case you're wondering there are no fans in the costumes.

GARY Oh look who's come out of her air-conditioned office to walk amongst us little people.

ICE PRINCESS Hello everybody. Please keep doing your stretching exercises. I just wanted to let you all know that according to the thermometer outside the entertainment office... it's only ninety-nine degrees, so I'm afraid that means full sets again today. Also the face character auditions have been postponed again due to budget cutbacks. Well, back to work everyone... and remember, keep smiling!

GARY It's a good thing they keep that thing in the shade, it keeps the mercury from popping out.

JASON I took one out with me once in Brer Bear it went up over 115 degrees man, Fahrenheit!

NARRATOR With the face character auditions postponed again I was still in the Mad Hatter. I was out on set with the White Rabbit one day. They still hadn't replaced Tammy. So it was just me and the rabbit. People didn't get who we were. The Alice unit without an Alice. They thought I was some kinda magician.

MAD HATTER You wanna see me pull this rabbit out of my hat? I'm sorry I don't have medical insurance. You like my teeth? Well, they only cost a dollar. They're buck teeth don't cha know. Didja like that one rabbit?

ZEKE Hey is that a boy or a girl rabbit?

MAD HATTER Well his name's Mr. White Rabbit, you figure it out. Nice tie, what happened somebody couldn't guess your weight? I have an excellent idea, let's change the subject.

ZEKE Uh, where does he see out of?

MAD HATTER He sees out of his… mouth! Yeah, it's from all those carrots he eats, they act like "fiber optics" don't cha know. What's that, Rabbit? You're not feeling very well? Well, that was a pretty bad joke… OH! You're not feeling very… WELL, look at the time, we've got to go, we're gonna be late.

ZEKE Hey, is it hot in there?

MAD HATTER Hot in where? Excuse us we've got to go, we don't want the rabbit to lose his head, the queen's a stickler for punctuality, and those are the things that upset her!

ZEKE Inside that costume. It must be hot in there?

MAD HATTER Hot? Did you say hot? Now just a second Rabbit. C'mere Zeke. Picture this… It's a hundred and ten degrees in the shade like today, right. You're wearing ski boots, oven mittens and a sleeping bag. On your head you've got a football helmet and earmuffs. You can't see, partly because the dark glasses you're wearing have fogged up due to your humid perspiration condensing on the lenses, but mostly because of the sweat trickling down over your eyes. You can't breathe because there's no wind and you're standing in the blazing heat waiting for some moron to remove his lens cap so he can take your picture because he's got some thing for bunnies. On top of it all you've got a fever because you've got the flu. Hot? You could fry an egg on his ass brain boy. I don't know if the Pulitzer Prize people have a category for understatement, but I'd check it out if I were you.

ZEKE I guess, I just didn't think—

MAD HATTER Well, if you don't think you shouldn't talk.

NARRATOR Just then the White Rabbit threw up. It came dribbling out of his head, forming a miniature Jackson Pollock on the pavement in front of the wishing well. I needed a vacation. I made a wish.

LAST DAY

NARRATOR A few days later I went down to the Zoo Crew board to check the schedule and request some time off. But they hadn't posted it yet. When Gary came by.

GARY Ding Dong the witch is gone. Did ya hear? They got rid of the Ice Princess. So, she was Snow White back in the seventies… who cares. The new guy is a real piece of work… He canned Jason this morning for bein' one minute late, on his birthday. Foods department… entertainment… what's the difference? I heard he used to flip burgers wit' his bare hands. You wanna get on his good side? Tell 'em we're gonna be formin' a character union.

> *Flips 'em the bird and says as Donald Duck:*

"Quack you" (*Quack-laughing as Donald Duck.*) Oh, hey, there's a picture up there for you kid… You know, you probably shoulda stayed over there in Limeyland.

NARRATOR I went over to the corkboard and in between some of the Crayola creations that kids had sent to Mickey Mouse were a couple of pictures… one was of three blurry characters going behind a waterfall and someone had written on it "going, going, gone." But another picture caught my eye. It was of Scotty and Pluto at the baseball game. (*Picks photo off the board and flips it over.*) Scotty Green March 4th 1984 to… (*Beat.*) September 12th 1991.

> *A moment of silence. He replaces it on the board. Wipes away a tear.*

Just then, Jimmy came out of the lead office and posted the new zoo crew schedule. I wasn't on it.

JIMMY Well, there's been a slight change of personnel. Management did a little house cleaning. New faces, new costumes…

NARRATOR I was trying to picture myself as a gummi bear, when Jimmy said…

JIMMY The uh… new boss wants to see you… in his office.

THE BOSS'S OFFICE

NARRATOR I'd never been up to the Boss's office before. I expected to see a bright emerald green light and a man behind a curtain. But it was a small office. There was hardly any light and the big man in the cheap suit behind the desk was no wizard. He said...

BOSS I've been looking through your file.

NARRATOR I'd never even seen my file. It was pretty thick.

BOSS You've been here for a while, so why didn't you go full time?

TREVOR Well, I have school. I'm studying theatre at UCLA—

BOSS Well, you have your priorities, and we've got ours. We've been here for you. But you just haven't been here for us. You're just not a team player. You've got an attitude problem. This is an "at will" state and well, you're terminated, now go clean out your locker...

NARRATOR Suddenly, I jumped up on his desk. I don't know what got into me.

> *Angry as Jimmy Stewart.*

Now doggone it... You're just a warped frustrated old man Mr. Kessler. You sit up here in your comfy, air-conditioned office and you think that you can replace people like me because we just fit the suit, but you're wrong see... this isn't about money and unions it's about Magic and Imagination and you just can't take that away from me and... and... (*Pause.*) Well, all right that's not what I said, that's what I WANTED to say. What I actually said was... "Oh... Okay." (*Sniff.*)

THE END

NARRATOR I cleaned out my locker. But instead of leaving through the employee exit like cast members were supposed to... I heard this little voice in the back of my head say....

MICKEY'S VOICE You've just been fired from the Happiest Place on Earth, where ya gonna go?

NARRATOR So... I went to Disneyland. I went back into the park and I went on the Peter Pan attraction. I hadn't been on it in years. As the lap bar came down, I was still numb. The pirate ship took off, I was flying. But for the first time I looked up and I saw the track overhead. And I looked down at the miniature London and I remember seeing the real thing and I saw the crumpled pieces of plastic they used for clouds. I looked at the stars and I saw Christmas tree lights. The ride ended and I got off. As I left Fantasyland behind me and I walked down Main Street, I thought "I'm never, never coming back." (*Beat.*) Just then something fell out of the sky and landed right in front of me. It bounced once and then twice.

> *Catches it.*

It's a baseball. I looked around. Nobody else had seen it. On it was written "Property of the MAD HATTER." It was my Imaginary Baseball. It wasn't theirs. They didn't want to play anymore. So, I took my ball and went home.

> *He tosses the imaginary baseball up in the air and catches it. He smiles and exits the stage with the ball. The Peter Pan whistle is heard from somewhere off stage.*
>
> *Blackout.*

End of play.

LOLITA ROADTRIP

BY

TREVOR ALLEN

Lolita Roadtrip

This darkly comic play follows Julia (a rebellious Stanford graduate student researching her thesis) and Danny (a hitchhiking teenaged runaway she picks up) as together they retrace novelist and lepidopterist Vladimir Nabokov's actual 1941 roadtrip from New York to Stanford. A series of cross country adventures ensues, as they confront their own dark pasts and discover what really causes a chrysalis to transform into a butterfly.

Production Information

Originally commissioned and developed by PlayGround/ Jim Kleinmann. Originally co-produced by San Jose Stage Company.

World Premiere: April 2011 San Jose Stage Company.

Executive Director:	Cathleen King
Director:	Lee Sankowich
Artistic Director, San Jose Stage Company:	Randall King
Artistic Director, Playground:	Jim Kleinmann

Cast

Julia Martin	Chloe Bronzan
Mrs. Mary Drake/Vera Nabokov/ Night Clerk/Tour Guide/Betsy/ Viki / Detective Hayes	Stacy Ross
Danny "Jackson"/Dmitri Nabokov	Patrick Alparone
Paul Drake/Vladimir Nabokov/ Union Soldier/Man in Hood/Bert	Julian Lopez-Morillas

LOLITA ROADTRIP

CHARACTERS

MAN (50's) PROFESSOR PAUL DRAKE, Professor of English Lit. / VLADIMIR NABOKOV, Novelist and lepidopterist / UNION SOLDIER / MAN IN HOOD / BERT

WOMAN (40's) MRS. MARY DRAKE / VERA NABOKOV, Wife of Nabokov

NIGHT CLERK / TOUR GUIDE / BETSY / VIKI, the Female Relaxation Specialist / DETECTIVE HAYES

WOMAN (20's) JULIA MARTIN, a graduate student from Stanford doing her thesis on V. Nabokov while tracing his 1941 roadtrip from NY to Palo Alto

TEENAGER (17–but can look a little older) DANNY "JACKSON" a teenager that Julia picks up in NY and gives him a ride to California / DMITRI NABOKOV, son of Vladimir and Vera

BACKGROUND

The famous novelist Vladimir Nabokov was also a well-known lepidopterist and a noted authority on "American Blue" butterflies. After fleeing occupied Europe and escaping to America, Nabokov, his wife and their son were driven in a brand new Pontiac from New York to California by Dorothy Leuthold, a young woman he had met through the New York Public Library. Stopping at the Grand Canyon on their way out to Stanford, where he was to teach Russian Literature, he discovered, described and named previously unknown types of butterflies: Cyllópsis pertepída dorothéa (which he named for Dorothy) its holotype is located at the California Academy of Sciences in San Francisco.

BUTTERFLY FUGUE

The four actors playing: JULIA, DANNY, PROF. DRAKE and MRS. DRAKE appear. There is a projection of a net across their bodies. They speak from behind a gauze-like curtain or scrim.

PROF. DRAKE Butterflies—

MRS. DRAKE Must have—

DANNY Four wings—

JULIA For flight—

PROF. DRAKE Butterflies.

MRS. DRAKE Butterflies.

DANNY Butterflies.

JULIA Butterflies.

DANNY Must have—

JULIA Two sets of wings—

PROF. DRAKE They need both—

MRS. DRAKE To fly.

DANNY One before—

JULIA One behind.

ALL To escape the mud.

> *Blackout.*

JULIA'S STORY 1

> *JULIA begins to tell a story as one might tell a bedtime story to a child.*

JULIA What if I told you a story? "Once upon a time, there was a little girl... who loved to tell stories and to listen to stories. She knew a man who was a friend of the family and a teacher at the nearby college. When he came to visit us he would say, "Come sit on my lap and I'll tell you a story." So the little girl would do as she was told. And he would begin, "Once upon a time," he'd say, "There was a beautiful little girl. Not as beautiful as you are, my dear. Just pretty enough to be a princess. Whereas you are as gorgeous as a queen." She liked that someone who used words like "whereas" thought that she was attractive enough to become a Queen.

> *Cross fade.*

DRAKE'S LOLITA LECTURE: SEX AND DEATH

> *PROF. DRAKE. Stands at the podium delivering his lecture from notes on 3x5 cards.*

PROF. DRAKE All right, all right. Hello? Eyes up here people. (*Shouting.*) Sex and death! Do I have your attention now? How inexpressibly wondrous a thing it is to be heard by one's very own bright eyed undergraduates. Greetings, I'm Professor Drake. For those of you new here... Welcome to the University. You made it. Now get over yourselves. I'd like to make one thing abundantly clear. We're all adults here. My courses start on time and I would appreciate it if you respected us both enough to be here in your seats and ready to participate accordingly. Thank you ever so much. Now, where are my assistants? Hiding? There you are. Excellent. This is Jeff and this is Mutt. Matt, sorry. If you have any questions, ask them. Well, take good notes, you'll need to know this for your study groups and for the poor schmucks who miss the lecture. That clock is slow by the way, just so you know. For those of you taking me for the first time... that didn't sound right did it? "What did he say?" Please note I do have posted office hours... although I'm never there, if I can help it. Nothing personal. All grad students report to the assistants for assignments and before any of you ask... No, I will not be your thesis advisor. Enough stalling. Let's talk about sex and death.

Cross fade.

NEW YORK PUBLIC LIBRARY

JULIA is wearing a white dress, a pair of white gloves and carrying a huge stack of old books. She stops and stares into the distance as if she has seen a ghost. She lets the books fall to the floor. She stands in a trance.

JULIA Drake?

She catches herself staring at nothing and snaps out of it. She begins picking up the books that have fallen to the floor. DANNY appears and begins helping her retrieve them.

JULIA Thank you... for helping me with my books, uh—?

DANNY Danny. Of course, I'm happy to.

JULIA (*Laughs.*) I can't believe I just said that, I sounded like a schoolgirl.

DANNY You are, aren't you? I like your glasses... um?

JULIA Julia. You're cute. Shouldn't you be in class somewhere?

DANNY I don't do that anymore.

JULIA Really?

DANNY I'm eighteen, it's time to live!

JULIA In a library?

DANNY I've spent more time here since I got out of school—

JULIA Graduated?

DANNY G.E.D.! What's with the gloves... practicing to be a mime?

JULIA No! My mother always told me that "Mime, does not pay."

DANNY That's bad—I like it. Sad going through life, not feeling—

JULIA They're to protect the books from my hands.

DANNY Right, because of the oil, I get it.

JULIA And the acids. They're very fragile.

DANNY Is that why you threw them all over the library?

JULIA They slipped—

DANNY (*Handing her back a book, he reads the cover.*) Who is Maria Sibylla Merian?

JULIA An extraordinary woman from the sixteen hundreds. An illustrator, painter and a scientist who studied the transformation and metamorphoses of the... I'm sorry, I just go right into that mode...

DANNY It's cool, I asked. Best way to learn, right?

JULIA Sometimes... or by doing... something for yourself.

DANNY Who's "Drake?"

JULIA What?

DANNY I thought that's who you called out to... before you dropped—

JULIA Oh? No... that's just an Old English word... for dragon.

DANNY That's cool.

JULIA No, it's stupid, I just thought I saw—

DANNY A ghost?

JULIA Yeah! "Who ya gonna call?"

DANNY Huh?

JULIA "Ghost-Bust-Ers?"

DANNY Oh, I don't watch old movies, sorry.

JULIA Thanks, Danny? I'm fine now. I have to go return these.

DANNY I overheard you talking to that research librarian—

JULIA Are you... stalking me?

DANNY Please, who has that kind of time? I was just behind you in line.

JULIA Too bad, it would have been a nice change from my regular guys. Fat, bald and clingy.

DANNY You're driving to California?

JULIA You have very good hearing—

DANNY And eyesight, also good hygiene and enough gas money to make it all the way to Los Angeles. But I don't have a car. And since you're going my way, I was wondering if you'd give me a lift?

JULIA I'm not going to... L.A. I'm going to Palo Alto.

DANNY Close enough. I'll pay for gas and half of our expenses. I never snore, I don't talk too much and I won't sing "bottles of beer on the wall" because I also don't drink. Here's my I.D.

He hands her his Student I.D.

JULIA "Sacred Heart?"

Handing it back.

DANNY Our lady of perpetual heartburn.

JULIA That's nice but—

DANNY I could help drive, unless it's a stick. Here's my licence (*He flashes it.*) Ew, bad hair day. I have references and people you can call that can vouch for me. I was a good boy-scout, until I discovered girls.

JULIA That happens—

DANNY I don't have a police record and I always say no to drugs, when asked. But most importantly of all, I need to leave New York before Monday.

JULIA Monday... because?

DANNY I hate Mondays!

JULIA Me too. But I have to make a lot of stops along the way—

DANNY That's cool, I don't have to be there until the end of the month.

JULIA For?

DANNY A reality TV show audition. Well... what do you say?

JULIA Where's the camera?

DANNY I know you don't know me but I really mean it.

JULIA You're cute but this is entrapment.

DANNY Please, take me with you.

JULIA Seriously?

DANNY I can at least help carry your books...

Picking them up.

JULIA (*She smiles.*) You don't smoke, do you?

DANNY Only after, ya know...

He smiles.

JULIA (*She studies him.*) That would be a "no" then?

DANNY Right. No… smoking.

JULIA When can you leave?

DANNY Before you can say—

JULIA Don't you need to pack?

DANNY (*Pats his backpack.*) Say that! I've got mine right here.

JULIA (*Pointing to a book.*) All right. Don't forget that one…

DANNY Lolita?

JULIA That's mine. She's coming with us.

> *Cross fade.*

MRS. DRAKE IN BED

> *MRS. DRAKE lies in a hospital bed in her own house. She is propped up with pillows. Over her is a thick green comforter and a hand sewn quilt, both of which are wrapped around her and tucked beneath her as if she were in a cocoon. On a side table is a small bell which has fallen over. She is trying to reach it but can't quite make it.*

MRS. DRAKE Honey? Are you there? I can't reach the bell. Can you hear me? (*Pause.*) Paul? Please, can you come in here? It's Carla's night off. I need you to change my… Paul, I need you! (*Pause.*) I'm on fire! (*Pause.*) Won't you come anymore when I call? There was a time when you wouldn't leave my side. Now… Honey, please? No?

> *She makes a longer reach for the bell, misses it.*

Can't you ever stop writing? I'll be gone soon enough and then you can stay in your den forever and never come out.

> *She grabs the bell.*

There.

> *She rings it vigorously with both hands. The small bell makes a loud tolling sound as of a cathedral bell. PROF. DRAKE enters the room.*

MRS. DRAKE It's just you and me tonight remember?

PROF. DRAKE Yes, of course. Is it that time already?

MRS. DRAKE It's past time, it's been four hours. Where were you?

PROF. DRAKE I was just working on the last chapter—

MRS. DRAKE Is it finished?

PROF. DRAKE Not yet… soon.

MRS. DRAKE And then you'll read it to me?

PROF. DRAKE Patience. Yes, I promise.

Cross fade.

DANNY'S STORY 1

DANNY tells his story in a bright light directly out to the audience.

DANNY I grew up in California. But my parents were from New York. They're dead. Car accident when I was two. I never knew them. I just came back to Manhattan to trace my roots. Never been here before. I did the usual things. I saw the Statue of Liberty, she's shorter than I imagined. Stayed at the Y, went to a Yankees game, got spit on, got lost on the subway, ended up in the financial district and blew stock brokers in bathroom stalls for cash. Same old, same old. So that's me, foot loose and fancy free on my way back to the west coast and my home by the sea.

Cross fade.

MAY 26: GETTYSBURG, PENNSYLVANIA, MOTOR COURT LEE-MEAD GETTYSBURG MOTEL

JULIA and DANNY sit in the Pontiac.

JULIA We're here.

DANNY This… is it?

JULIA Definitely.

DANNY How can you tell?

JULIA According to the GPS—

DANNY Uh, huh—what's the address?

JULIA There is no address. But that sign over there says "Gettysburg!"

DANNY Address?!? (*Laughing.*)

JULIA What's so funny?

DANNY Gettysburg… Address.

Laughs louder.

Nevermind.

JULIA Are you… on something?

DANNY I'm sorry. I'm really tired. No sleep and low blood sugar… makes me loopy. I need to lie down.

JULIA Right… well. I'm going to go see if that Motel might have been the "Motor Court" they stayed in… and you…

DANNY Can carry your luggage?

JULIA Can get your own room.

DANNY Did I mention that I have "gas money" not "lodging money?"

JULIA Or… you can sleep in the car.

DANNY So… that's how it is, huh?

JULIA Exactly.

DANNY You're just gonna leave me out here?

JULIA If you don't like it… you can hitch another lift.

DANNY But… I thought we were, you know—

JULIA No.

DANNY Oh?

> *Grins at her.*

JULIA Not a chance.

DANNY What's up?

JULIA I called your references… a pet store, a movie theatre and a mortuary? Former employers?

DANNY Guess which job was the most fun?

JULIA None of them knew who you were—

DANNY I'm shocked… I didn't think I was that forgettable—

JULIA I've taught much better liars than you… try again.

DANNY I didn't think you'd call. I don't have anyone, all right?

JULIA It's all right with me… just don't bullshit me again.

DANNY Deal. It's kinda cold out here…

JULIA There's a sleeping bag in back seat.

DANNY Thanks?

JULIA It's really warm.

DANNY It'd be even warmer with two…

JULIA I'm going now—

DANNY Can I use the heater?

JULIA Sorry, I don't think so—

DANNY I wouldn't run the battery down too much—

JULIA The car keys are coming with me.

DANNY I'm not gonna steal your car, I can't drive a stick!

JULIA Let's just say... I have trust issues.

DANNY I see... well, you wanna... *(Moves closer.)* talk about that?

JULIA I don't really know you—

DANNY Well, then come over here and I'll tell you all about me—

JULIA *(She laughs.)* You know... I'm old enough to be your—

DANNY Teacher?

JULIA Goodnight, Danny.

DANNY Aw, come on... I was only—

JULIA Sweet dreams.

> *She exits.*

See you in the morning.

> *She exits the car and enters the motel. The night clerk is played by the same actress as MRS. DRAKE.*

JULIA I know it's late, but your sign said "vacancy" and I'd like to get a room for the night.

NIGHT CLERK Uh huh. Sure is late. Yer lucky the office is still open. Just one... Mrs?

JULIA "Miss." Martin. Yes. A single room.

NIGHT CLERK Uh huh. I thought I heard ya talkin' to someone outside.

JULIA No, just me.

NIGHT CLERK Only... one night?

JULIA Yes... indeed. I was wondering did this... hotel... used to be known as the "Lee-Meade Motor Court?"

NIGHT CLERK Well I wouldn't know 'bout that. I'm not really the night clerk. I'm just filling in for Pauline. She's got the cancer. Doin' the Chemo. Can't keep nothin' down, poor thing. As bald as a plucked chicken. Bless her soul.

JULIA Would this establishment have been open, in say... 1941?

NIGHT CLERK Well honey, I really don't know but I don't think so. The owner bought this place back in '76 and it were practically new. Why? You some kinda journalist?

JULIA I'm doing some research on Vladimir Nabokov for my dissertation… he stayed somewhere around here once. I thought that—

NIGHT CLERK You mean that fella who wrote that (*hushed voice*) "Lolita" book?

JULIA Yes, the same. Have you read it?

NIGHT CLERK It was banned.

JULIA What was "bad" about it?

NIGHT CLERK No, BANNED. It was a dirty book, wasn't it?

JULIA Oh? Well, not really but I can see what you—

NIGHT CLERK Yer writing 'bout that pervert, for school?

JULIA Yes, you see my premise asserts that his wife actually—

NIGHT CLERK I don't need to read smut to know what it's all 'bout. The "good book"'s all I need. You familiar with the gospels, dear?

JULIA I read it cover to cover when I was twelve. The Old Testament with all the begatting at the beginning was a bit rough to get through but by the end of the New one, it mellowed out. The ending was a little over the top though. All that blood.

NIGHT CLERK Ah honey, I am so sorry but we don't have a room to spare. I was lookin' at the wrong day. We're booked solid. There's a "War between the states" reenactment convention comin' in to town this weekend and we're just packed.

JULIA But your sign says…

NIGHT CLERK (*She flips a switch and a large neon "NO" can be seen through the window.*) Sorry. I know you're a workin' girl just tryin' to get by. But why don't you and whoever you got hidin' in the car go down Race Horse Alley and follow the train tracks to the sleazy 8. They're always open. Ask for their special hourly rate.

> Cross fade to the car. There is the sound of wind. There is the sound of knocking. Three loud raps on the window. DANNY sits up, half awake. He is zipped inside the sleeping bag. He stares out the windshield. He mutters to himself.

DANNY Blue? (*He rubs the sleep out of his eyes.*) Cops? (*He wipes the windshield to see through it.*) Just a second! (*He rolls down the window.*) Hello officer, I was just sleeping… long day on the road… (*He stares at the figure that has stepped into the light.*)

UNION OFFICER (*Played by the same actor as PROF. DRAKE.*) Indeed. The road is long and it has no end.

DANNY Hey, you're not a cop. What's with the outfit?

UNION OFFICER 2nd Cavalry Division, Army of the Potomac.

DANNY Right… you lookin' for somethin'?

UNION OFFICER My little girl.

DANNY Excuse me?

UNION OFFICER Last I can recollect, I had just raised my saber to signal the charge and my men all followed me across the field. The shells were exploding all around us but I could see the fear in the gunner's eyes as we came down the slope upon them. The Rebs shot my mount right out from under me and down I fell. When I woke, I was pinned under my horse. There was nothing but the sound of dying men all around me and the calls of the crows. I heard the enemy sound a retreat in the distance… but I could not move. There was blood in my eyes and then the darkness came. Now I have done my duty, for God and country. I seek only for my girl. My "J" bird.

DANNY Dude, you're good. You should be on the History Channel—

The UNION OFFICER disappears as JULIA enters and climbs into the driver's seat.

DANNY It's not morning already is it?

JULIA Change of plans, no room at the inn.

DANNY Hey, did you meet the General? (*Looking back out the window.*) Sorry, I didn't get your rank, what are you?

JULIA Who are you talking to?

DANNY The guy in the Civil War costume? Weird, you didn't see him?

JULIA No… What did his face look like?

DANNY I don't know, middle-aged guy. I thought he was a cop at first.

JULIA Were his eyes… blue? (*She is shaken.*)

DANNY Hard to tell in that get up.

JULIA What did he say?

DANNY He launched into some Ken Burns-y spiel about the war, got all spooky and said he was looking for a little girl called "J"?

JULIA Drake! (*Turns the key in the ignition.*) Hold on to something!

Blackout. The sound of the car peeling out is heard.

LIFESTYLE OF A BUTTERFLY: INTRO

NABOKOV is standing with his back to the audience in front of a huge chalkboard. He writes the word "cycle" on the board. He adds the word "uni-" in front of "cycle." He pauses, erases it and replaces "uni" with "bi-". He pauses. He chuckles and then erases "bi-" and replaces it with "tri-". He quickly erases "tri-" and replaces it with "quad-". He quickly erases "quad-" and writes "lepi-"then he erases that and writes "life-" he stares at the word "life-cycle" and then writes next to that "of a lepidoptera." He chuckles to himself and replaces the word "cycle" with "style." He then quickly draws freehand the outline of a butterfly's four wings. He turns around and 'notices' his audience. It looks as if the wings behind him are his.

NABOKOV Good evening and welcome. My name is Vladimir Nabokov. Don't bother trying to pronounce my last name correctly, just call me Vladimir. For those of you here to hear me speak of my books, I fear that you will be disappointed. Pardon me, I feel that they speak for themselves and I do not wish to contradict them. For those of you seeking advice on writing, I want you to simply know that I was once like you, out there in the dark, listening to someone like me. It was not until I went out there and listened to what was in here (*Touches his heart.*) that I became a writer. No. No words about my words tonight. I want to speak to you about my true passion, one that has gripped me since I was a boy. The cause I would pursue, were it financially possible and climatically practical, everyday for the rest of my life. Yes, I am speaking of butterflies.

Cross fade.

QUILT FUGUE 1: JULIA/DANNY/MRS.DRAKE/PROF. DRAKE

JULIA begins to tell a story as one might tell a bedtime story. MRS. DRAKE speaks as if to herself, wearing a brightly colored quilt. DANNY tells his story in a bright light directly out to the audience. PROF. DRAKE stands at the podium delivering his lecture from notes on 3x5 cards. The four characters speak their monologues directly out to the audience. The pace should feel quick, with lines dovetailing one after the next. The effect should feel like a quartet of musicians each playing their own notes but aware that they are part of a group.

JULIA Later, when the girl was old enough, she began to baby-sit for the man, who had to attend many functions at the university with his wife. So she would look after his young boy who was very well behaved, for a nine year old.

DANNY I got named "Danny" not after "Daniel" but after a bug: Nymphalidae, Danainae, Danaus, Plexippus.

MRS. DRAKE A slender thread. A tenuous grasp. One strand severed and I'm free.

PROF. DRAKE Please, and I can't stress this enough… Don't ask me to autograph anything, especially a copy of my book, *The Chrysalis.*

JULIA When the man would return, but before she would get on her bicycle to peddle the six blocks to her house, he would ask her to read to him.

DANNY Can you believe it? They named me after an insect?

MRS. DRAKE But not yet. Can't move. Tied down. Trapped under the weight of this quilt I've created.

PROF. DRAKE I used to do that… until I found some for sale online. I wouldn't have minded so much, except that the inscriptions on three of them all read "to my favorite student."

JULIA He said it soothed his nerves to have someone else read to him besides his wife, who was upstairs reading stories to their son.

DANNY Apparently they were living in the East Village.

MRS. DRAKE Hand sewn. Each stitch. The imperfections visible to the naked eye.

PROF. DRAKE Things like that tend to bring down the value of the object on auction, not to mention my artistic integrity. Which I'm thinking of having surgically removed. I hear it's covered by my insurance under elective surgery like moles, warts and polyps.

JULIA But then came a time when the man's wife wasn't there very much and he needed her to baby-sit more often.

DANNY My real mother was a second generation flower child and my father was studying to be some kind of biologist.

MRS. DRAKE A labor of love. The last act of a desperate woman.

PROF. DRAKE Where was I? Oh, that's right, murder and pedophilia in the Eisenhower era? Correct!

JULIA The man had her read longer and longer books to him.

DANNY They must have seen it as a compromise.

MRS. DRAKE Before my fingers became useless because of the trembling and the pain.

PROF. DRAKE A novel by one of the greatest writers ever to have worked in the English language.

JULIA Until one day she began reading a curious book to him.

DANNY Our son, the butterfly.

MRS. DRAKE Before my mind wandered out of the present and into the past.

PROF. DRAKE A brilliant Russian exile who fled the communists, lived in Germany, until he fled the Nazis and eventually came here.

JULIA It had a little girl's name on the cover. She was called, Lolita.

PROF. DRAKE *Lolita*… which you've all read by now yes? Don't look at me like that. It was on the syllabus.

Cross fade.

MAY 27: LURAY, VIRGINIA, PARKHURST INN & COTTAGES

JULIA and DANNY are parked.

DANNY Yes Virginia, there is a small cottage called Parkhurst!

JULIA This should be the place. I think. It kinda looks like it.

DANNY Great. I'm hungry. Now if you don't mind I'd like to get out and stretch my legs, get some air, maybe go water the bushes—

JULIA I'm sorry about that back there… I just got a little um…

DANNY No, you got a lot… um! I really appreciate the lift but—

JULIA Where are you going?

DANNY To California… but I want to get back there alive—

JULIA I mean right now…

DANNY Just for a walk—

JULIA With your bag?

DANNY It's been fun and you seem like a nice lady but—

JULIA Don't call me that!

DANNY Nice?

JULIA That four letter "L" word should be banned. I'm fine with like, love and lust… but call me that again and…

DANNY You okay with "Lesbo?"

JULIA That's five. What makes you think I'm—

DANNY My mistake.

JULIA Just because I'm not interested in you that way—

DANNY Listen I didn't—

JULIA You're way too young—

DANNY I'm gonna go now.

JULIA What, you're going to hitchhike?

DANNY That or maybe catch a bus?

JULIA Really?

DANNY Or a train...

JULIA I'm sorry I scared you...

DANNY I'm not scared of you... you're just a little intense—

JULIA Yeah, I get that way sometimes. I just thought... but it couldn't be him.

DANNY Who's this guy you're running from? An ex?

JULIA A dragon. Look. Let me make it up to you. I'll pay for a room for you for the night. You can decide if you want to come with me in the morning. If not, I'll drive you to a station.

DANNY Where are you gonna sleep?

JULIA In my own room.

DANNY I wouldn't want you to be tempted to take advantage of me—

JULIA I just want to stare at the inside of my eyelids for a good eight hours.

DANNY Cool. They look like they have a couple of vacancies—

JULIA Hey, thanks for coming with me this far... I just didn't want to be alone, you know what I mean?

DANNY I feel you. You mind if I borrow some reading material?

JULIA Aren't you tired?

DANNY Insomnia. But words put me to sleep.

JULIA Here... sleep through this (*hands him* Lolita).

    Cross fade.

LIFESTYLE OF A BUTTERFLY: EGG

NABOKOV appears. A slide is projected on the chalkboard behind him, a photograph of a green monarch butterfly egg on a large green leaf.

NABOKOV Which came first the butterfly or the egg? Well, let's say eggs for now. Butterfly eggs come in all shapes and sizes. From the most ornate, bejeweled intricate constructions to the most bland little brown splotches of goo. If you've spent anytime outdoors in butterfly country, you have seen them. They are generally camouflaged to blend in with the particular plant that the young will inhabit. After a short amount of time the newborn will emerge from it's shell, eating it's way out and then eating everything else in sight.

Cross fade.

QUILT FUGUE 2: JULIA/DANNY/MRS DRAKE/PROF. DRAKE

MRS. DRAKE No grand plan. No blueprint to follow. All of it pieced together.

JULIA There were nights when she would bring her bathing suit and she would go swimming in the man's pool while he was away.

DANNY I was adopted when I was three and my "new parents" moved us to L.A. That's where I spent the quality years of my youth. Smog-bound in Santa Monica.

PROF. DRAKE *Lolita*? All right, so it was a fiction but was it entirely fictional? It was based on some facts.

MRS. DRAKE A piece here, a scrap there. Using all my old fabric.

JULIA One night the man came home early and caught her in the hot tub. But rather than tell her to get out… he just laughed and said "that's a good idea."

DANNY I didn't know any of this until I found out right around the holidays.

PROF. DRAKE For example, the Sally Horner case, 1950. The eleven year old girl who was kidnapped in New Jersey and driven all over the U.S. by a man who had witnessed her steal a five cent notebook from a drugstore on a bet.

MRS. DRAKE All my old abandoned sewing projects incorporated into this.

JULIA The man got into the hot tub, too. But he didn't wear a bathing suit.

DANNY I was going through some papers that the creep, I called "Daddy," kept in a locked part of his desk. I wasn't going to steal anything.

PROF. DRAKE The man who took her, threatened her—but not in the way you might think. He told the girl that he would turn her over to the police if she didn't get in his car.

MRS. DRAKE A swatch from the bolt you bought me in Florence.

JULIA His wife was still away but he would not say where. He said that since it was his house, he got to make the rules and that as far as he was concerned, clothing was optional.

DANNY He'd caught me smoking weed in the garage, after he beat the shit out of me, he confiscated my stash.

PROF. DRAKE So she went with him. And they drove and they drove and they kept driving. It wasn't until two years later when they were stopped by a traffic cop just half an hour from here in San Jose that the ride ended.

MRS. DRAKE The cornflower blue from the dress that I wore when we first danced through the night.

JULIA He liked to go "skinny dipping" in his own pool and he hoped that the girl didn't mind. She said that she didn't.

DANNY I heard him pretending to flush it down the john.

PROF. DRAKE His story didn't check out and the authorities arrested, tried and convicted the sexual predator. This pervert who had kept little Sally a prisoner during their long road trip said he loved her.

MRS. DRAKE That white taffeta ribbon from my wedding gown.

JULIA She used to swim nude at camp when there was no one around.

DANNY The bastard threatened to turn me in for possession and I said if he did, I'd tell child protective services everything.

PROF. DRAKE When asked why she didn't run away or call for help… and there had been several opportunities for her to do so. Sally said she was "afraid that she would get into trouble…" because of the notebook.

MRS. DRAKE That ragged pale blue, a torn patch from our boy's blanket before he got sick…

JULIA It made her tingle all over as if she were on fire.

DANNY But I knew he'd hidden it away somewhere.

PROF. DRAKE Can you believe that? In order to avoid a misdemeanor for shoplifting, she endured unimaginable torments at the hands of this psycho.

MRS. DRAKE The green there, the color of your eyes, to gaze at me when you are gone. Like now. Like always.

PROF. DRAKE True story. That was one of the models for Nabokov's book. Truth is often sicker than fiction, just read the newspapers... preferably, before they all go out of business.

Cross fade.

MAY 28: BRISTOL, VIRGINIA, MOTEL GENERAL SHELBY

JULIA and DANNY stand in a cavern in near darkness. There is the sound of dripping water.

DANNY Sweet. You were right. This is a really big cave.

JULIA These caverns go for miles.

DANNY So besides holes in the ground what's this place got?

JULIA It's the birthplace of country music.

DANNY That would explain the fashions and giant guitar we passed—

JULIA That's a radio station—

DANNY I thought I was hallucinating.

JULIA Just look at those stalactites and stalagmites.

DANNY What's the difference?

JULIA One goes up and one goes down. I don't know which is which.

TOUR GUIDE *(Played by same actress as Mrs. Drake.)* Good question. The answer is, the one with a "c" is on the ceiling and the one on the ground is spelled with a "g". The Stalactites's are the result of millions of years of water dripping down from the vaulted roof of this cathedral of stone and depositing minute amounts of limestone, slowly descending to the chamber's floor below. Each drop that falls, adding to the growing stalagmite rising to meet it. This process can take millions of years but eventually they will come together and become one calcified whole. A column of stone that has stood erect since before the pyramids were built. Impressive isn't it? Are you on vacation with your... family?

JULIA *(Laughs.)* What? Oh, sure. Just passing through.

TOUR GUIDE Well, don't forget to stop at the gift shop. We've got a wonderful selection of dinosaur toys and some lovely fossil earrings.

Exits.

JULIA Yeah, thanks for the perspective.

DANNY They look like teeth.

JULIA You look like death…

DANNY Thanks, Mom!

JULIA What made you change your mind and come with me?

DANNY Your sparkling personality, good looks… and a free ride.

JULIA I have that effect on zombies.

DANNY I didn't sleep.

JULIA Oh, I'm sorry—

DANNY You should be. Your choice of literary sedatives is to blame—

JULIA How far did you get?

DANNY I finished it just before you knocked on my door—

JULIA What'd you think?

DANNY It's pretty messed up, you know? Why, do you like it?

JULIA Well, I'm writing about its creation—

DANNY You're writing about a guy who wrote a book about a guy who wrote a confession about a little girl he had sex with?

JULIA That's why I'm traveling. I'm doing some more research for my dissertation.

DANNY Following the route of the characters in the book?

JULIA No, although I thought of that. I'm actually just retracing Nabokov's first trip out to California. He, his wife and son were driven by this woman that he met…

DANNY At the New York public library—

JULIA You have been listening to me—

DANNY Only to the good bits—

JULIA They made stops along the way and I'm interested in seeing—

DANNY That's what all those red crosses on the map are for?

JULIA Bingo!

DANNY Yea, I guessed right! What do I win?

JULIA Well, what do you want?

DANNY Can't you guess?

JULIA Danny!—

DANNY Swing and a miss—

JULIA You'll have to do better than that—

DANNY Well according to the signs we could stick around and take in the "DukeFest." Are you a fan of the Hazzard boys and their rebellious doin's?

JULIA No, I never watched the TV show.

DANNY TV show?

JULIA Uh… did they make a movie?

DANNY To you popular culture in this century is just something that happens to other people, isn't it?

JULIA I'm not going on a movie date with you—

DANNY How do you feel about Nascar?

Cross fade. There is the sound of a loud engine and the twangy guitar of a country tune.

LIFESTYLE OF A BUTTERFLY: CATERPILLAR

NABOKOV is standing in the middle of a projected photograph of: a monarch caterpillar eating a large leaf.

NABOKOV After emerging from their egg, the caterpillar is on a mission to consume several times its weight in a matter of weeks. This handsome fellow will become a monarch in time. A prince in potentia. They eat the toxic milkweed, which helps them build up a poisonous taste as an adult and discourages predators from thinning their populations. But they are very vulnerable. Poor vision, a thin skin, through which they breath and jaws that are not much good as a defence. They are simply eating machines. They must store up as much mass as possible to be able to accomplish the startling transformation which lies ahead.

Cross fade.

QUILT FUGUE 3: JULIA/DANNY/MRS DRAKE/PROF. DRAKE

MRS. DRAKE sighs and speaks as if to herself, pushing the plunger on a morphine drip.

MRS. DRAKE The patches, the pieces. All part of a whole. Wrapped around me. For comfort from the cold. But those red stripes. I never did like those. They remind me of barber poles and hair that won't grow back. Of candy canes and Christmases that won't come again. Too late now to pull them off and start over.

JULIA The man even got her to shed her own inhibitions and swim in the nude, when he wasn't looking.

DANNY "Daddy" locked me in my room for a couple of days until my step-mom let me out while he was passed out drunk.

PROF. DRAKE Speaking of psychos, there was the case of Edward Grammar who killed his wife Dorothy planted her body in the car and almost got away with it.

MRS. DRAKE Those blue birds though. Where did they come from? Damn these meds. They mute even my thoughts.

JULIA "Naked as a Jay bird." As he used to say.

DANNY His first wife left him for a lawyer when he started drinking too much.

PROF. DRAKE Writers steal and this author was an exceptional magpie with an eye for shiny objects.

MRS. DRAKE Their pattern is familiar, like the jays that used to visit us in the spring.

JULIA She would swim around and around and then ask him to close his eyes when she got out and then she would drop her towel and join him in the hot tub where the bubbles would create a foam so thick that nothing could be seen.

DANNY He said he was a consultant, but I never knew what, if anything, he was supposed to be an expert about. He only taught me about pain.

PROF. DRAKE We all know how the book was received here in the U.S. It was called filth. It was claimed to be a complete fiction. But you may not know that Nabokov wrote a previous version, in Russian, entitled "the Enchanter."

MRS. DRAKE Where did you come from little ones? Yes, I got those from the shop in the village with the calico cat in the window.

JULIA And they would sit there in the steaming water and listen to jazz playing on his big stereo system with speakers the size of the slabs of Stonehenge.

DANNY His new wife wasn't too bad, at least she had a heart. But she was only nine years older than me and didn't want a teenaged son, not one that wasn't hers.

PROF. DRAKE He personally knew men who were "nympholeptics." However, his own personal leanings do not point toward him being a sexual predator… but suspicion was cast upon him.

MRS. DRAKE There's that small patch of grey, so out of place in my colorful quilt. That was from… mother's old house coat… faded and worn. Her uniform. No. Not today. Not now.

JULIA And the man would tell the girl of the world. The big wide world and all of the places that he had visited in his travels to foreign lands.

DANNY She saw the bruises and finally broke down and told me everything. I didn't believe her, at first.

PROF. DRAKE Because those who lack imagination cannot possibly understand those who can imagine the unthinkable. Deflowering a twelve year old girl! There. I said it. Are you awake now?

MRS. DRAKE Where is the gold from the curtains in our old house? So sparkle-y so shimmery, hidden under a fold? No doubt.

JULIA He told her stories about his life before he came to teach story writing or whatever it was called, and where he might take her someday... if she was good.

DANNY Then I found the paper trail in his desk. He never threw anything away.

PROF. DRAKE Yes, she wasn't a teenager as the movie suggests. She was a child. But little Dolores Hayes wasn't a virgin when Humbert absconded with her.

MRS. DRAKE There's that dark patch. Where did that come from... oh yes, from the mourning dress I wore after our son... So black, like a hole... that's getting bigger... and bigger... so deep... to swallow me up. No!

PROF. DRAKE He says that she seduced him. And he was right. Disturbed? Good. Let's talk about this.

Cross fade.

MAY 29: THE SMOKY MOUNTAINS AND BELVA, TENNESSEE, MAPLE SHADE COTTAGES

JULIA and DANNY are sitting on the ground with a "take-away" picnic lunch between them. They are eating ribs and gazing off into the distance.

JULIA So that's why they're called the "Smoky Mountains?"

DANNY I guess Misty Mountains sounded too Middle Earthy?

JULIA I loved those—

DANNY Movies? Me too!

JULIA Books... I read them all when I was... your age.

DANNY That long ago?

JULIA Nice day for a picnic, huh?

DANNY Thanks for treating.

JULIA Ned's carry out.

DANNY Best reason to visit... um... where are we?

JULIA Belva. It was named after Belva Lockwood, suffragette and the first woman to run for president of the United States. Twice.

DANNY I take it she didn't win... or she'd be on the money.

JULIA She was for Equality and World Peace in the eighteen eighties.

DANNY How'd that work out for her?

JULIA A strong woman in a weak-minded world?

DANNY That well huh?

JULIA She was before her time—

DANNY A nice way of saying the world wasn't ready for her, huh?

JULIA Would you vote for a woman for president?

DANNY That would depend... on the woman.

JULIA And the party?

DANNY Who the woman in my life was voting for...

JULIA Oh, really?

DANNY Yeah, I wouldn't want to cancel out her vote.

JULIA That's considerate... are you snowing me?

DANNY No, I figure a woman in the White House would be a nice change.

JULIA But only if she wasn't a complete and total—

DANNY Exactly. This has got to be the best picnic I've ever had.

JULIA You don't get out into nature much, do you?

DANNY I'm a city boy. Great ribs—

JULIA You've got some sauce on your... well, all over actually.

DANNY How's this?

> *He sticks his tongue out all around his mouth.*

JULIA Baby wipes?

DANNY Do they really use those on babies? Or is it like "doggy bag?"

JULIA Do you want some?

DANNY Babies?

JULIA Wipes.

DANNY Oh, yes. Thanks. Do you… want babies?

JULIA Do I want to further populate an overpopulated planet?

DANNY Put that way—

JULIA Depends on the man.

DANNY Really?

JULIA And his genes—

DANNY You've got a thing for guys in denim?

JULIA Genetics… ya know, if I want to help him… pass them on.

DANNY I knew it, you're a hopeless romantic!

JULIA C'mon. We've got miles to go…

DANNY Before we sleep?

JULIA You do read?

DANNY Surprised?

JULIA We'll hit someplace cheap, you can pay for your room this time.

DANNY One room's fine…

JULIA Now listen I told you—

DANNY I don't need one… I like the back seat, it's comfy.

JULIA You can use my shower… in the morning, before I check out.

DANNY Thanks… for keeping me clean.

> *Cross fade.*

CAKE WITH PAUL AND MARY DRAKE

MRS. DRAKE lies in a hospital bed in her own house. She is propped up with pillows. Over her is a thick green comforter and a hand sewn quilt, both of which are wrapped around her and tucked beneath her as if she was in a cocoon.

MRS. DRAKE Paul? Are you there? I smell smoke. Something's burning!

> *PROF. DRAKE enters through the door, he is carrying a pink birthday cake with a lot of candles burning on top.*

PROF. DRAKE Where's the birthday girl? There she is!

MRS. DRAKE You remembered?

PROF. DRAKE Was there any doubt?

MRS. DRAKE Always… but it vanishes when you are near, my love.

PROF. DRAKE Quick, blow out the candle before it melts.

She blows them out.

PROF. DRAKE Did you make a wish?

MRS. DRAKE Everyday.

PROF. DRAKE Here, I'll cut you a piece.

MRS. DRAKE I thought you were burning the house down.

PROF. DRAKE I almost did. This is my second attempt at "cakery."

MRS. DRAKE What happened to the first?

PROF. DRAKE Charcoal. But that was from a box… this is—

MRS. DRAKE From scratch?

PROF. DRAKE Would you believe me if I told you…

MRS. DRAKE Yes, always—

PROF. DRAKE This is from that little bakery you loved so much.

MRS. DRAKE Loved?

PROF. DRAKE What?

MRS. DRAKE Past tense, loved. I'm still capable of loving… cake!

PROF. DRAKE Oh, honey. I only meant… that you used to. When we would… Here, have some, it's your favorite, I think—

He gives her a forkful. She eats it.

MRS. DRAKE Mmmmmmm. I am going to miss this…

PROF. DRAKE Shhhhh, not now. Have your cake—

MRS. DRAKE And eat it too? (*She laughs*). I'm sorry, I just—

PROF. DRAKE I know. Me too.

Cross fade.

MAY 30: CROSSVILLE, TENNESSEE, CUMBERLAND MOTOR COURT

DANNY and JULIA have parked and they are standing outside the car staring across the road at something.

DANNY Crossville courthouse? What's with the statue garden over there?

JULIA This is what happens when free speech turns into sculpture.

DANNY I get it, someone must have put up a nativity and then…

JULIA There's a cross and there's all the other faiths—what's that?

DANNY The Flying Spaghetti Monster. He's new.

JULIA Are those giant… meatballs?

DANNY Don't make fun of the pasta-farians.

JULIA Where's blind justice and her scales?

DANNY She usually goes topless, they probably drew the line at that.

JULIA Well this all wasn't here in the forties.

DANNY So you're doing your dis-thing on this dead Russian guy and his dirty book because, why?

JULIA It's not pornographic. It's tragic.

DANNY You're saying it's not porn… if it's artistic?

JULIA I'm saying… that the novel is art not smut, yes.

DANNY He's a pedophile, but he's a good storyteller, so it's OK?

JULIA It's fiction! The author wasn't into kiddie porn—

DANNY How do you know?

JULIA I've done years of research on him… he wasn't like that… I can't believe I'm having this discussion with you—

DANNY Because you think I'm ignorant or because you don't know—

JULIA My point is that although the narrator is morally repugnant and he's a sexual predator and it doesn't show women in the best light and the author's motives for telling the story may even be suspect… the work itself has socially redeeming qualities that elevate it above the level of merely exploitative… pornography.

DANNY What'd Mrs. Nabokov think of it?

JULIA She's the one who made him publish it.

DANNY Wait, what?

JULIA She actually saved it from the fire. He was in the process of burning the only copy of the manuscript in their backyard when she physically stopped him and removed it from the flames. She gave *Lolita* a chance for life.

DANNY Why was he burning it? Guilty conscience?

JULIA The same reason the Beatles broke up, artistic reasons.

DANNY The who?

JULIA Sir Paul McCartney's first band?

DANNY Paul... who?

JULIA Stop! How old are you, again?

DANNY Relax, I'm legal. I was just messin' with you. I thought they split because of that woman, "Yo-Yo" what's-her-bucket?

JULIA You're cute when you're acting like an idiot—you are acting?

DANNY How come his wife kept him from destroying his masterpiece?

JULIA Vera understood that it would sell. It was controversial, but it made him famous. The proceeds from the book allowed Nabokov to write full time, provide for his family, collect butterflies and eventually to return to Europe.

DANNY Butterflies?

JULIA He was a world class lepidopterist.

DANNY You are so making this up.

JULIA Why, don't you believe me?

DANNY You're a writer, you like a good story even if it's not true.

JULIA Point taken but it happens to be a fact. He loved butterflies.

DANNY So behind this book-burning, porno-mongering misogynistic-lepidopterist was a good woman pushing him to make great art?

JULIA You're not as dumb as you look.

DANNY Just exhausted—

JULIA Why don't you take a nap in the backseat? They won't be open for a couple of hours.

DANNY Aren't you gonna read me a story?

JULIA What do want me to read?

DANNY Nothing... Russian.

JULIA Have you ever read the last chapter of *Ulysses*?

DANNY It's not about the Civil War is it?

JULIA Different Ulysses.

DANNY Is it long?

JULIA It has one of the longest sentences in the cannon.

DANNY Spoken by a woman, right?

JULIA It was written by a man.

DANNY Is it arty or dirty?

JULIA You decide. Shhhh. Be quiet and listen. "Yes…"

> *He puts his arms behind his head and lays back closing his eyes as she picks up a book and begins to read.*
>
> *Cross fade.*

LIFESTYLE OF A BUTTERFLY: PUPA/CHRYSALIS

> *NABOKOV is standing in the middle of a projected photograph of: a monarch chrysalis.*

NABOKOV The chrysalis. After gorging itself for weeks on milkweed, the caterpillar is ready to shed its larval stage and begin to pupate. It will crawl to the top of a high branch and attach itself to it with a silken thread, before splitting it's exoskeleton and shedding its skin for the last time. It will grab hold of the branch with its cremaster and the newly exposed pupa will dry, harden and become a shiny green and gold speckled shell. Beneath this armor, protecting it from the outside world, it will become liquid and go through an unbelievable metamorphoses. Going from a creature of earth to one of the air.

> *Cross fade.*

QUILT FUGUE 4: JULIA/DANNY/MRS DRAKE/PROF. DRAKE

JULIA So the girl wrote stories and the man would read them. He even gave her a leather bound journal to write in. And she filled it up with her thoughts about life, love and the pursuits of a happy-go-lucky "Queen to be."

DANNY I tracked down my "biologicals" and found their death certificates.

MRS. DRAKE My candle. The only illumination tonight. Something soothing. Calming about the flame. My love. Gone again. In the other room as usual. Door closed.

PROF. DRAKE If you're looking for a cheap thrill, and who isn't? You'll notice that the actual description of the act itself is, to be fair, very mild by today's standards.

JULIA She shared with him the monumentally important things that preoccupy a young girl's mind.

DANNY It was such a relief knowing that I wasn't related to those people.

MRS. DRAKE You're probably contemplating the intricacies of the psychological structure of certain verses in an original manuscript in the hopes that it will provide further insight into your own already overdue efforts.

PROF. DRAKE Go to any bookstore, find the "romance" section, pick up a book at random. Yes you can judge them by their covers.

JULIA The man encouraged her to write and gave her more and more books to read. Big ones with big words.

DANNY I'd found some meth in his drawer too and some kiddie mags. Sick bastard.

MRS. DRAKE I wish he would just lie here with me, to me, for me. A simple lie is all I ask. Whisper to me that it will all be all right. That we will be together like in the old days.

PROF. DRAKE Chances are it'll be some variation of a bodice ripper. Flip it open, pick a page somewhere about three quarters of the way in and start reading.

JULIA And so it went on for what seemed like forever but it was really only as long as a summer.

DANNY As far as I was concerned I had done my time. When I left, I made an anonymous tip to the local DEA office and gave them his name.

MRS. DRAKE Just say that the light will continue to burn. But you can't even give me that can you?

PROF. DRAKE I bet you that you will run across a passage that is filled with throbbing innuendo which is far more graphic than the language used by Nabokov.

> *Cross fade.*

MAY 31: JACKSON, TENNESSEE, GEORGE ANNA HOTEL

> *JULIA is standing outside the car. DANNY is jacking up the back wheel, changing a flat.*

JULIA Are you sure you don't want some help with that?

DANNY No, I'm good. Just relax, that blowout was gnarly.

JULIA I could call a tow truck. I've got roadside—

DANNY What for? Take it easy. I got this.

JULIA You don't have a car but you know how to change a tire?

DANNY It's genetic.

JULIA Male pattern stubbornness?

DANNY It's a guy thing—

JULIA No arguments here.

DANNY Relax, I wrote a paper on this—

JULIA Oh, really?

DANNY To get my GED. We got to pick one of the essay topics—

JULIA You chose "fixing a flat?" No wonder our education system sucks.

DANNY I picked a step by step methodical process that I knew I could make sound good using all the vocab I could muster.

JULIA You're instilling me with a lot of confidence, jack boy.

DANNY You've got a full-sized spare, so this should work.

JULIA Smile.

> *She snaps a photo with her cell phone.*

I'll call it "Jacking in Jackson."

DANNY Were you intending that double entendre?

JULIA It's not my fault if you willfully misconstrue my meanings.

DANNY Just checking—

JULIA Is that why you're helping me… because you think I'll—

DANNY C'mon now. I just want to pay you back. Let me?

JULIA Fine. Fix it.

> *A man wearing a dark hooded jacket and dark glasses appears out of nowhere.*

MAN IN HOOD *(Played by same actor as DRAKE)* Well hello, miss. Havin' trouble with your car?

JULIA Oh, where'd you come from?

MAN IN HOOD I been watchin' you and I came over to offer my services—

JULIA That's nice of you but I don't need help—

MAN IN HOOD *(He takes out a knife.)* Good then you won't be stupid and call for any.

JULIA What? No! Danny—

MAN IN HOOD *(He moves toward her.)* Gimmie your purse or I'll cut your face—

JULIA *(She goes for her purse.)* All right, here it is—

She reaches into it and pulls out a pistol.

This what you were looking for?

MAN IN HOOD Crazy bitch!

He runs off.

DANNY (*Coming out from behind the car holding a tire iron.*) He's got a point. Whoa, don't shoot—

JULIA Where were you?

DANNY Down there, are you okay?

JULIA It happened so fast—

DANNY You couldn't just wait for me to sneak up on him?

JULIA I thought you ran away…

DANNY Nah, I was just about to get all ninja on his ass.

JULIA Feel free to go after him and avenge my honor Galahad.

DANNY Where did you get that?

JULIA (*She pulls out her cellphone.*) Family heirloom. My dead Uncle's. Don't freak, it's licensed.

DANNY Who are you calling?

JULIA The media to let them know that this much maligned town actually does deserve it's standing on the top 25 most dangerous cities list. Who knew?

DANNY No, seriously.

JULIA 911, what do you think?

DANNY Why? He's gone. Let's just get out of here.

JULIA Give me a good reason why I shouldn't report this.

DANNY I'll give you seventeen reasons… and they'll probably give you a couple… for transporting me over state lines.

JULIA (*Hanging up.*) I knew it!

DANNY I'm gonna be eighteen… in September.

JULIA What else did you lie to me about?

DANNY What do you want to know?

JULIA Everything… but first, fix that.

Cross fade.

THE DRAKES IN THE DARK

MRS. DRAKE lies in a hospital bed in her own house. She is propped up with pillows.

MRS. DRAKE *(She cries out in pain.)* No. Where is it? Paul!

PROF DRAKE enters through the door, he has a glass of whiskey in his hand.

PROF. DRAKE What's wrong?

MRS. DRAKE Pain… can't find the—

PROF. DRAKE I'll find it for you—

MRS. DRAKE So dark…

PROF. DRAKE Here's light… *(He turns on the light.)* There, you see?

MRS. DRAKE Pain, so sharp…

PROF. DRAKE *(He picks up the morphine drip control.)* Here it is… here you go…

MRS. DRAKE *(She pushes the plunger and sighs.)* Ah… that's better.

PROF. DRAKE *(He toasts her with his glass.)* Here's to killing the pain.

MRS. DRAKE Here's to you… my light-bringer.

Cross fade.

JUNE 1: HOT SPRINGS, ARKANSAS, WONDERLAND MOTOR COURTS

JULIA and DANNY are sitting side by side in bathrobes, slightly steaming. There is the sound of bubbling water and the reflected blue light suggests a nearby hot tub.

JULIA I never thought I'd be happy to hit Arkansas.

DANNY Who knew they had hot springs… in "Hot Springs?"

JULIA Mmmm hmmmm. Hometown of Bill Clinton. Explains a lot.

DANNY Thanks for treating me to this "hot spa action" and chilaxin'!

JULIA *(Laughing.)* For the record, I didn't touch you. In case you fell asleep and don't remember, that was a professional.

DANNY Yeah, I got that feeling, she was very good with her hands.

JULIA Glad you had a bathing suit? I didn't think I'd be wearing mine on this trip… funny how plans change.

DANNY Who says I'm wearing mine under this robe?

JULIA You're like that stupid pink bunny, you don't stop do you!

DANNY Sorry. I have another confession to make…

JULIA You waited until I was completely blissed out for this huh?

DANNY I've never done this before…

JULIA You've never been pampered, exfoliated and oiled before?

DANNY Not that either. I haven't… been with a woman… like you.

JULIA My therapist could probably back me up on this… but I don't think there are many women like me, at least not walking free.

DANNY I meant… I haven't been with… you know…

JULIA What about your many clients… or was that all crap too?

DANNY My gentlemen callers?

JULIA All men?

DANNY Not many little old ladies trolling the streets for ass.

JULIA So… you've never…

DANNY This was the first time I've ever felt a woman's hands on me.

JULIA I don't know what to say… I'm sorry, I mean—

DANNY I had this rich dirty old bastard once, real eccentric queen. He was into spankings with giant lollipops. One time, I cracked this enormous rainbow sucker on his bony butt. The pieces went everywhere stuck to the walls, got buried in his plush carpet. He gave me a real big tip. I told him the same thing. He said, "when you don't know what to say… just say 'piffle.' Keeps 'em guessing!"

JULIA So, you're not… that way?

DANNY You make it sound like a direction. No, I was born straight as an arrow. It's not a choice, you know?

JULIA In theory, but in practice you're… bi?

DANNY Not even bi-curious, I just do it for the money.

JULIA Piffle.

> The RELAXATION SPECIALIST enters. She is played by the same actress as MRS. DRAKE.

RELAXATION SPECIALIST (*Spoken to JULIA with a southern drawl.*) I beg your pardon?

JULIA Oh, I'm sorry. Nevermind—

RELAXATION SPECIALIST How y'all doin? Ma name's Viki and I'll be your "relaxation specialist" today. Your mud bath will be ready in just a few minutes. Takes a little while for that stuff to get a goin'. Would you like anything to drink while you wait?

DANNY Bourbon on the rocks, a dash of seltzer and a twist of lemon.

JULIA Water, please?

RELAXATION SPECIALIST (*She ignores DANNY's request.*) Water comin' right up. I'll bring you a pitcher. Would you prefer still or sparkling?

JULIA Still… and could I get some lemon slices in that?

RELAXATION SPECIALIST Well of course you can, honey. My pleasure.

DANNY On second thought, make that a double straight up—

JULIA Straight up, on an empty stomach?

RELAXATION SPECIALIST (*She ignores DANNY's request.*) Come again?

JULIA Oh, nothing. Thank you… uh, Viki.

RELAXATION SPECIALIST Namaste.

> *She exits.*

JULIA Serves you right for being chronologically challenged.

DANNY Piffle!

> *Cross fade.*

LIFESTYLE OF A BUTTERFLY: EMERGING ADULT BUTTERFLY

> *NABOKOV is standing in the middle of a projected photograph of: a newly emerged monarch butterfly.*

NABOKOV After a couple of weeks, the adult butterfly emerges from its chrysalis. Discarding the husk of its former self. Pumping fluids into its new virgin wings. Hanging onto it's parent plant and drying in the sun. Gone are the massive jaws replaced by a long proboscis for gathering the nectar from flowers far less colorful than itself. What was once a massive, bloated body has become an insubstantial frame work defining four magnificently hued wings. The transformation complete, the new born butterfly launches itself into the sky for its maiden flight. Forsaking forever its past pedestrian life.

> *Cross fade.*

QUILT FUGUE 5: JULIA/DANNY/MRS DRAKE/PROF. DRAKE

JULIA Then one night when the man got home late, the boy was upstairs in bed and had long ago gone to dreamland.

DANNY I don't know if they picked him up or not. I called once… but the phone had been disconnected.

MRS. DRAKE Fire has no memory; its elemental appeal lies in its destructive capacity coupled with its light and heat.

PROF. DRAKE However, it's the "idea" of the taboo that is being broken that makes the book "dirty" in the eyes of some.

JULIA The man smelled of alcohol and smoke and a little like a skunk.

DANNY As far as I'm concerned, I have no family. I'm only going back there because I know where everything is.

MRS. DRAKE Everything is flammable in this world from paper to people from cars to cities even carbon in its most compressed form, diamond will catch and burn white hot if enough heat is applied.

PROF. DRAKE He gives us an unreliable narrator, a manipulative pervert who acts out of a self deluded sense of love for an idea of the girl that he loved when he, himself, was just a boy.

JULIA He spoke in a very loud voice and laughed more than usual.

DANNY I'll be able to get by on my own.

MRS. DRAKE I think of the sun… and all of us here on this great big rock, this molten metal ball with its continental shell and liquid hydrogen shroud. These massive tectonic scabs drifting across its face would all burst into flames if we were to just spiral in toward the sun.

PROF. DRAKE He believes he is in love with his little Lolita. And who's to say he's not? In many cultures girls marry young and there's nothing wrong with it. Remember, she was the one who seduced him.

JULIA He stumbled onto the patio and took off all his clothes and just dove into the electric blue of the swimming pool.

DANNY Besides, at least it's warm down there.

MRS. DRAKE That would be something. I'd love to be alive to see it.

PROF. DRAKE Sorry. Where was I? Humbert's delusions. Right. Excuse me.

Cross fade.

JUNE 2: DALLAS, TEXAS, GRANDE TOURIST LODGE

JULIA and DANNY have just rolled into Dallas. JULIA turns off the ignition and launches into a very energetic impromptu song.

DANNY Are we there yet?

JULIA "The stars at night are big and bright—"

She turns to look at DANNY as if asking him to clap.

DANNY (*He looks at her as if completely bored then he rolls his eyes, sighs and claps four times.*) Yee Haw!

JULIA "Deep in the heart of… Dallas!"

DANNY Finally, tall buildings! That's better.

JULIA You really are a city boy—

DANNY I'm not a boy. When you gonna buy me a drink?

JULIA No. I think I'll buy you an "I shot J.R." T-shirt.

DANNY Who's "Junior?"

JULIA Stop it. TV show? Come on—

DANNY Sorry, I don't get your references—

JULIA Do me a favor? Say… "Right on!"

DANNY Okay. (*ahem*) "RIGHT on."

JULIA See? I say right OOOON! We even stress different words.

DANNY Toe-MAE-toe Toe-MAH-toe! That doesn't mean we can't—

JULIA We're completely different generations.

DANNY What? Like you're a "boomer?"

JULIA Bite your tongue—

DANNY Gen-X-er? Whatever?

JULIA And you're a—I don't even know what you are. Gen. Y? Z?

DANNY What's supposed to come after Z? They gonna start over?

JULIA You are a "man-grub" from the planet metro-sexual.

DANNY Metro? Oh please, that was so four years ago.

JULIA Was it, really? Even my hip references would be in preschool now.

DANNY I'm just sayin' that's stupid to label people like that.

JULIA You think?

DANNY It's like the Zodiac—

JULIA The killer?

DANNY What killer?

JULIA Stop! You're giving me arthritis of the brain.

DANNY Just fuckin' with you. I saw that movie—

JULIA That's what I mean, it wasn't just a movie. I lived through that. People we're scared to death for years. You weren't even born yet, were you?

DANNY You're such an ageist!

JULIA Sorry, I have to keep reminding myself you're only—

DANNY You throw everybody from a certain age into the same box.

JULIA If it fits—

DANNY Astrology, right? Total bullshit! People born in the same month, under the same sky, so what?

JULIA All right, I think I'm following you, but that's different—

DANNY I mean, what if you were born down in South America where they can see a totally different bunch of stars and Christmas is in the summer? And what happens now that Pluto's just a rock and not a planet anymore? Doesn't that mess things up?

JULIA All right that's crap… but you have to admit that sometimes—

DANNY Or with the types of years, like the year of the rat or pig or whatever? That's even more stupid. People who happen to be born in the same year aren't alike at all, you know?

JULIA You've been saving this up haven't you?

DANNY Take two people born in Europe on April 20, 1889. One was Albert Jean Amateau, a famous Turkish Jew who grew up to become a Rabbi, a lawyer and a social activist. The other was Adolph Hitler, a totaly evil-fascist-nazi-mother-fucker!

JULIA How do you know—

DANNY That Hitler was a mother-fucker?

JULIA No, about the other guy, Albert what's it's—

DANNY I had to do a paper on him when I was a freshman—

JULIA See, when I hear you say "freshmen" I think "college" but then I look at you and I think… "shoved in a locker."

DANNY My school didn't have lockers.

JULIA Well, Turkey's not really in Europe, is it?

DANNY All I'm sayin' is, labeling whole generations? That's fucked up!

JULIA Your "generation" uses that word like a punctuation mark.

DANNY It's just to get attention.

JULIA You're kinda cute when you're not being indignant.

DANNY You're kinda hot when you're not being patronizing.

JULIA What about college?

DANNY Not interested.

JULIA Don't you want to do something?

DANNY I am.

JULIA With your life?

DANNY I'm living my life, what are you doing?

JULIA I'm doing research for my—

DANNY You're writing about somebody else's life who happened to write about other people's lives except they didn't even exist. Is that really living?

JULIA I can't believe that I don't have a refill on my meds, my therapist is over a thousand miles away and my appointment isn't for two weeks!

DANNY You'll have a lot to talk about. Now, if I was to—

JULIA If I "were to" Please, "was ta?" That makes my ears hurt.

DANNY If I "were to" over-generalize, I would say your generation was over-educated, over-medicated and over-analyzed.

JULIA Ouch. "Are we there yet?" Said the mute monkey to the blind monkey as the deaf monkey eavesdropped.

DANNY What? Was that supposed to be offensive?

JULIA No, it's just something that somebody used to say to me… when I was a girl. I'm sorry, Danny. I didn't mean that you were like the rest of those…

DANNY You don't even know what to call us do you?

JULIA I don't suppose "teens" works?

DANNY Nope. Do you think there are a lot of big Texas oil men who'd like to have a little fun in the evenings?

JULIA You can't shock me anymore—

DANNY If you won't buy me a drink, I'm sure somebody will.

JULIA What you do is your own business. Just be careful—

DANNY I'll be safe, I always am.

JULIA This car is leaving tomorrow morning at eight a.m. Okay?

DANNY I'll be back here and ready to go.

JULIA I'm going to check out the Grand-E Tourist-E Lodge-E.

She begins laughing to herself.

DANNY What's so funny, Gran-E, remember a joke-E?

JULIA I was just thinking of the title for this chapter of your memoir… "Danny does Dallas."

DANNY I don't get it.

JULIA Now I know you're fuckin' with me.

DANNY I don't plan to write a memoir… I'll let you do that.

He exits.

JULIA Deal!

Cross fade.

LIFESTYLE OF A BUTTERFLY: MIGRATION

NABOKOV is standing in the middle of a projected photograph of a monarch butterfly flying in a deep blue sky.

NABOKOV I know a thing or two about migration. I've had to do enough of it in my own life. Not all butterflies migrate. But the ones that do are a mystery to us. We can only guess at the mechanisms involved. Here in North America, when the weather gets colder, the Monarchs begin their annual pilgrimage flying thousands of miles to their wintering grounds in California. They flock to the same eucalyptus trees year after year. Then in the spring they return North and the cycle repeats itself. The strange thing is that many generations will pass during this annual occurrence and it is often the grandchildren or great grandchildren of the originals that see the journey's end. The instinct for survival is strong and it is as old as time itself.

Cross fade.

QUILT FUGUE 6: JULIA/DANNY/MRS DRAKE/PROF. DRAKE

JULIA The girl had brought the man her journal and offered to read her latest, greatest story. That's when the man began to cry.

DANNY I just got sick of the city. Dirty old men, the smells, the people.

I was ready for rude locals but I wasn't ready for the tourists. It was like, the suburbs must be empty, you know?

MRS. DRAKE I hear the sound of wind outside. A place I'll never go again.

PROF. DRAKE It is a tragedy... comic, but tragic none the less. But who's story is it? The man, the girl, the playwright and part time pornographer, Quilty?

JULIA She went over to the side of the pool where he was weeping and she reached out her hand but then he grabbed her and she lost her balance and she fell, screaming into the sky.

DANNY I'm one to talk, right? But I was just a working boy. Hustling, pick-up, delivery. Anything, you know?

MRS. DRAKE I hear the water dripping in the sink because he hasn't got it fixed. Busy forging a life onto paper. The pan of water must be full by now.

PROF. DRAKE The narrator tells us that it is his story. But the story is named after the girl that he violated. She has her innocence taken from her, her youth and then she dies in childbirth. That's tragic. Doesn't it make it her story?

JULIA The water, air, chlorine and night flooded her lungs and everything began to go dark.

DANNY I just finished this catering gig where I got paid under the table. These marketing freaks needed a model, for color, at a classy Vodka party uptown.

MRS. DRAKE Stop. Let it go. Breathe. I feel the wind. I feel the water.

PROF. DRAKE Or... is it the author's own inner tragedy? Was he writing from his own truth? Did he really like little girls, whether he acted on his feelings or not?

JULIA Then he pulled her up and out coughing and sputtering onto the side of the pool.

DANNY I said sure, so they stripped me and spray painted me gold all over, like a statue.

MRS. DRAKE The image of the pool is fractured and refracted when the wind breaks the surface into a multifaceted image mosaic.

PROF. DRAKE Was there something dark and sinister behind this book. Or was his earlier attempt in Russian, *The Enchanter* closer to the dark sticky truth?

JULIA He said he was sorry. He didn't know his own strength. He didn't mean to pull her in. He offered to dry her clothes.

DANNY My "costume" was just a little gold thong. Fucking surreal.

MRS. DRAKE It is only when the wind is calm and the water is still can one see into the pool.

PROF. DRAKE Or is that all a load of crap?

JULIA The young girl waited for her dress, socks and panties to finish drying and she listened to her shoes tumbling in the dryer out in the garage and wondered what they looked like all spinning in there together.

DANNY I got paid to just walk around and have my picture taken with rich, drunk, beautiful people.

MRS. DRAKE When one is no longer distracted by the show on the water, one can concentrate on what lies in the water.

PROF. DRAKE Was he such a good writer that he had absolutely nothing in common with his characters.

JULIA Those dirty shoes dancing with her clean, white dress.

DANNY They can be really ugly, when you're just a thing to them.

MRS. DRAKE I am in the water. Floating on my back. Not drowning.

PROF. DRAKE What do you think? You tell me. That's your assignment for next time.

Blackout. Intermission.

JUNE 3: LUBBOCK, TEXAS, MOTOR HOTEL

JULIA is sitting on hood of the car staring into the sky. DANNY is laying on his back on the roof of the car. He has a bag of ice on his right eye. JULIA points up at a constellation.

JULIA And that one is Hercules. You see it?

DANNY He doesn't look like his pictures.

JULIA Does he look like the guy that did that to you?

DANNY I won't say this again. "I got drunk and fell down, a lot."

JULIA Is that why I found you crying in the lobby and refusing help from anyone?

DANNY I didn't need their help—

JULIA You just need a free ride, no questions asked, right?

DANNY Thanks for the ice. I think the swelling's gone down.

JULIA You were out for a while—

DANNY (*Pointing at the sky.*) What's that one?

JULIA That's Ophiuchus the god of healing. It's supposed to be a figure holding a snake… hence "Serpent Holder." They say it's the 13th sign of the—

DANNY Nevermind—

JULIA You asked—

DANNY Is there anything you don't know?

JULIA Yes, what happened to you, really?

DANNY Mistaken identity.

JULIA You mistook some burly cowboy for a John and he—

DANNY Mistook my face for a sack of potatoes that needed mashing.

JULIA Poe-TAY-Toes, Poe-TA-Toes.

DANNY So I called the whole thing off… but he had a few friends who met me in the alley and they made me see the error of my ways—

JULIA You were lucky—

DANNY Yeah, nothing broken.

JULIA That you weren't killed.

DANNY They all ran when a cop drove by—

JULIA What did he do?

DANNY Kept driving, maybe he didn't see me behind the dumpster.

JULIA You look like—

DANNY I've had worse. (*He winces.*) Not much, but I'm still goin'—

JULIA Very lucky, pink-bunny-boy.

DANNY (*Points up at the sky.*) What was that?

JULIA I have no idea?

DANNY C'mon—

JULIA No, really.

DANNY Was that a shooting star thing, you know, uh… meteorite?

JULIA They're meteors when they're up there, meteorites when they—

DANNY I knew you knew—

JULIA Actually, it was a UFO looking for a place to land.

DANNY They've come to take me home!

> *BERT and BETSY, a couple played by MR. and MRS. DRAKE,
> dressed in matching sweat outfits, enter and walk up to them.
> JULIA is so surprised by their sudden appearance she jumps off the
> hood and stands behind the car. DANNY stays on the roof. Silent.*

BERT I wouldn't joke about that if I was you.

BETSY They can hear you, you know. So… be careful.

JULIA Where did you two come from?

BERT How do. Name's Bert, this is my wife, Betsy.

BETSY That's our RV over there, the big green one.

BERT Home on the road. So, what's doin'?

BETSY You havin' car trouble, sweetie?

BERT Need a jump? Some gas? Want me to look under the hood, Miss?

JULIA Julia. That's very kind of you, but we're fine.

BETSY Who's "we" dear?

JULIA Danny and I—

BERT Now, sweetie, don't pry.

JULIA We just wanted to… do a little star gazing.

BETSY Well, you picked a nice night for it.

BERT No chance of tornados. Knock wood.

JULIA Is that Lubbock off there, in the distance?

BETSY Why, it sure is. Here for the UFO convention. Are you?

BERT Celebratin' the Lights… you know. (*Looks up.*) Up there!

JULIA No… sorry, we're just passing through.

BETSY Oh? Well, you have a good trip, then. Uh… both of you.

BERT Best to you and your uh… well, enjoy the view.

> *They exit.*

DANNY Friendly folks around here, huh?

JULIA Thanks for leaving me hanging, Man-grub.

DANNY I wasn't in the mood for company. Sorry.

JULIA Hey, there goes another one… make a wish.

DANNY Mine already came true.

> *Cross fade.*

LIFESTYLE OF A BUTTERFLY: MATING

NABOKOV is standing in the middle of a projected photograph of two blue butterflies copulating.

NABOKOV Having myself made a very thorough investigation of the minute genitalia of various lepidoptera species... I can say that no two are exactly alike. The specifics may differ from species to species, but in the broadest sense they go to it like males and females the world over. Mating takes place abdomen to abdomen. He in she, she around he. This is the romantic part. He grabs hold of her with special "claspers" and will pass her a spermatophore for safe keeping, which she will use to fertilize her eggs, or not. If they are interrupted by a predator, they take to their wings. Locked together in the air. Some species only mate once. Others are as promiscuous as it is possible to be. Receiving the protein rich packet but removing the sperm and going on to the next hopeful. Making a living through deception. Some males will also insert a cap into the female to prevent her from accepting anyone else, kind of a "chastity cork." But there is a dark side to these beautiful creatures. Some Monarchs won't wait for a female to accept them. They have these very sharp points and they will clasp onto a newly emerged helpless, young female and just stab her with it, sometimes causing serious damage. Sad but true.

Cross fade.

QUILT FUGUE 7: JULIA/DANNY/MRS DRAKE/PROF. DRAKE

JULIA When the girl came back inside, the Man was sitting on the long couch in the TV room.

DANNY After the soiree in the sky, this old guy brought me back to his very own penthouse to party.

MRS. DRAKE There was something I meant to do... today.

PROF. DRAKE Today I want to call your attention to the imagery in *Lolita*.

DANNY He laid out a lot of cash and coke.

JULIA He was watching a movie with lots of pretty people who were not wearing very many clothes.

DANNY So, I let him scrub the gold paint off of me.

MRS. DRAKE Thank you for the bath. I feel new again.

PROF. DRAKE A level of attention to the quotidian bordering on obsession.

JULIA The girl herself was only wearing a long white bathrobe that smelled of vanilla and coconut which belonged to the man's wife.

DANNY It wasn't so bad.

MRS. DRAKE Not enough strength to say or do what I want to—

PROF. DRAKE The motels, the towns, the landscape of a young America all rendered through the mind's eye of this monster, Humbert.

JULIA He said that she wouldn't mind her wearing it because she was in the hospital for an operation and that she would be staying there for a while and that they gave her other kinds of robes to wear.

DANNY But then he had me do favors for all his friends who just happened to show up when the clubs let out. That was a long night.

MRS. DRAKE All through the night you write and write and write—

PROF. DRAKE Seeking beauty, he finds it in the end, only to lose it.

JULIA She sat down and watched the TV with him.

DANNY I just kept thinking, I'm using them. Like I used all the others. For money, for drugs for a place to stay.

MRS. DRAKE But you never read to me anymore do you? Not like you used to.

PROF. DRAKE Humbert standing above that ridge listening to the sounds of children at play in the innocent valley below.

JULIA The girl watched as the pretty people in the movie did things that she had only seen the neighbors' dogs do in their backyard when she was looking over the fence from her bedroom window one night.

DANNY But for the first time. It rang hollow. The truth cut through me. I felt like I was completely alone.

PROF. DRAKE That passage alone is worth writing the book for. Tragic not only in it's description but in his realization of what he has done.

MRS. DRAKE Before the sickness and the dark times when we were alive. This bed is not enough. This life is not mine anymore. I just want to be free.

    Blackout.

JUNE 4: SANTA FÉ, NEW MEXICO, EL REY COURTS

    JULIA and DANNY are not visible through the windshield. Occasionally a foot comes into view and it seems as if they are doing something inappropriate. Actually, JULIA is teaching DANNY to drive by showing him how the clutch and the pedals work. They are both down on the floor boards looking at the pedals.

JULIA Okay, okay, that's it. Gently…. Don't rush it!

DANNY I'm not. Just don't make me nervous—

JULIA Okay, now put it in!

DANNY Like this?

JULIA No, see it popped out… try again!

DANNY There!

JULIA That's it. There you go… smooth, see?

DANNY Oh, yeah!

> *JULIA and DANNY appear above the dash again a little flushed. DANNY is sitting in the driver's seat.*

JULIA You wanna try this for real now?

DANNY Um… sure… why not?

JULIA Now that I've shown you with your hands… you can picture doing it with your feet. All right?

DANNY Now?

JULIA Of course!

DANNY What if somebody sees?

JULIA People do this all the time—

DANNY (*He starts the car.*) Wow. All right, here we go!

JULIA Good now press down on the clutch.

DANNY Like this?

JULIA That's the gas. The clutch. Like I showed you—

DANNY There… now what?

JULIA All right now gently shift it and get ready…

DANNY Okay…

JULIA Pop it—

DANNY Yeah!

JULIA Give it some gas… not too much—

DANNY Shit!

JULIA That's okay. These things happen. Everybody stalls sometimes.

DANNY What about that beer now?

JULIA Deal was if you could learn stick I would buy you a six pack.

DANNY Right—

JULIA You have not mastered the art of shifting…

DANNY Fine. Take two—

JULIA Okay. Push it in. Get it. Let it out. Go. Go. Go!

DANNY There!

JULIA Good enough, I could use a drink. But move over, I'm driving.

DANNY We saw that little tequila shack back by the turquoise graveyard. Sound good?

JULIA I said beer.

DANNY You said six drinks—

JULIA I said six pack!

DANNY Ever notice that guys who drink six packs don't have six packs?

JULIA You are not doing six shots of anything—

DANNY C'mon we've got to celebrate. You got some good stories about—

JULIA If they're true. They seems to be but I suspect that old man was just telling me what he thought I wanted to hear—

DANNY Pshaw! You think that about all guys, don't you?

JULIA Not about all men… only the ones I've met in this life.

DANNY What about in other lives?

JULIA Just because we're deep in the heart of Santa Fe, don't go all Shirley MacLaine-y on me. There must be something in the air.

DANNY Do you believe?

JULIA No, I think. There seems to be a big difference between those two things—

DANNY Thoughts and beliefs?

JULIA I think for myself… therefore I do not need to believe what other people believe.

DANNY In anything?

JULIA All right… I believe in me. What I experience. Beyond that…

DANNY What about me?

JULIA We were talking about me—

DANNY Do you believe in me? That I exist?

JULIA I think that you exist... you appear to be alive... so?

DANNY What if... I didn't?

JULIA I believe... that I think... that I'd like that drink now.

Cross fade.

DRAKE'S LOLITA LECTURE: MELTDOWN

He stands at the podium, visibly shaken. He can barely bring himself to speak.

PROF. DRAKE All right. Can I have your attention. Thank you. Excuse me... I... was going to... speak to you about... *Lolita* and her conclusion... however, I've just received some urgent news... and I... I'm afraid that... I won't be able to... It would be better if... where's my assistant? There you are... all the way in the back? I'm not that frightening am I? Well, I suppose I am... but I promise I won't bite. C'mon down. I need you to fill in for me now. I know you weren't expecting to be up here today... but now you're going to have to earn your stripes. Here are my lecture notes... don't worry about the chicken scratch in the margins... I can barely read those myself. Just stick to the main points... and give them the assignment at the end, all right? (*back to his students*). I leave you in... capable hands. As you recall... We were discussing... tragedy... as an intellectual exercise... a narrative construct... a well worn cliche. Now... I hate to be dramatic... you know me... but I believe it is fair to say... that I must go play a part in my own now. Goodbye.

He exits. Cross fade.

JUNE 6: HOLBROOK, ARIZONA, FOREST COURT

DANNY is staring at JULIA, in the backseat of the car. She clearly has a fever.

DANNY I've never seen anybody drink that many shots of tequila—

JULIA You're very young.

DANNY We may have to get you to a doctor—

JULIA No, you don't go to the hospital to get better—

DANNY You're burning up—

JULIA You go there to get sick, there are germs everywhere—

DANNY You have a fever—

JULIA Strains of things they can't cure, resistant, deadly—

DANNY I can't take your temperature but I can tell—

JULIA There's a first aide kit in the glove compartment—

DANNY Really?

JULIA What'd ya think I kept in there? Gloves? (*She laughs.*)

DANNY (*He pulls over. He stops the car. He opens the glove compartment and takes out the kit.*) There's even a thermometer in here. This is very organized!

JULIA You should see my kitchen—

DANNY (*Turning back towards her.*) Okay, open up!

JULIA Sterilize that!

DANNY We're in the middle of the desert it's about as sterile as you can get!

JULIA You want me to catch something?

DANNY (*He grabs a bottle from the back seat, pours some alcohol on the thermometer.*) Here.

JULIA Oh, you spilled it—

DANNY We can either do this the easy way or the hard way—

JULIA That's not funny, how'd you like it if I shoved it up your—

DANNY C'mon, "J" just put this under your tongue—

JULIA What'd you call me?

DANNY There she is. Good girl.

JULIA (*Spoken with thermometer in her mouth.*) M'm Mnom m mmood mmirl! (I'm not a good girl.)

DANNY All right. Now let's see where we are?

    JULIA is humming "Ain't She Sweet?" softly to herself.

DANNY That's west… So, if we head that way… we should probably make it to this next "X" on your list… assuming you don't die on me here. And if you pass out, I'm taking—

JULIA (*She stops humming.*) MMMking MMMammtage mov mmmme? (taking advantage of me?)

DANNY I'm taking you to the nearest hospital—

JULIA (*A buzz and she spits out the thermometer.*) What's it say?

DANNY (*Reading it.*) It wasn't in that long—

JULIA Long enough, it beeped—

DANNY One hundred and one, you've got a fever!

JULIA Barely, it's a flu. Gimme those pills.

DANNY You don't want to get help?

JULIA You're helping me.

DANNY What if I wasn't here—

JULIA Where are you going?

DANNY Nowhere. I just meant—

JULIA Two of these and some rest and I'll be just fine…

DANNY Hey, listen. I've got something I need to tell you. "J"?

> *JULIA has passed out. DANNY looks at the map, stares out the windshield and turns the key in the ignition. Cross fade.*

LIFESTYLE OF A BUTTERFLY: LAYING EGGS

> *NABOKOV is standing in the middle of a projected photograph of a female butterfly laying eggs on the underside of a leaf.*

NABOKOV With the male long gone, the pregnant female searches for a suitable place to lay her eggs. When the magical moment arrives she will usually conceal them under the leaves of the plants that her brood will consume. Sometimes hundreds or sometimes only a single egg per plant. This gives her offspring an opportunity to eat as much of the host vegetation as possible. Once finished, the mother will die. Unless it is a more hearty species, built to last a few more months. But in essence, once fertilized, she becomes an egg delivery device. Her reason for being is to create the next generation. After that, nothing awaits her but oblivion. These are butterflies that I am speaking of, of course.

> *Cross fade.*

JUNE 7: THE SOUTH RIM OF THE GRAND CANYON, ARIZONA, SOUTH RIM, BRIGHT ANGEL LODGE

> *JULIA seems to wake from sleep as if from a fever dream. She rubs her eyes and steps out of the car. There is a shift in light as if the first rays of the sun were coming up over the rim of the Grand Canyon. She blinks her eyes and walks forward staring amazed at the sight.*

JULIA There is a God… and she can paint.

> *Three figures stand silhouetted against the colorful sunrise. They are each carrying a butterfly net in their hands. The youngest has*

two nets. He comes forward revealing that he is DANNY, wearing a long fake fur coat. He hands JULIA a net. She takes it. She realizes she is still dreaming.

JULIA Duh-duh—?

DANNY/DMITRI Dmitri.

JULIA Of course—

DANNY/DMITRI Here, come see the pretty-flies—

JULIA The butterflies?

DANNY/DMITRI Papa says that dawn is the best time to catch them—

JULIA Why is that?

DANNY/DMITRI Because they are cold and slow to fly away.

JULIA How did you get here?

DANNY/DMITRI You drove us in the "Poinka" (Pontiac), silly!

JULIA Where... do you live?

DANNY/DMITRI I am alive, here!

JULIA Where is your home?

DANNY/DMITRI I don't have a home, we live in little houses by the roadside.

VERA/MRS. DRAKE (*In a thick Russian accent.*) Dmitri, come here. It is very cold. Get back in the car.

DANNY/DMITRI (*He turns to go.*) Da!

JULIA Thank you!

VERA/MRS. DRAKE Dorothea!

JULIA I'm not—

VERA/MRS. DRAKE Vladimir Vladimirovich requests that you accompany him down the canyon on some mule path. He believes he has seen a prize specimen. You know how he can be. Like a big boy. Please go.

JULIA Sure, why not?

VERA/MRS. DRAKE We will be in the car attempting to keep warm. Tell him not to be too long. It won't help but tell him I said so.

Exits.

NABOKOV/PROF. DRAKE Come, my little bird. There is a prize on the wing.

JULIA Vlad—Uh… Mr. Nabokov?

NABOKOV/PROF. DRAKE Nyet. Call me Volodya, please. Only don't let Vera hear you.

JULIA What are we doing?

NABOKOV/PROF. DRAKE Well, I am hunting for a rare and possibly undocumented Neonympha to add to my collection and you are assisting me.

JULIA I am undergoing a massive psychotic episode with auditory and visual hallucinations in 3D surround sound.

NABOKOV/PROF. DRAKE Please, Dorothea…

He creeps towards her with his net raised.

Hold still—

JULIA You're a product of my fevered imagination—

NABOKOV/PROF. DRAKE (*He holds his net above his head.*) Shhhh. Don't move.

JULIA You don't even look like him—

NABOKOV/PROF. DRAKE (*He sweeps the net down over her head.*) Gotcha!

JULIA Wait!

NABOKOV/PROF. DRAKE (*He removes the net and reaches into it with his hand. He produces a butterfly.*) There she is! I christen thee, Cyllópsis Pertepída Dorothéa.

JULIA Poor thing, she's frightened.

NABOKOV/PROF. DRAKE Hand me the jar in my bag, quickly.

JULIA (*She does so.*) She's so beautiful—

NABOKOV/PROF. DRAKE (*He pops it into the jar.*) Now it will be preserved for posterity.

JULIA (*Watching the butterfly.*) But… she's dying.

NABOKOV/PROF. DRAKE That is why it is called a "killing jar." How typically English. Not an "euthanasia enclosure" or a "transformation chamber." Kill-jar. So blunt and literal. There, it's done.

JULIA You killed her?

NABOKOV/PROF. DRAKE (*He puts the jar back in his bag and turns to walk away.*) A small price to pay for immortality.

There is a shift in light. JULIA wakes from sleep as if from a fever dream. She rubs her eyes. She is standing outside the car, lit as if the first rays of the sun were coming up over the rim of the Grand Canyon. She blinks her eyes and walks forward staring amazed at the sight. DANNY is standing on a glass observation deck.

DANNY Hey sleepy, you're back among the living. You all right?

JULIA Bad dreams. It's all out of my system now.

DANNY Your temp's down. I didn't want to wake you but now that you're up... this is totally worth it.

JULIA It's beautiful... and you can't put it in a bottle.

DANNY C'mon out here. It puts the "grand" in canyon.

JULIA What... are you standing on?

DANNY Glass. Relax, it's strong. (*jumping*) See?

JULIA You won't ride a donkey... but you'll do that?

DANNY I don't trust 'em. I don't think they like people on their backs all day. I don't blame 'em.

JULIA I can see fine from here—

DANNY (*He holds out his hand.*) Live a little. You came this far, I'll meet you half way.

JULIA (*She takes hold of his hand.*) All right...

DANNY Look out at the horizon.

JULIA (*She looks down and falls to her knees.*) That... is... a long way down.

DANNY Don't look down.

JULIA It's like... looking back in time.

DANNY Yeah, it's something huh?

JULIA You have a gift for understatement.

DANNY I know you don't want to hear this... but I think I love you.

JULIA And overstatement... you're not in love with me. Trust me.

DANNY I totally am—

JULIA No. You just want me.

DANNY So...

JULIA Let's go to Vegas.

Cross fade.

DRAKE'S GOODBYE TO THE LOVE OF HIS LIFE

DRAKE is in his dressing gown. His wife is sitting up in bed. She is heavily medicated. There is a morphine drip by her bed. The "trigger button" is in her hand. She stares at him. He holds a book.

PROF. DRAKE You wanted to hear it. Well here it is. *The Chrysalis.* "In the autumn of—"

MRS. DRAKE Too late... my love. No time... my dove. It's over now.

PROF. DRAKE Hush, don't say that. The hospice staff said—

MRS. DRAKE You would hush... my last breath... wouldn't you?

PROF. DRAKE I know that's the med's talking. Now, I promised to read you—

MRS. DRAKE Turn the lights on—

PROF. DRAKE They are on—

MRS. DRAKE Want to... see your eyes. You had... beautiful eyes.

PROF. DRAKE So do you—

MRS. DRAKE Hazel. Not one constant color. Blue, Green and Gold swirled.

PROF. DRAKE Rayleigh scattering. Do you want me to do something for you?

MRS. DRAKE Listen... to me... before I go... I need you to...

PROF. DRAKE I'll get Carla.

MRS. DRAKE NO! Stay with me... take this... I can't do it... I just can't—

PROF. DRAKE What are you asking me to do—

MRS. DRAKE You know... you promised...

PROF. DRAKE You're not—

MRS. DRAKE You always make them... You always break them—

PROF. DRAKE All right. (*He takes the trigger from her.*) Just tell me when.

MRS. DRAKE You were... the love of my life...

PROF. DRAKE And you are my life...

MRS. DRAKE I want you to know... I didn't blame you...for Peter's death.

PROF. DRAKE (*Visibly shaken.*) Please don't—

MRS. DRAKE I blamed you for her—

PROF. DRAKE You knew?

MRS. DRAKE You have… a tremendous capacity… for self deception…

PROF. DRAKE Is that why you burned it?

MRS. DRAKE I destroyed it… to save you… from yourself.

PROF. DRAKE I always wanted to tell you— but I just couldn't—

MRS. DRAKE The pain… It's time. You're on your own now. Please, Paul?

PROF. DRAKE (*He presses the button assisting her suicide.*) Farewell, Mary-Leigh… my love.

> *She sighs as if life were draining out of her. She closes her eyes for the last time. He weeps. Cross fade.*

JUNE 9: LAS VEGAS, NEVADA

DANNY and JULIA stare in awe as the great neon way is reflected in the windshield and all around them.

DANNY I've died and gone to neon hell… look at all that!

JULIA I've booked us a room in the one with the volcano.

DANNY Isn't that a bit pricey?

JULIA I found it through one of those cheap travel sites.

DANNY Capt. Kirk or the little gnome with the pointy hat?

JULIA Even cheaper… I told them I was reviewing for a blog.

DANNY And… are you?

JULIA I'm also selling ocean front property in Greenland, interested?

DANNY Are you going to write about this?

JULIA Sure… if I don't like their service. I got us a suite.

DANNY Oh, please—

JULIA I said I was doing a piece on honeymoon destinations and I needed accommodation for myself and my—

DANNY Don't even—

JULIA Photographer. How fast can you grow a beard?

DANNY How long do you plan on staying?

JULIA What if you didn't shave for a couple of days?

DANNY I haven't shaved all week.

JULIA There's no way they're going to let you into a casino—

DANNY I don't gamble—

JULIA Because you can't, peach fuzz—

DANNY I don't fly because I can't, I don't gamble because I won't.

JULIA What if you wore a wig and I called you my sister?

DANNY That's not funny.

JULIA I'm sorry I was just "messin' wit ya." You got all serious.

DANNY Can we stop at a drug store?

JULIA Sure. Are you feeling all right?

DANNY I need to buy a few things.

JULIA Like what? I'll pay for whatever you—

DANNY Love gloves?

JULIA You're so cute. (*Laughing.*) I picked up a pack at the last gas station. There was a dispenser in the ladies room.

DANNY How many?

JULIA Three… but if we need more I can always—

DANNY You don't get it. How am I supposed to turn tricks? John's don't bring their own. Oh, that's right you've never had to work for a living "that way" have you?

JULIA Hey, wait a minute… you don't have to—

DANNY I don't? Where do you think I got this money? The kindness of strangers? That's how I earn my way—

JULIA I thought you were exaggerating about… all that.

DANNY No, I'm "nice" to men and they pay me. It's that simple.

JULIA And you were just planning on—

DANNY There's money to be made. Look out there. You can smell it.

JULIA Don't do this…

DANNY Why? Do you want me all to yourself tonight?

JULIA Yes, how much?

DANNY That depends on what you want—

JULIA Let's see, honesty, loyalty, sincerity—

DANNY That's gonna cost you extra…

JULIA Will you take a check?

DANNY I don't know... ask my pimp. (*He breaks into a grin.*)

JULIA You little shit!

DANNY (*Laughing.*) Wow, I had you goin' didn't I?

JULIA I should have known when you said "The kindness of strangers?" That was way too Tennessee.

DANNY So how much would you have paid me?

JULIA Would you really have accepted money for...

DANNY Not a check. Boy's gotta have some standards.

JULIA Seriously, you don't have to—

DANNY Unless the Devil's having a barbecue, I think we're here.

JULIA This certainly wasn't here when they passed through.

DANNY Pirates and clowns and hookers—

JULIA Oh my...

DANNY Remember, whatever happens here...

JULIA Ends up in my book.

DANNY Am I in it?

JULIA You'll have to sign a release, you know?

DANNY Uh huh. Try and make me.

> He starts to kiss her, she moves.

JULIA Fetch the bags... you're also supposed to be my assistant.

DANNY I want a raise.

JULIA Oh, I'll give you one... if you're good.

> Cross fade.

DANNY'S STORY: FLYING

DANNY tells his story in a bright light directly out to the audience.

DANNY I went into the old guy's master bedroom to cleanup. I stood there in his private bathroom which was bigger than all the bathrooms I'd ever been in, put together. I saw my reflection in the gold mirrors as I wiped the rest of the gold and sticky stuff off of my chest. When I came out, dressed in my street clothes, all his friends were gone and he was sacked out on the leather sofa drooling out the side of his mouth. I Just looked at the art on the walls, at the grand piano, at the way these people lived. And it hit me. What I was, what I'd turned into. I went outside on the balcony. I watched the sunrise from the rooftop of a building so tall that there were clouds below me and for a moment all I wanted to do was step off and fly.

Blackout.

LIFESTYLE OF A BUTTERFLY: DEATH

NABOKOV is standing in the middle of a projected photograph of a once beautiful butterfly with its wings in tatters, torn to shreds by time.

NABOKOV Butterflies are not built to last. The adult can live a few days, or weeks, maybe months. But they cannot abide the cold. An unseasonable frost can be devastating. Predators abound, even for the toxic species. There's always something stupid out there with teeth willing to bite anything that flies. Diseases are rampant. Parasites, including the kind that consume the insect from the inside out, all take their toll. They cannot replace their dead cells or repair their wing scales. After the briefest of lives, the ravages of time are evident on the wing tips of even the heartiest of flyers. You can see them in the autumn. Tattered flags valiantly flapping against the breeze. Unless captured and collected by a rabid entomologist, they succumb to the inevitable entropy of the world as it slowly wears them down. A brief but beautiful existence.

Cross fade.

JUNE 10: SAN BERNARDINO, CALIFORNIA

The car has just pulled up and there is a cloud of dust. JULIA steps out of the car and stares off into the distance. DANNY opens his door and stares over the top of the car at her and the view.

JULIA Here we are.

DANNY Out of the desert and into civilization.

JULIA La-La-Land!

DANNY Correction. San Bernardino. Big difference.

JULIA I can see why they would have stopped here.

DANNY I fail to see the appeal?

JULIA Pit stop. There's a cafe over there.

DANNY If I ever see another cactus, I swear I'll take a hostage.

JULIA Speaking of... how are you doing?

DANNY Just a little sore. How 'bout you?

JULIA Yeah, that was...

DANNY What a difference a bed makes—

JULIA And a hot tub and a chandelier, and an ironing board—

DANNY Hey, this is one of your dots on the map!

JULIA And then he changed the subject—

DANNY Do you wanna sleep here tonight? Assuming, you want to sleep?

JULIA No, we can head down to Santa Monica. It's not that far.

DANNY You sure?

JULIA That's also on the list and you said—

DANNY What about your doctoral-quest thingy, local color?

JULIA I think I preferred Arkansas. (*Looks around.*) This can wait. I promised to take you there and I will.

DANNY Yeah, so... what's the rush. Tomorrow is good, too.

JULIA What happens tomorrow?

DANNY The sun comes up back there and eventually it wakes up this side of the continent. People get up, they live their lives—

JULIA What happens when you get to where you're going?

DANNY You drop me off. We go our separate ways. You go North, back to your college and academia and I... stay here—

JULIA Doing what?

DANNY Is this a trick question?

JULIA No, I really want to know—

DANNY I hustle, I trick, I hit the library looking for older women—

JULIA Stop it.

DANNY I take my back pack and go sleep in this little spot I know down by the pier. It's close to the beach showers and toilets. There's a couple of restaurants that always have clean leftovers and they don't lock their dumpsters. The weather's nice, the tourists provide a steady source of—

JULIA And that's what you want?

DANNY That's not what you asked—

JULIA What am I to you?

DANNY You're the writer, not me... I don't know what to say.

JULIA Fine. Let's get some coffee and get back on the road.

DANNY "No green straws…"

JULIA "No burned beans!"

DANNY I'll never forgive you.

JULIA "Forgive" me for what!

DANNY I said, "forget you."

JULIA Oh, sorry! I thought you said…

DANNY We'll need to hurry if you want make the coast before dark.

JULIA You know, I'll miss you.

DANNY I've got your number.

JULIA But… no phone.

Cross fade.

JULIA'S STORY "AND THEN THEY…"

JULIA tells a story as one might tell a bedtime story to a child.

JULIA Then the man looked away from the skin on the screen and said to the girl that he was sorry about the pool, sorry that she fell in and that he would drive her home, after he sobered up. Then she told him that it was okay, that it was an accident, and then he cried some more. So then she went to him, and kissed him on the forehead because she had always wanted to do that… and then on the cheek and then on the mouth and then he… and then she… and then they…

Cross fade.

JUNE 11: SANTA MONICA, CALIFORNIA, MISSION COURT

DANNY and JULIA are parked. They gaze out at the Santa Monica pier. There is the sound of seagulls, and children and life on the beach.

DANNY This is it!

JULIA The People's Republic of Santa Monica. This where ya live?

DANNY Survive… sometimes. I wouldn't call it a living.

JULIA Could be worse. Could be snowing.

DANNY Before I caught the train East… it was the rainy season.

JULIA Yeah, but it's a warm rain, right? Cheer up!

DANNY What do you want from me?

JULIA According to the map, there's a motel over there.

DANNY So? Did the Russians sleep there?

JULIA No… but I'm going to. And I don't want to sleep alone.

DANNY And what happens in the morning?

JULIA I leave and we never see each other again. Come dance with me?

DANNY I can't dance the way you do…

JULIA Ballroom? It's easy, I'll teach you—

DANNY What about him?

JULIA Who?

DANNY You know who. HIM. The professor. The author of your story?

JULIA No.

DANNY Aren't you going back up to Palo Alto?

JULIA I can't—

DANNY Why not—

JULIA I'm not ready—

DANNY How many years has it been?

JULIA You're too young, you don't understand—

DANNY Fine then, teach me that—

JULIA I'm not your teacher, all right?

DANNY Stand up to him!

JULIA I'm not strong enough—

DANNY Call the cops—

JULIA This isn't some prank where I can make an anonymous call.

DANNY You want to stay scared? Then keep it secret—

JULIA He never really hurt me—

DANNY What he did was wrong—

JULIA And what am I doing with you?

DANNY You're defending him?

JULIA No… I just can't face him alone.

DANNY I'll come with you.

JULIA You will?

DANNY Yes.

JULIA Just to the motel or…

DANNY All the way to his house and right up to his front door.

JULIA Come here.

She grabs him and pulls him to her.

DANNY Maybe we should get a room first?

Cross fade.

METAMORPHOSIS: A MONARCH IS BORN

NABOKOV is standing in front of an image of thousands of butterflies.

NABOKOV An egg is laid. A new life born. The larva hatches. Ugly, misshapen and alone. Instinctively, the caterpillar begins to feed on the toxic leaves where its absent parents have deposited it. It grows enormous. Bloated and poisonous it inches through life until it can eat no more. It becomes too big for its own skin, which splits open. The pupa emerges and it hangs itself, upside down, Houdini-like from a branch and becomes liquid life inside it's new shell. Frozen in time. Then an ageless metamorphosis occurs, its mystery still undiminished though we can now study its progress with an electron scope and see the very molecules dance within the chrysalis. The days fly past. The beautiful jade green fades, becoming translucent. The colors of the flyer trapped inside showing through, like stained glass. Membranes and veins. A perfect symmetry of form and function. The case is cracked, the life within released. Four wings folded now unfurl and dry in the sunlight, waiting for flight. The tarsi grip the husk of its old skin now unrecognizable. The scales of gold shimmer in the heat haze between the dark veins and ivory spots. A treasured thing. All gossamer, ethereal and unreal. On a breeze no stronger than a whisper, the butterfly takes wing. It lets go the bonds of its former terrestrial existence and soars into the air. It is suddenly swallowed by a crow! Which promptly spits it out, not liking the taste. But the Monarch flies on, with tattered wings, now wise in the ways of the world and grateful for its bitterness and toxic upbringing.

Cross fade.

JUNE 12: FRESNO, CALIFORNIA

JULIA and DANNY are in the car. There is the sound of wind and other cars doppler-ing into the distance. The radio is blaring "dance hall days." DANNY is staring at an oversized map of California. JULIA has her cell phone headset in her driver's side ear.

JULIA Dance Halls Days? You know that song's about Lolita, don't you?

DANNY Wang Chung was literary?

JULIA I just saw a sign… something about raisins?

DANNY Fruit stand that way—

JULIA Where are we?

DANNY (*Points to map.*) Right here. But your next Red X is over there, toward Fresno—

JULIA Fuck Fresno!

DANNY All of it… or just the raisin lovers?

JULIA (*She dials a number on her phone.*) We're going North!

DANNY Who are you calling?

JULIA I'm ordering a pizza—

DANNY Yeah, right!

JULIA I got his number—

DANNY You're calling him?

JULIA It's ringing—

DANNY What are ya gonna to say to him?

JULIA I don't want to talk to him—

DANNY So what happens when he picks up?

JULIA (*She hangs up.*) Answering machine—

DANNY You're not a good con, your eyes do that thing when you lie—

JULIA All right, I wanted to make sure he was home—

DANNY He picked up?

JULIA I hung up right when he answered—

DANNY You're unbelievable! What about caller ID?

JULIA He's a Luddite, I doubt he even has a push button phone let alone—

> Her cell phone rings.

DANNY Your dinosaur just "star sixty-nine'd" you (*He grabs her cell phone.*) Let me talk to him—

JULIA No, wait!

DANNY Hola? (*There is the sound of a man's voice.*) Que? (*The man's voice is louder.*) Who-lee-ah? La señora allí no es ninguna mujer aquí (*The man's voice is louder.*) Número apesadumbrado, incorrecto, Gringo!

He hangs up the phone.

JULIA That was—

DANNY Brilliant?

JULIA Really, very... offensive!

DANNY Oh, come on, I just said he had the wrong number—

JULIA Give me that!

She grabs her cell phone back.

DANNY If you're gonna make an omelette... it doesn't matter if the eggs are white or brown.

JULIA That's just stupid. You don't think your little high school Spanish and Bandito impression fooled him, do you?

DANNY Look, I was just trying to help—

JULIA I know but you'll have to let me—

The cell phone rings.

DANNY Answer the phone? Go right ahead—

JULIA (*She stares at it, then silences the phone.*) There.

DANNY Why don't you put it on vibrate and in your pants? Maybe he'll finally be able to make you happy.

JULIA Are you turning green?

DANNY I'm not sick—

JULIA Jealous?

DANNY Of your previous... pervert?

JULIA You're sweet.

DANNY Why? Should I be?

JULIA Honey, I have to deal with him on my own.

DANNY But I can help you—

JULIA You'll have to wait in the car. Trust me.

DANNY If you say so... I'll always be here if you need me.

They kiss. Cross fade.

JULIA'S STORY END

JULIA tells a story as one might tell a bedtime story to a child.

JULIA When the world stopped spinning and her breath returned. The girl was lying on the carpet, the open robe beneath her. The man had gone upstairs into the bathroom. She stared at the ceiling and heard his footsteps up above, pacing. The buzzer for the dryer called to her. She got up, wearing nothing and looked down and saw the drops of blood on the nice, clean, white robe. She felt as if she had been torn in two. And then she dressed and he came back down and he drove her home… in silence. She said goodbye to the man and he let her out. Her clothes were only slightly damp but her shoes were still wet and left footprints on the driveway. She watched as he drove away and she remembered her stories. All those damaged, sad and lonely, twisted and torn, lovely heartbroken stories she had written for him had gone into the water with her and now lay soaking, on the floor of his room along with the stained robe. And the girl never went back to see the man ever again. Until today.

Cross fade.

DRAKE'S HOUSE

Night. DRAKE is in his study. JULIA appears through the french doors. DRAKE has been drinking too much. He has a glass of red wine in his hands. He turns and sees her there, he nearly collapses.

PROF. DRAKE You?

JULIA Yes.

PROF. DRAKE You're really…

JULIA Young and innocent? No. Not anymore.

PROF. DRAKE You look…

JULIA Little girls grow up.

PROF. DRAKE So… beautiful.

JULIA Still? After all these years?

PROF. DRAKE Your hair…

JULIA Disheveled. I've been traveling. Yours is…

PROF. DRAKE Slowly disappearing… like my memories. Care for a drink?

JULIA Where is she?

PROF. DRAKE She… passed… the cancer finally…

JULIA You're free, then.

PROF. DRAKE No. I am trapped in the body of an old man.

JULIA There are worse punishments.

PROF. DRAKE My sweet little "J" bird please, forgive me.

JULIA I hated you... for... for so long...

PROF. DRAKE I'll pay for my sins... but you must know that I loved you—

JULIA No, I loved you. But you can't call what you did "love."

PROF. DRAKE I looked for you...

JULIA I see you everywhere—

PROF. DRAKE On campus... I heard that you had enrolled—

JULIA You're always in my mind—

PROF. DRAKE I keep expecting to see your face out there—

JULIA I can't eat—

PROF. DRAKE Looking up at me with those eyes—

JULIA I can't sleep—

PROF. DRAKE And now you're here with me—

JULIA You're always there like a burned image on my brain.

PROF. DRAKE I've never stopped loving you—

JULIA No!

> *She pulls out her gun and points it at him.*

Not love!

PROF. DRAKE That was rather overly dramatic don't you think? Is that real?

JULIA Make your peace with whatever you believe in—

PROF. DRAKE You... can't be serious—

JULIA Because you took advantage... You took my innocence, my journal and my life. Now I'm taking them all back. Where is it?

PROF. DRAKE Your journal was ruined. The water damage—

JULIA (*She holds up the book by PROF. DRAKE.*) *The Chrysalis* by Paul Drake. (*Reading the jacket.*) "A breathtaking exploration of the labyrinthine thought patterns of a disturbed child. He shows tremendous insight into the secret life of an adolescent girl on the edge..." Explain how my words got into your book. Do you have a photographic memory?

PROF. DRAKE I dried it out. The ink smeared, the words were blurred. But I managed to save it. To copy it out. Word by word. Late at night. Like a monk in a cell. After the drugs had finally forced her to sleep through the pain. I intended to return it to you as a gift.

JULIA I liked the happy ending you contrived for me. Touching.

PROF. DRAKE I kept waiting for you to… but then you went away. You wouldn't return my calls. It was all I had of you… I began writing it and I couldn't stop. It all just flowed out of me into the story.

JULIA Where is it?

PROF. DRAKE Burned… She did it… after she got sick… She found it… and understood what I had done… I think she was trying to save me from exposure. I saved you the ashes… you're welcome to them.

JULIA And the rest?

PROF. DRAKE Your innocence? Well, you weren't really, were you? Remember, it was you who seduced me.

JULIA Is that what you believe?

PROF. DRAKE I heard that you moved away to become a writer? When you came back for your doctorate, I was so proud. But I left you alone because I respected your—

JULIA Privacy?

PROF. DRAKE Your wishes. I swore that if you ever came to see me… I would give you this—

Taking out an envelope from a book.

JULIA The ashes?

PROF. DRAKE You share of the royalties from… our book.

JULIA (*She lowers the gun.*) You think this is about the money?

PROF. DRAKE Here, take it.

JULIA (*She takes the envelope full of cash.*) I never felt like a whore, until now—

PROF. DRAKE I can't undo the past but consider it a partial reparation?

JULIA (*She sets the gun down to open the envelope.*) So… How much for my soul?

PROF. DRAKE Not enough, but there's more—

JULIA If I act now do I get a set of steak knives too?

PROF. DRAKE The publishers want a sequel… collaborate on it with me—

JULIA Like before? No. I want full disclosure. You tell them everything!

PROF. DRAKE I know you hate me—

JULIA You don't get it! I don't hate you, but you hated yourself... and then you made me hate myself—

PROF. DRAKE Why are you here?

JULIA I came to scare you—

PROF. DRAKE Congratulations, mission accomplished—

JULIA To show you that you have no power over me anymore—

PROF. DRAKE I never did. You were the one who had the all the power. I couldn't stop myself. Do you know what my life has been like?

JULIA Haunted? Anguished? Filled with thoughts of suicide?

PROF. DRAKE You could have gone to the authorities. I expected you to tell someone. Everyday, I waited for the knock at the door. Thinking, "this is it." The day of reckoning. Here come the cameras, the media circus. There goes my life!

JULIA I only told one person and she didn't believe me—

PROF. DRAKE Please, "J" forgive me—

JULIA I do forgive you, not because you deserve it but because I do.

PROF. DRAKE Thank you.

JULIA You should have thanked your wife.

PROF. DRAKE You told her...

JULIA Yes. Just like you're going to tell the world. Or I will.

PROF. DRAKE I'm sorry—

JULIA Me too.

PROF. DRAKE (*He picks up the gun points it at her*) I can't do that.

JULIA Keep it. It's not loaded anyway. Goodbye.

PROF. DRAKE Julia, please don't... not after all we've—

JULIA (*Holding the book with the money tucked inside.*) Shared? No. "This is the only immortality you and I may share."

> *JULIA exits. DRAKE watches her go. He slumps back down in his chair. Heart racing. He looks down at the gun. He brings it up to his head looking at it. Blackout. There is a loud gunshot.*

POLICE INTERROGATION. JULIA AND DETECTIVE HAYES

> *JULIA is sitting in a chair. It is dark all around her. There is a bright light on her face blinding her. The voice of DETECTIVE*

HAYES standing in the room is heard. Her face is hidden in shadows.

JULIA "This is the only immortality you and I may share—"

DETECTIVE HAYES Right, you said that line from that book, turned to leave and then he grabbed you?

JULIA We struggled and the gun went off. I thought it wasn't loaded.

DETECTIVE HAYES I see. All right, one more time from the top, Julia. Please?

JULIA How many times? I told you. I did it.

DETECTIVE HAYES Yes, you did. But that's what doesn't make sense to me.

JULIA Detective, I can't help what does or doesn't make sense to you—

DETECTIVE HAYES Call me Charlotte, please. Calm down. You want some more tea?

JULIA No, thank you.

DETECTIVE HAYES We've got all night if necessary. You say you shot him, accidentally. At close range…

JULIA I was frightened, I cleaned up and was going to take off when that patrol car pulled up—

DETECTIVE HAYES Just washed the powder off, huh? You were pretty clean—

JULIA I've watched enough cop shows to know how—

DETECTIVE HAYES Really? Can't stand 'em myself. Too violent. Your prints were found on the weapon all right. It was registered to your deceased uncle? But there were other prints too.

JULIA I pulled the trigger—

DETECTIVE HAYES Just like that? You killed this man… this Professor Drake? Blew his mind all over his study walls… Because?

JULIA Self-defense.

DETECTIVE HAYES You keep saying that… but there was no sign of a struggle.

You know who else's prints we found on the pistol?

JULIA My uncle's?

DETECTIVE HAYES Nice try. No. Who do you think?

JULIA Danny's?

DETECTIVE HAYES Sure… Your little boyfriend's baby fingers were all over it. Care to tell me why?

JULIA He's not my boyfriend—

DETECTIVE HAYES Well, he is a boy, isn't he?

JULIA Where is he?

DETECTIVE HAYES We've uh… got him in the other room down the hall.

JULIA Danny's here?

DETECTIVE HAYES Afraid so. You see, we couldn't send him off to juvenile detention until we got some straight answers from you—

JULIA I told you—

DETECTIVE HAYES A story… now I just want the truth. Why would you lie to us… to protect your—

JULIA No, it's not like that—

DETECTIVE HAYES And the money was what? Blackmail?

JULIA It was guilt money—

DETECTIVE HAYES About what?

JULIA Past sins—

DETECTIVE HAYES Did you think that Danny would shoot him?

JULIA I didn't want him to—

DETECTIVE HAYES He didn't. And neither did you. Julia, listen to me. It's over. The forensic folks say that after you left, your late literary man put the pistol in his mouth and just squeezed. That's how we found him. You didn't even see the mess did you?

JULIA No. I didn't know there was a bullet in the chamber… he—

DETECTIVE HAYES Yeah, the next-door neighbor heard the gunshot, immediately came out on her porch and saw you crying, alone in the car.

JULIA Danny was gone—

DETECTIVE HAYES You thought he'd just wait in the car like a puppy?

JULIA He didn't even leave a note—

DETECTIVE HAYES So then you thought Danny shot Drake?

JULIA I didn't want him to get into any more trouble—

DETECTIVE HAYES You took the blame yourself, to cover for him?

JULIA Yes. So now you know I'm not guilty of murder… just an unwitting accomplice to a suicide.

DETECTIVE HAYES And transporting a minor across state lines…

JULIA What's going to happen to Danny?

DETECTIVE HAYES (*She slides a photo across the table to JULIA*) Julia… I need you to tell me who you see in this photograph.

JULIA You want me to identify him?

DETECTIVE HAYES Danny… Jackson? That's what it says on the back…

JULIA (*She takes the photo*) That's not his last name that's where we were when we…

DETECTIVE HAYES All I see is your car with its wheel jacked up. What do you see?

JULIA I… I don't understand. Did you photo-shop him out? He was right there—

DETECTIVE HAYES No. No, he wasn't. Listen to me very carefully. We've done a lot of digging and I can tell you for a fact that Danny… doesn't exist.

JULIA You're lying!

DETECTIVE HAYES Wait. Stop. Listen to me. We checked with the motels where you stayed. The registries. He wasn't there—

JULIA He slept in the car—

DETECTIVE HAYES Nobody saw him. Not even in Virginia where you paid for two rooms. The other room was unoccupied. The manager was quite clear with me on that point.

JULIA What are you saying? That I—

DETECTIVE HAYES I know this must be very hard for you to accept. I didn't believe it myself, at first. I'm sorry I had to string you along about holding him here. I had to know for sure.

JULIA He's not?

DETECTIVE HAYES I've personally been in contact with your psychiatrist. She didn't appreciate having her vacation interrupted. Can't blame her. But we did have a little chat. And I think I understand now.

JULIA What did she say…

DETECTIVE HAYES Not much. Confidentiality, you know. Been off your meds for a while?

JULIA That's not... Danny's not...

DETECTIVE HAYES (*She hands her another photo.*) Now I want you to look at this one. The description you gave of Danny matches the body of a young John Doe found in Manhattan the day you left. All over the news. You must have seen it. Kid jumped from a penthouse balcony, also a suicide.

JULIA And you think that I...

DETECTIVE HAYES No. I'm saying that you've been in a very impressionable state of mind. We're not going to charge you with anything.

JULIA What now?

DETECTIVE HAYES Drake had no surviving family and his publishers are trying to cover it all up. They want to speak with you, of course.

JULIA What about me...

DETECTIVE HAYES You need help. But I don't think you're a danger to yourself or others, now. You're free.

JULIA Thank you.

DETECTIVE HAYES Drake left you a note. Just two words. The last word is "me." The first one starts with an "f". Care to guess which one? (*Pause.*) Julia, why did he need to be "forgiven"?

JULIA God knows.

DETECTIVE HAYES Do you?

JULIA What if I told you...

DETECTIVE HAYES What if—?

JULIA What if I told you... a story? "Once upon a time, there was a little girl... who loved to tell stories." (*She cries.*)

> *Blackout.*

THE DRAKES EXIT

> *PROF. DRAKE lies slumped over his desk. The echo of a gunshot is heard. He stands amazed that he is still alive. Looks back down at the desk and the gun. He looks down at his hands. He realizes he is dead. MRS. DRAKE appears in a halo of white light. She smiles at him. He stares at her.*

PROF. DRAKE It was actually... loaded?

MRS. DRAKE I wish I had a new life for every time I've heard that—

PROF. DRAKE I don't remember... pulling the trigger—

MRS. DRAKE I guided your hand, it was your time—

PROF. DRAKE You… you… killed me?

MRS. DRAKE Let's just say… I assisted you. Now, we're even.

PROF. DRAKE Mary, can you forgive me for… for everything?

MRS. DRAKE It's not for me to forgive.

PROF. DRAKE God, I missed you—

MRS. DRAKE I've been waiting.

PROF. DRAKE Where are we… is this…?

MRS. DRAKE No more words. I'll show you. Come fly with me.

> *She takes him by the hand. There is a rush of air as of the sound of wings.*
>
> *Cross fade.*

JULIA AND DANNY'S GOODBYE

DANNY and JULIA stand in a pool of light.

DANNY I tried to tell you.

JULIA Why should I listen to you? You don't exist.

DANNY Not anymore. Will you tell my story now?

JULIA Yes. How about that dance?

DANNY Teach me?

> *She holds out her arms. He comes to her. Waltz music begins to play. JULIA places DANNY'S hands in the "right places" but then she changes her mind and decides to lead. They begin to waltz around the interrogation chamber. At the height of their duet, DANNY silently steps aside and JULIA continues dancing on her own as if DANNY was still there. DANNY exits as if unseen. The music builds to a crescendo. JULIA stops and looks around for DANNY. She smiles.*
>
> *Blackout.*

End of play.

THE CREATURE

BY

TREVOR ALLEN

The Creature

No green skin, no neckbolts—this is an elegant, presentational production based on Mary Shelley's novel. Told from the Creature's point of view and juxtaposing the stark first years of his existence with the scientist's denial of his creation, *The Creature* breathes new life into this timeless supernatural tale in a fugue-like cacophony of horror, revenge, and redemption.

Production Information

World Premiere: October 2009 Black Box Theatre, San Francisco

Producer:	Karen McKevitt
Director:	Rob Melrose
Stage Manager:	David Young
Artistic Director:	Trevor Allen

Cast

The Creature	James Carpenter
Victor Frankenstein	Gabriel Marin
Captain Walton	Garth Petal

THE CREATURE

CHARACTERS

CAPT. WALTON: The captain of a frozen ship (and other characters).

VICTOR FRANKENSTEIN: A man haunted by his past.

THE CREATURE: A "monster" in search of his creator.

TIME

Tonight... we tell this story.

ACT 1 SCENE 1

CAPT. WALTON To Miss Margaret Saville. March fifteenth, St. Petersberg. You will be happy to hear that no disaster has occurred which might hinder the commencement of my voyage. One which you have regarded with such dark foreboding. Do not worry about my safety. Think of the benefit to mankind... the discovery of a northern passage, near the pole. A shorter route to those lands which at present takes so many months to reach. The ship is strong, the crew good and the weather clear. If we should meet again, after I have crossed these immense seas, and returned home... then perhaps I will give up this wandering life. However, if you should never hear from me again... then remember me with tenderness and affection. Captain Robert Walton.

July first. We are under way. I had hoped to sail much earlier and avoid the shifting pack ice as much as possible but one catastrophe has followed another. If I were a superstitious man I would have turned back many times already. But a kind of divine madness hurries me on. I know that you may never read this, but it comforts me to think that I am speaking with you. Love Robert.

August eleventh. I celebrated my thirtieth birthday with moldy bread, salted pork, and the last of the Scotch. But, I could not be more overjoyed at the prospect of completing this voyage. We sighted our first iceberg, at some distance, though still a bit too close for my liking. I wish that I were able to describe the terrible beauty of this place. The northern lights are awe-inspiring and there is life here, of a kind that is both odd and wondrous. I wish that you could see these sights with your own eyes... My spirits are high even though the cold is severe... the ink freezes as I pen these words.

September fourth. Somewhere in the Arctic Ocean. So strange an incident has occurred that I must record it. We are nearly surrounded by ice, it has closed in around the ship on all sides, scarcely leaving her room to float. Our situation is somewhat dangerous, especially since we are encompassed by a very thick fog. We have dropped anchor. Yesterday the mist cleared away, and I saw, stretching out in every direction a vast plain of ice, it seems to go on forever. I went below deck, and was endeavoring to get some rest since I had been on watch all night… when the crew began calling to me. They said that they saw something on the ice. I went forward and a strange sight met me. What looked like a sled drawn by dogs, passed us at the distance of half a mile to the north. Something… sat in the sled. It was shaped like a man, but it seemed distorted somehow… I watched the rapid progress of this traveler with my telescope, until it was lost among the distant inequalities of the ice. That night, the ice cracked, and freed our ship. However, we lay to, fearing to encounter those huge masses in the dark. In the morning, as soon as it was light, I went on deck and found all the sailors busy on one side of the vessel, apparently talking to someone in the sea. I peered over the side… floating on a large fragment of ice I saw a dogsled… none of the dogs remained alive.

But there was a man covered in ragged furs standing there. The sailors were trying to persuade him to come aboard. The stranger addressed me…

FRANKENSTEIN Before I come on board your vessel… tell me where you are bound?

CAPT. WALTON You can imagine my astonishment on hearing such a question from a man on the brink of destruction. It was only when I told him that we were on a voyage of discovery towards the pole that he consented to come on board. He was nearly frozen, and dreadfully emaciated by fatigue and suffering. I have never seen a man in such a wretched condition. I asked him why he had come out so far on the ice?

FRANKENSTEIN To seek… one, that fled from me.

CAPT. WALTON Did the man that you pursued also travel by sled?

FRANKENSTEIN It did.

CAPT. WALTON Then… we have seen him.

FRANKENSTEIN Which direction? Tell me—

CAPT. WALTON Due north—

FRANKENSTEIN Good… good… I will rest now… but then I must continue…

    He blacks out.

CAPT. WALTON September fifth. My guest has rested and recovered somewhat. Today he asked me about my intention of going North.

FRANKENSTEIN North? What do you hope to find there?

CAPT. WALTON It's been my lifelong ambition… to cross uncharted seas… to conquer the unknown. I seek a course through the ice…to the lands beyond… this expedition may fail… but one man's life is a small price to pay for the acquirement of knowledge.

FRANKENSTEIN Do you share my madness?

CAPT. WALTON Madness? I merely wish to explore—

FRANKENSTEIN That is only the beginning—

CAPT. WALTON You don't understand—

FRANKENSTEIN On the contrary my dear Captain… I understand all too well.

CAPT. WALTON What do you hope to find out there?

FRANKENSTEIN I go north because… I must.

CAPT. WALTON Who are you following?

FRANKENSTEIN Not who, Walton… What. My death… it's out there.

CAPT. WALTON I see—

FRANKENSTEIN I hope you've posted a guard?

CAPT. WALTON That won't be necessary… if anyone is out there, he'll freeze—

FRANKENSTEIN Do you wish to die a horrible death?

CAPT. WALTON No, of course not—

FRANKENSTEIN Then listen to me—arm your men… and set a watch, day and night—

CAPT. WALTON What should I tell them to look for?

FRANKENSTEIN They'll know it when they see it.

CAPT. WALTON It?

FRANKENSTEIN Yes…

CAPT. WALTON The other man… on the sled? He must be drowned by now.

FRANKENSTEIN I hope to God you're right.

CAPT. WALTON You need some rest, we'll discuss this in the morning—

FRANKENSTEIN My friend… I was once like you… You have hope, and the whole world before you. You have no cause for despair. But I—I have lost everything, and cannot begin my life again. There is only one thing left for me to finish… and it is waiting for me out there. When my strength has returned I will attend to it—

CAPT. WALTON This creature… can you tell me why you—

FRANKENSTEIN You may perceive, Captain Walton, that I have suffered greatly. I had decided that the memory of my deeds should die with me… but you have persuaded me otherwise. You seek for knowledge and wisdom, as I once did… a noble goal. But I hope that the gratification of your wishes will not be a serpent to sting you, as mine has been. If we were among the tamer scenes of nature, I might fear to encounter your disbelief, perhaps even your ridicule… but many things may appear possible here… at the end of the world.

CAPT. WALTON He told me that he would begin his story tonight. Strange and harrowing must be his tale and frightful the storm which embraced this gallant vessel on its course, and wrecked it thus.

Blackout.

ACT 1 SCENE 2

THE CREATURE It is with considerable difficulty that I remember my creation…

FRANKENSTEIN I was born in Geneva.

THE CREATURE All the events of that period are confused… in my mind.

FRANKENSTEIN My family is one of the most well known of that republic. My father was the local magistrate.

THE CREATURE I remember the cold… the hunger and pain…

FRANKENSTEIN There was a great difference between the ages of my parents, but that seemed only to bring them closer together.

THE CREATURE Waking in a dark room… and you were there… Frankenstein.

FRANKENSTEIN I was their oldest child. Their plaything and their idol.

THE CREATURE Your face was the first thing I saw—

FRANKENSTEIN The innocent and helpless creature given to them by God…

THE CREATURE Filled with horror and disgust.

FRANKENSTEIN A being whose future was in their hands to direct toward happiness or misery.

THE CREATURE A strange cacophony of sensations seized me. I saw, felt, heard, and smelt all at the same time...

FRANKENSTEIN For a long time I was their only child. But my mother had always wanted a daughter—

THE CREATURE It was a long time before I learned to distinguish between the operations of my various senses—

FRANKENSTEIN When I was about five years old, they spent a week on the shores of Lake Como.

THE CREATURE I remember, a strong light... I had to shut my eyes.

FRANKENSTEIN Their benevolent natures often made them enter the cottages of the poor to help in any way they could.

THE CREATURE Darkness overcame me—

FRANKENSTEIN One day when my father was away, my mother and I found a peasant and his wife distributing a scanty meal to five hungry children.

THE CREATURE I remember hearing your voice...

FRANKENSTEIN There was one which attracted my mother, an orphan—

THE CREATURE But when I opened my eyes again and the light poured in... you were gone.

FRANKENSTEIN When my father returned, he found a beautiful young girl playing with me in the hall of our villa.

THE CREATURE I stood, with a little difficulty and looked around for you.

FRANKENSTEIN With his permission my mother adopted her.

THE CREATURE I found you... stretched out on your bed and I tried to speak... but all that came out was a groan...

FRANKENSTEIN And so Elizabeth Lavenza became the inmate of my parents' house. My more than sister. My childhood companion and the love of my life.

THE CREATURE I reached out for you—but you ran away from me, taking the light with you—

FRANKENSTEIN On the birth of a second son, Earnest, my parents gave up their wandering life and settled in Geneva.

THE CREATURE I walked and I believe I descended to the ground... and so I left the place of my birth and went out into the world.

FRANKENSTEIN By the time my youngest brother William was born, my parents lived in considerable seclusion.

THE CREATURE I found a great alteration in my senses. Before, dark shapes had surrounded me... but now I found that I could wander anywhere—

FRANKENSTEIN I was predisposed to avoid crowds, and to attach myself to only a few.

THE CREATURE But after a while the light became more and more oppressive. The heat made me weary as I walked. Until I found a place to rest in the shade. This was the forest near Ingolstadt...

FRANKENSTEIN I was indifferent to my schoolmates but I had one close friend, Henry Clerval.

THE CREATURE I spent days walking in the woods... until I finally arrived at a village. It was miraculous. The huts, the cottages, and the stately houses amazed me... I entered one of the best of these.

FRANKENSTEIN I have to admit that my temper was sometimes violent, and my passions extreme.

THE CREATURE I hardly placed my foot inside the doorway... when the children shrieked, and one of the women fainted.

FRANKENSTEIN I was driven from an early age by a need to understand things... I confess that it was the secrets of heaven and earth that I desired to learn—

THE CREATURE Soon the whole village was roused. Some ran away... but some attacked me with stones or anything else they could throw. I escaped into the forest... battered and bruised by the hands of men—

FRANKENSTEIN When I was fifteen. I witnessed a violent thunderstorm.

THE CREATURE I hadn't experienced fear before.

FRANKENSTEIN I watched a stream of fire strike a beautiful old oak which stood about twenty yards from my window.

THE CREATURE It was blinding...

FRANKENSTEIN As soon as the dazzling light vanished... I saw that the tree had disappeared. I dreamt of harnessing this power.

THE CREATURE When I couldn't run any more I took refuge in a small hovel.

FRANKENSTEIN When I visited the tree the next morning...

THE CREATURE It was quite bare...

FRANKENSTEIN I found it shattered. Nothing remained but a blackened stump.

THE CREATURE A wretched sight after the palaces I had seen in the village.

FRANKENSTEIN It was not just splintered by the shock… it was entirely reduced to thin ribbons of wood.

THE CREATURE The hovel joined onto a cottage. But, after my dearly bought experience… I knew I shouldn't enter it.

FRANKENSTEIN I have never seen anything so completely destroyed… (*Laughs.*) except my soul.

THE CREATURE I retreated to a deserted pigsty and lay down in the straw. I was happy just to have found a shelter from the storm but still more from the barbarity of men.

FRANKENSTEIN When I was seventeen, my parents decided that I should become a student at the university.

THE CREATURE I heard a step, and looking through a small hole in the wall, I saw a beautiful young creature, carrying something heavy, walk past me.

FRANKENSTEIN My departure date was set. But before the day arrived, the first misfortune of my life occurred.

THE CREATURE When all of a sudden another creature came up to her and uttered a few soft sounds. Then he took the log and carried it to the cottage himself.

FRANKENSTEIN My mother became sick with a fever. The looks of her doctors predicted the worst…

THE CREATURE In one wall of the cottage was a window but it had been boarded up. There was a crack in one of the boards. I looked through it and I could see a small room…

FRANKENSTEIN On her death-bed she joined the hands of Elizabeth and myself and said—"Children, my hopes of future happiness were placed on the prospect of your marriage. This expectation will now be the consolation of your father."

THE CREATURE In one corner, near the fireplace, sat an old man. The young girl took something out of a drawer and sat down beside him. He picked up a piece of wood, he began to blow through it, such sounds came out of it… sweeter than the voice of the nightingale.

FRANKENSTEIN She passed away quietly… and even in death her face showed affection…

THE CREATURE He played a lovely mournful tune, which drew tears out of the eyes of the woman. But the old man took no notice, until she sobbed out loud. Then he made a few sounds, and the fair creature, stopped crying. He smiled at her with such kindness and affection that I felt sensations of a peculiar and over-powering nature.

FRANKENSTEIN I can't describe the feelings of sorrow which I felt. My mother was dead and I couldn't bring her back. But I still had duties to perform… Elizabeth comforted me…

THE CREATURE I felt a mixture of pain and pleasure, such as I had never experienced before, either from hunger or cold, warmth or food… and I turned away from the window, unable to bear these emotions.

FRANKENSTEIN The day of my departure for Ingolstadt came. When I descended to the carriage… they were all there… my father to bless me, Clerval to shake my hand one last time, and my Elizabeth to kiss me good-bye.

THE CREATURE I lay on my straw, but I couldn't sleep. I thought about the day. What struck me most was the gentle manners of these creatures… I wanted to join them, but I didn't dare.

FRANKENSTEIN I threw myself into the coach that was to convey me away and once I was out of their sight… I wept like a little child.

THE CREATURE I remembered too well the treatment of the villagers. I decided to remain quietly in my hovel, watching.

FRANKENSTEIN Eventually I saw the high white steeple of the town and was conducted to my solitary attic apartment, to spend the evening as I pleased. All alone.

THE CREATURE The cottagers rose the next morning before the sun. The young woman prepared the food and the young man chopped wood for the fire. The old man was blind. A condition I did not understand at first. When I realized that he was without sight and that he relied on the two young creatures for help, I was amazed. It was my first glimpse of kindness. I wanted to help too. Before, I had taken food from their garden and water from their trough. When I understood how little they had… I went into the forest at night and gathered berries and nuts and drank from the stream. I even began stacking firewood outside their shed every morning before they woke up. I was learning.

Blackout.

ACT 1 SCENE 3

FRANKENSTEIN The next morning I delivered my letters of introduction and paid a visit to some of the professors. Chance, or the influence of some angel of destruction, led me to Doctor Waldman, professor of chemistry.

CAPT. WALTON (*as PROFESSOR WALDMAN*) Victor, the ancient alchemists, promised impossibilities, and performed nothing. The modern masters promise very little, they know that lead cannot be transmuted into gold, and that the elixir of life is an illusion. But these scientists, whose hands seem only made to dig in the dirt, and their eyes to look through the microscope... have indeed performed miracles.

FRANKENSTEIN These were the words of fate spoken to destroy me.

CAPT. WALTON (*as PROFESSOR WALDMAN*) They penetrate into the recesses of nature, and show how she works in her hiding places.

FRANKENSTEIN I felt as if my soul were fighting with a palpable enemy.

CAPT. WALTON (*as PROFESSOR WALDMAN*) They ascend into the heavens. They have discovered how the blood circulates, and even the nature of the air we breathe.

FRANKENSTEIN One by one the various locks were opened which guarded my mind.

CAPT. WALTON (*as PROFESSOR WALDMAN*) They have acquired new and almost unlimited powers.

FRANKENSTEIN Chord after chord was sounded—

CAPT. WALTON (*as PROFESSOR WALDMAN*) They can command the thunders of heaven, mimic the earthquake, and even mock the invisible world with its own shadows.

FRANKENSTEIN Soon I was filled with one thought—

CAPT. WALTON (*as PROFESSOR WALDMAN*) Fear...

FRANKENSTEIN One idea—

CAPT. WALTON (*as PROFESSOR WALDMAN*) Fear of the unknown

FRANKENSTEIN One purpose.

CAPT. WALTON (*as PROFESSOR WALDMAN*) That is all that holds us back—

FRANKENSTEIN So much has been done, but I will achieve far more.

CAPT. WALTON (*as PROFESSOR WALDMAN*) What new discoveries await us...

FRANKENSTEIN Walking in the footsteps already marked…

CAPT. WALTON (as PROFESSOR WALDMAN) If we only have the will to search?

FRANKENSTEIN I will pioneer a new way, explore unknown powers, and unfold to the world the deepest mysteries of creation.

CAPT. WALTON (as PROFESSOR WALDMAN) Who knows… perhaps the answers to life itself?

> *He exits.*

FRANKENSTEIN The madness had won.

ACT 1 SCENE 4

THE CREATURE I made a discovery of great importance. I found that these creatures possessed a method of communicating their experiences and feelings to each other by articulate sounds. I saw that the… words… they spoke sometimes produced laughter or sadness. This was a godlike art. I wanted to learn how to speak and become more like them—

FRANKENSTEIN At first my labor was fluctuating and uncertain—

THE CREATURE In the beginning I failed at every attempt I made—

FRANKENSTEIN But I gained strength as I proceeded, and soon I became so caught up in my work that the stars often disappeared in the light of morning while I was working in my laboratory.

THE CREATURE Their pronunciation was quick and the words they uttered had no apparent connection with any visible objects.

FRANKENSTEIN My progress was rapid. At the end of two years, I made some discoveries which procured me great esteem and admiration at the University.

THE CREATURE At first I was unable to discover any way to unravel the mystery of their language.

FRANKENSTEIN I had become as well acquainted with the theories and practices of the day as any of the professors.

THE CREATURE By great concentration of will, after having spent several cycles of the moon in my hovel, I discovered the names that were given to some of the most familiar objects.

FRANKENSTEIN My residence there being no longer conducive to my improvement, I thought of returning to my native town.

THE CREATURE I learned the words—

FRANKENSTEIN My home—

THE CREATURE Wood—

FRANKENSTEIN Family—

THE CREATURE Bread—

FRANKENSTEIN Elizabeth—

THE CREATURE And fire.

FRANKENSTEIN When an incident happened that prolonged my stay and sealed my fate.

THE CREATURE My life would never be the same again.

FRANKENSTEIN One of the phenomena which attracted my attention was the organization and structure of the human animal... and indeed, any creature endowed with life.

THE CREATURE I also learned the names of the cottagers themselves.

FRANKENSTEIN I often asked myself, "What was the principle of the creation of life?"

THE CREATURE The young man and woman each had several names.

FRANKENSTEIN How many questions are we on the brink of answering, if cowardice or ignorance did not restrain our inquiries.

THE CREATURE He was, Brother, Son and Felix. She was called Sister, Daughter or Agatha.

FRANKENSTEIN I applied myself more particularly to the problems associated with the spark of life itself.

THE CREATURE But the blind old man had only one name... Father.

FRANKENSTEIN Where does it come from, why does it end... could it be prolonged or even artificially created?

THE CREATURE It was a long time before I understood what that word meant—

FRANKENSTEIN I was driven by an almost inhuman enthusiasm. My experiments were called grotesque by my fellow students. So I began to work alone, at night, in secret.

THE CREATURE Each new discovery drove me on.

FRANKENSTEIN In order to examine the cause of life, I first studied the causes of death.

THE CREATURE I can't describe how I felt—

FRANKENSTEIN I quickly mastered the science of anatomy and even though the university provided me with lab animals and cadavers... these were not sufficient for my needs.

THE CREATURE When I learned the idea behind each new sound and was able to pronounce them… I wept like a little child.

FRANKENSTEIN I had to observe the natural decay of the human body. And so I was led to examine… graves and forced to spend days and nights in charnel-houses.

THE CREATURE I learned so many words.

FRANKENSTEIN I watched the corruption of death.

THE CREATURE I heard many more like—

FRANKENSTEIN How the fine form of man—

THE CREATURE Good—

FRANKENSTEIN Was degraded and wasted.

THE CREATURE Evil—

FRANKENSTEIN I saw how the worm inherited the wonders of the eye and brain…

THE CREATURE But I didn't understand their meanings, yet.

FRANKENSTEIN I became determined to never end up like that.

THE CREATURE My life in the hovel became routine. I slept while my friends were out working in the fields. I watched and listened as the old man told stories or played his flute. I learned all I could.

FRANKENSTEIN It was late at night… I was standing over a corpse, dissecting, examining and analyzing all the minute details of the change from life to death.

THE CREATURE At night, when they slept I would collect my own food and do the chores that I had seen the son do… like clearing their path of snow or bringing water from the well.

FRANKENSTEIN In the midst of this darkness a sudden light struck me—a light so brilliant and wondrous and yet so simple, that I became dizzy at the thought of it.

THE CREATURE Afterwards I found that these labors being performed by an invisible hand, amazed them.

FRANKENSTEIN I had discovered the secret of creation.

THE CREATURE Once I heard them speak the words "guardian angel"…

FRANKENSTEIN I was surprised, that among so many men of genius I alone should be reserved to discover such an astonishing secret.

THE CREATURE I didn't know that they were talking about me.

FRANKENSTEIN After months of incredible labor and fatigue, I became capable of bestowing animation upon lifeless matter.

FRANKENSTEIN *(Directed to CAPT. WALTON.)* Remember Captain, I am not relating the visions of a madman. The stages of my discovery were very distinct and were all set down in my journal.

CAPT. WALTON I see... and where is this journal?

FRANKENSTEIN I... lost it.

CAPT. WALTON How?

FRANKENSTEIN The creature that destroyed my life took it and it is lost. My friend, I see by the look in your eyes, that you expect me to tell you this secret. Listen to me and you will understand why I am... reserved upon that subject. I will not lead you on, as innocent as I was then, to your own destruction. Learn by my example, how dangerous the acquirement of knowledge at any price can be.

> *Blackout.*

ACT 1 SCENE 5

THE CREATURE In the midst of their poverty... these people were happy. I watched the brother carry the first little white flowers that peeped out from beneath the snowy ground to his sister.

FRANKENSTEIN When I found such an astonishing power placed in my hands...

THE CREATURE They were like me... but not like me—

FRANKENSTEIN I considered for a long time how I should use it...

THE CREATURE I wanted more than anything else to be one of them—

FRANKENSTEIN It never occurred to me that I shouldn't—

THE CREATURE I didn't know who, or what... I was. You never told me.

FRANKENSTEIN I possessed the capacity to bestow animation, but to prepare a frame for the reception of it, with all the intricacies of nerves, muscles, and veins... still seemed like a work of inconceivable difficulty.

THE CREATURE In the day, the young man worked in the fields, but after dinner he would read to the old man and young woman. This reading puzzled me at first—

FRANKENSTEIN —At first I doubted whether I should attempt the creation of a being like myself, or one of simpler organization...

THE CREATURE But I discovered that he made many of the same sounds when he read as when he talked.

FRANKENSTEIN But my mind was on fire…

THE CREATURE I guessed that he saw symbols for sounds on the paper which he understood.

FRANKENSTEIN I was propelled from one success to another.

THE CREATURE I wanted to know these too, but I didn't even understand all the sounds yet…

FRANKENSTEIN I knew that I had the ability to give life to an animal as complex as man…

THE CREATURE He was teaching his sister to read… and as I listened, I began to learn too.

FRANKENSTEIN Why shouldn't I?

THE CREATURE Language came easily to me.

FRANKENSTEIN I began a journal of my greatest experiment—

THE CREATURE On one of my nightly wanderings I came across a satchel filled with papers like I had seen in the cottage. I carried them off before their owner returned.

FRANKENSTEIN The raw materials within my command didn't seem adequate for such an undertaking.

THE CREATURE The papers were *Plutarch's Lives*, *The Sorrows of Werther* and *Paradise Lost*… My history, my philosophy and my bible.

FRANKENSTEIN I didn't doubt that I would ultimately succeed, but I prepared myself for many setbacks.

THE CREATURE These books became my sole possessions and I spent many months deciphering them…

FRANKENSTEIN I thought about the advances which take place in science every day—

THE CREATURE I applied my whole mind to it and I improved greatly in this science, but not enough to have any kind of conversation.

FRANKENSTEIN I hoped that my attempts would at least lay the foundations for future success.

THE CREATURE I wanted to show myself to the cottagers.

FRANKENSTEIN I began the creation of a human being in a solitary chamber at the top of the house. My own laboratory.

THE CREATURE But I decided not to… until I could speak their language.

FRANKENSTEIN I kept my filthy workshop a secret.

THE CREATURE This might make them overlook my deformity.

FRANKENSTEIN Since the minuteness of the parts hindered my speed, I decided to make the thing of a gigantic stature… about eight feet in height, and proportionally large.

THE CREATURE I admired the perfect forms of my friends… their grace, beauty, and delicate movements.

FRANKENSTEIN I spent months collecting and arranging my materials.

THE CREATURE But then one bright moonlit night as the snow began to melt…

FRANKENSTEIN I took bones from crypts and vaults.

THE CREATURE I saw my face reflected in a clear pool.

FRANKENSTEIN The dissecting room and the slaughter-house also furnished many of my materials—

THE CREATURE At first I stepped back, unable to believe that the thing in the water was really me.

FRANKENSTEIN It was hard work and I often turned with disgust from my labor.

THE CREATURE I was filled with disgust when I became convinced that I really was a monster.

FRANKENSTEIN Only the moon watched as I tortured living animals, to animate this lifeless clay.

THE CREATURE What possessed you to do this?

FRANKENSTEIN A frantic impulse urged me on and I lost all perspective. I thought only that a new species would bless me as its creator and that many happy creatures would owe their lives to me. No father could claim the gratitude of his children as completely as I would be able to.

THE CREATURE Behold the great creator at work.

FRANKENSTEIN If I could bestow animation on lifeless tissue… in time I might be able to prolong life indefinitely. To stop death.

THE CREATURE What gave you the right to play God?

FRANKENSTEIN I pursued my task with unremitting labor. My cheeks grew pale and I became emaciated. Sometimes, on the very brink… I failed. But I clung to the hope that the next hour or the next minute might bring success. I was urged on by a madness.

ACT 1 SCENE 6

THE CREATURE As the sun became warmer, and the light of day longer, the snow vanished, and I saw the bare trees and the black earth begin to blossom…

FRANKENSTEIN The spring passed while I worked.

THE CREATURE It was my first spring—

FRANKENSTEIN It was a beautiful season but I was insensible to the charms of nature. I also forgot my friends and family so many miles away. I hadn't seen them for such a long time and I knew my silence made them uneasy. My father's voice was always there—

CAPT. WALTON (*as FRANKENSTEIN'S FATHER*) I know that while you are pleased with yourself, you will think of us and we shall hear from you regularly. However, I will regard any interruption in your letters as proof that your other duties are equally neglected.

FRANKENSTEIN Father you're wrong…

CAPT. WALTON What's wrong?

FRANKENSTEIN (*Realizing he's speaking to WALTON.*) Walton? I thought he was wrong… but now… I'm convinced that he was justified and that I shouldn't be free from blame.

THE CREATURE My mind became more active. When I slept… I dreamed of the old blind father, the strong young man and the beautiful woman.

FRANKENSTEIN A man should always try to preserve a calm and peaceful mind, and never to allow passion or desire to disturb that tranquillity.

THE CREATURE They seemed like superior beings, who held the keys to my future.

FRANKENSTEIN I don't believe that the pursuit of knowledge is an exception to this rule.

THE CREATURE In my imagination… I saw a thousand images of how I would present myself to them… and how they would react.

FRANKENSTEIN If your life's ambition has a tendency to weaken your affections, and to destroy your taste for the simple pleasures… then it is wrong…

THE CREATURE I imagined that they would be afraid at first, until by my gentle actions and kind words, I could first win their friendship and then their love.

FRANKENSTEIN That is to say... It is not befitting a human mind.

THE CREATURE These thoughts kept me going. My one goal was to acquire the art of speech. My voice was harsh, and not like their soft tones, but I pronounced the words that I understood well enough. I learned very quickly. I guess I should thank you... for my mind... father.

FRANKENSTEIN It was on a dreary night in November that I saw the accomplishment of my work.

THE CREATURE Knowledge is such a strange thing.

FRANKENSTEIN I was anxious and tired. I hadn't slept in days.

THE CREATURE It acts like a disease for which there is no cure.

FRANKENSTEIN When I collected the life giving instruments around me, to infuse a spark of being into the lifeless thing on the table it was already midnight.

THE CREATURE Sometimes I wanted to shake off all thoughts and feelings and forget myself... but I couldn't... not even in sleep.

FRANKENSTEIN The rain pattered against the panes, and the lightning flashed overhead.

THE CREATURE That's when the nightmares would start.

FRANKENSTEIN My candle was almost burnt out, when in that half light, I saw the dull yellow eye of the creature open... It breathed hard and shook its limbs...

THE CREATURE I found that there was only one way to overcome the pain of life, and that was in death. Which I feared.

FRANKENSTEIN I jumped back in fright, but as I did so... it fell back and just lay there... motionless. Like death itself.

THE CREATURE Because I didn't understand.

FRANKENSTEIN It was a catastrophe, not because I had failed... but because up until that moment I hadn't given any thought to the thing itself. It was hideous!

THE CREATURE I admired virtue and good feelings, and loved the gentle manners of my friends, but I was shut out from their lives because of the way I looked.

FRANKENSTEIN I had selected its features as beautiful...

THE CREATURE The music, the flowers and the stories were not meant for me...

FRANKENSTEIN Beautiful?.... God, its yellow skin barely covered the muscles and arteries beneath...

THE CREATURE I am a miserable... creature.

FRANKENSTEIN Its hair was long and black, and its teeth were pearly white but they only formed a more horrible contrast to its watery eyes. They seemed almost the same color as the yellow sockets they stared out of. It had a shriveled complexion and straight black lips.

THE CREATURE I learned about families.

FRANKENSTEIN I had worked for two years, with the sole purpose of infusing life into that inanimate body.

THE CREATURE Sons and daughters—

FRANKENSTEIN I didn't sleep—

THE CREATURE Mothers and fathers—

FRANKENSTEIN I didn't eat—

THE CREATURE I had none of these—

FRANKENSTEIN And now that I had come this far—

THE CREATURE I was none of these—

FRANKENSTEIN When I saw it move... the beauty of the dream vanished!

THE CREATURE Where is my family?

FRANKENSTEIN I was sick at the sight of it.

THE CREATURE Where did I come from?

FRANKENSTEIN I turned all the machines off and left my lab.

THE CREATURE No mother held me—

FRANKENSTEIN I threw myself onto my bed—

THE CREATURE No father watched over me—

FRANKENSTEIN Completely exhausted—

THE CREATURE My past is a blank.

FRANKENSTEIN And finally slept...

THE CREATURE I have always been exactly as I am now...

FRANKENSTEIN But nightmares haunted me—

THE CREATURE I have never seen anything that resembled me—

FRANKENSTEIN I thought I saw Elizabeth turn into a corpse as I held her in my arms.

THE CREATURE But I do remember you…

FRANKENSTEIN When I woke…

THE CREATURE I saw your face there in the dark—

FRANKENSTEIN A cold dew covered my forehead—

THE CREATURE Lit by flashes of light—

FRANKENSTEIN My heart stopped when, by the dim yellow light of the moon I saw the thing I had created—

THE CREATURE Filled with disgust while I writhed in agony, wracked with pain.

FRANKENSTEIN Standing over my bed staring down at me.

THE CREATURE I must have blacked out from the shock. When I woke… you were gone.

FRANKENSTEIN There was an evil expression on its face.

THE CREATURE I searched for you… and I found you sleeping on your bed—

FRANKENSTEIN Its jaws opened—

THE CREATURE What am I?

FRANKENSTEIN It made some inarticulate sounds—

THE CREATURE Where did I come from?

FRANKENSTEIN It might have spoken—

THE CREATURE Why am I alive?

FRANKENSTEIN But I didn't understand it.

THE CREATURE Please tell me—

FRANKENSTEIN One of its arms reached out to grab me—

THE CREATURE Who are you?

FRANKENSTEIN I escaped and ran downstairs.

THE CREATURE Don't run away—

FRANKENSTEIN I took refuge in the courtyard of the house.

THE CREATURE Soon after I came to my hovel, I discovered some papers in the pocket of the coat that I had taken from your lab.

FRANKENSTEIN I stayed there the rest of the night listening for any sign of the corpse to which I had given life.

THE CREATURE At first I ignored them but when I learned to decipher their symbols I studied them with great interest.

FRANKENSTEIN I couldn't bear the thought of it.

THE CREATURE It was your journal of the months leading up to my… creation.

FRANKENSTEIN A revived mummy wouldn't be as hideous as this creature.

THE CREATURE Everything in there which refers to my origin was written by you.

FRANKENSTEIN I had looked at it while it was still unfinished, and it was ugly then…

THE CREATURE All the details of that series of disgusting events which produced me are set down.

FRANKENSTEIN But it was just dead tissue..

THE CREATURE The description of my so called "odious and loathsome frame" is given, in language which made your own horrors clear and rendered mine indelible.

FRANKENSTEIN Raw meat.

THE CREATURE What I read made me sick. Why did you make a monster so hideous that even you turned away in disgust?

FRANKENSTEIN Now that those muscles and joints were moving, it was like something out of hell.

THE CREATURE God, in pity, made man beautiful, after his own image but my body is a filthy version of yours. It's more horrible because of the resemblance.

FRANKENSTEIN I stood there with my back to a tree and a scalpel in my hand… waiting… for the rest of the night.

THE CREATURE Even Satan had companions, fellow-devils, to encourage him. I am alone.

Blackout.

ACT 1 SCENE 7

FRANKENSTEIN Morning dawned and the thing hadn't appeared again. As soon as it was light I ran into the streets. I expected to see it around every corner. Just then a coach came towards me. When It stopped, and the door opened… Henry Clerval stepped out…

CAPT. WALTON (*as CLERVAL*) Victor, I'm so glad to see you! It's great of you to meet me here. How did you know I was coming? It was supposed to be a secret. Elizabeth sent me… to keep an eye on you.

FRANKENSTEIN (*to CAPT. WALTON.*) Clerval, it's so good to see you again I…

I suddenly felt calm for the first time in months. We walked towards my college. But the creature I had left in my apartment might still be there, alive, and walking around or dead on the floor. I was more afraid that Clerval would see it than I was of the thing itself. I asked him to wait at the bottom of the stairs, while I went up to my room. My hand was already on the door before I knew what I was doing. I threw it open, but nothing appeared. I went in… but the apartment was empty and my lab was free of its hideous guest. I could hardly believe my luck. When I was sure that it had gone… I ran down to Clerval. But I couldn't control myself. I jumped over the chairs, clapped my hands, and laughed out loud.

CAPT. WALTON (*as CLERVAL*) Victor! For God's sake, what's the matter? You're not well. What's the cause of all this? (*Shaking him by the shoulders.*) Victor, what's wrong?

FRANKENSTEIN Don't ask me, it can tell you. There behind you! Oh God, save me!

CAPT. WALTON It's all right…

FRANKENSTEIN Clerval?

CAPT. WALTON Walton.

FRANKENSTEIN Yes, of course. Walton.

CAPT. WALTON Everything's going to be fine…

FRANKENSTEIN It grabbed me…

CAPT. WALTON You're safe… it's not here. It was only a nightmare…

FRANKENSTEIN When the creature disappeared I had a nervous fever for months. Clerval nursed me back to health…

CAPT. WALTON That's right, now you get some sleep. I'll be up on deck, just call out if you need me.

　　　Blackout.

ACT 1 SCENE 8

THE CREATURE Autumn passed and I saw, with surprise and grief, the leaves decay and fall. The winter came again, and an entire revolution of the seasons had taken place since I awoke into life. My attention, was focused on my plan of introducing myself to my protectors. I decided, to enter the cottage when the blind old man was alone. One day the young man, and woman went for a walk. I approached the door of their cottage and knocked.

He knocks.

CAPT. WALTON (*as THE BLIND OLD MAN*) Who is there?

THE CREATURE Pardon my intrusion. I am a traveler in need of a little rest. You would greatly oblige me if you would allow me to sit by the fire for a few minutes.

CAPT. WALTON (*as THE BLIND OLD MAN*) Please enter, and I will try to help you. I'd be glad of the company. Unfortunately, my children are out, and I'm afraid my eyes aren't what they once were. But there is food—

THE CREATURE Don't trouble yourself... I have food. It is only warmth and rest that I seek.

CAPT. WALTON (*as THE BLIND OLD MAN*) Your accent... are you from here?

THE CREATURE No, but I understand the language... I am going to claim the protection of some friends, that I... love. But I am an unfortunate... man. I have no other relations in the world. These good people that I am going to have never seen me, and know nothing about me. But they're my one hope. I'm afraid that if I fail there, I'll become an outcast forever.

CAPT. WALTON (*as THE BLIND OLD MAN*) To be friendless is truly sad... but the hearts of men, are full of love and charity. Don't despair, if these friends are good and kind—

THE CREATURE They are kind— they are the best people in the world but... they might not see me for what I really am. My life has been harmless... even beneficial, but a fatal flaw might cloud their eyes. I am deformed... from birth... Where they should see a creature with feelings they would only see... a monster.

CAPT. WALTON (*as THE BLIND OLD MAN*) That is... unfortunate. But if you really are harmless, then can't you get them to see past your skin?

THE CREATURE I am about to try. That's why I'm so afraid. I really need these friends... For many months I have done good deeds for them, in secret. But if they saw me they might think I would hurt them.

CAPT. WALTON (*as THE BLIND OLD MAN*) Where do these friends live?

THE CREATURE Near... this spot.

CAPT. WALTON (*as THE BLIND OLD MAN*) (*Beat.*) I can't see your face… but there is something in your voice… If you will confide in me, I might be able to help. I'm poor, but I'd do anything I could to help my fellow man.

THE CREATURE How can I thank you? You are the first person ever to speak kindly to me. I will be grateful to you forever. Your help will assure me of success with my friends… that I am about to meet.

CAPT. WALTON (*as THE BLIND OLD MAN*) May I ask the names of these… friends?

THE CREATURE This was the moment of decision, which was to bestow happiness on me or rob me of it forever. I struggled to answer him, but the effort destroyed all my remaining strength. At that moment I heard footsteps outside. I grabbed the hand of the old man and said… Now is the time! Protect me! You and your family are the friends that I seek.

CAPT. WALTON (*as THE BLIND OLD MAN*) My god… what are you!?

THE CREATURE At that moment the door opened and his children entered. The horror on their faces still haunts me today. She fainted. He ran forward and tore me away from his father. Then he knocked me to the ground and struck me violently with a piece of firewood. I could have torn him limb from limb… But my heart sank inside me and I refrained. I tried to speak to him… but he just kept beating me until I was overcome and ran into the woods.

ACT 1 SCENE 9

FRANKENSTEIN The face of the creature I had created was always in my mind.

THE CREATURE No longer afraid of discovery, I howled like a wild beast.

FRANKENSTEIN A horrible monster. Distorted and twisted—

THE CREATURE The cold stars shined overhead and the voices of birds mocked my cries…

FRANKENSTEIN A fiend that I had loosed upon the world of men.

THE CREATURE The world of men was at peace but I bore a hell within me.

FRANKENSTEIN In my fever dreams I ranted about the beast.

THE CREATURE The sun rose and I crept back into my hovel. I thought that I might still be able to reconcile things. So I sat there silently, expecting my family to wake, like they always did.

FRANKENSTEIN My words surprised Clerval.

THE CREATURE I waited all day in utter… stupid… despair. The shadows grew long… but they didn't appear.

FRANKENSTEIN At first he thought my "illness" was due to exhaustion.

THE CREATURE My "Family" had left me in the night… breaking the only bond that held me to your world.

FRANKENSTEIN But the longer my recovery took, the more he became convinced that it was due to some terrible event.

THE CREATURE Hatred filled my mind and for the first time… I craved revenge. I didn't even try to control myself. When the darkness came, I piled firewood all around the cottage. A fierce wind rose and cut through me.

FRANKENSTEIN I lay insensible for a time with a kind of insanity.

THE CREATURE I set fire to a dry branch and danced around the hovel. I screamed at heaven until it hurt to breathe.

FRANKENSTEIN I remember the first time I became capable of observing the outside world again.

THE CREATURE When the moon went down… I torched the only home I have ever known. The wind fanned the flames—

FRANKENSTEIN The snow and fallen leaves were gone—

THE CREATURE And the trees outside—

FRANKENSTEIN And the trees outside—

THE CREATURE My hovel—

FRANKENSTEIN My window—

THE CREATURE Caught fire—

FRANKENSTEIN Came back to life.

THE CREATURE And then it all went up in smoke.

FRANKENSTEIN It felt like the nightmare was over.

THE CREATURE And now, with the whole world in front of me, where should I direct my steps?

FRANKENSTEIN I felt alive again.

THE CREATURE Your journal told me where to find your home… and family.

FRANKENSTEIN It was a divine spring—

THE CREATURE It was late in the fall when I left—

FRANKENSTEIN And the season contributed greatly to my convalescence.

THE CREATURE My travels were long and the sufferings I endured, intense.

FRANKENSTEIN I felt sentiments of joy and affection revive in my heart.

THE CREATURE Now and then something would show me the way to you—

FRANKENSTEIN After my recovery, I introduced Clerval to the professors of the University and he became a student of the Fine Arts. I decided to join him… and I sealed my laboratory. Forever. I stayed until the end of the term. The months passed and the nightmare faded.

THE CREATURE I rested during the day, and traveled only at night, when no man could see me. I found that my path cut through a deep forest. It was still light when I came to the other side and saw a deep river flowing past. I stopped, to drink… when a young girl ran past the trees where I stood… She was laughing and calling out… She was playing. I watched as she went along the riverbank—but then her foot slipped, and she screamed as she fell in.

I left my hiding-place and jumped into the cold water, even though I could not swim myself. Dragging her to the shore, I saved her. But she was breathless. I grabbed her to force the water out. She started to cough when I was interrupted by the man that she had been calling to. He saw me and ripped the girl from my arms, carrying her off into the woods. I tried to follow them, I don't even know why. But when he saw me, he pointed something at my body. There was a loud noise, fire and smoke and then there was pain. I fell to the ground. Broken flesh and bone. The compassion I had felt only a few moments before gave way to a burning rage. Since that day I have vowed eternal hatred and vengeance to all your kind.

FRANKENSTEIN The past year seemed unreal somehow. An improbable fiction.

THE CREATURE After some weeks my wound healed, and I continued my journey.

FRANKENSTEIN My return to Geneva was set for the spring.

THE CREATURE It was spring… when I reached Geneva.

ACT 1 SCENE 10

THE CREATURE Morning dawned when I arrived... so I found a hiding-place in the fields just outside town. I was thinking about how to approach you... when a young child came running through the tall grass. When he saw me he stopped and just... stared. As I looked at him... a thought struck me. This little boy was... unprejudiced. If I could reach out to him... ask him to be my friend... I wouldn't be so lonely on this peopled earth—

FRANKENSTEIN It was already May when the letter from my father arrived... But it was not what I expected...

CAPT. WALTON *(as FRANKENSTEIN'S FATHER)* My dear Victor. You have probably waited impatiently to hear from me... concerning your homecoming. At first I was tempted to simply tell you the day on which we should expect you. But that would be a cruel kindness, and I can't do it. Your brother William is dead. That sweet, gentle child was murdered. Last Sunday Elizabeth, your two brothers and I went out for a walk. It was after noon before we reached home only to discover that Ernest, who had run off with William, had reached the house before us... but he asked me where his brother was... A search was made... and at about five in the morning I discovered my boy, lying in the grass... His neck was broken... there was a hand-print.

Elizabeth insisted on seeing the body... She told me that she had let him wear a very valuable locket with a portrait of your mother in it. It was not found and was undoubtedly the temptation that caused his death. She needs you... She blames herself. Come home, son. Your unfortunate Father, Alphonse Frankenstein.

THE CREATURE I grabbed the boy and pulled him towards me. But as soon as I touched him... he screamed. I told him not to be afraid... I even smiled. But he bit my arm and called me a monster. I told him that I just wanted to be his friend... he said that he would tell his father—the Magistrate Frankenstein. Magistrate meant nothing to me... but your name...

FRANKENSTEIN It was completely dark when I arrived outside Geneva. I wanted to visit the spot where my brother was murdered. I left the coach and went on foot. I saw a storm passing the summit of the mountains making beautiful images in the air. Watching the tempest— I suddenly saw a figure in the clump of trees near me. I stood there, frozen... I couldn't be wrong... I saw it. A flash of lightning showed me... its face. The thing that I had created was still alive.

THE CREATURE He must have seen the hate in my eyes because he screamed more loudly than before and tried to run—I just put a hand over his mouth to keep him quiet—but then I heard a snap... I let go... but he just fell on the grass... and stopped moving...

FRANKENSTEIN Over a year had passed since the night I had loosed this demon on the world... How many people had it killed? I spent the rest of the night in the storm... My mind was filled with thoughts of misery and carnage... When morning dawned I ran to my father's house. I wanted to tell them the truth...to get help and go after the thing... to kill it. But I didn't. I knew how my tale would sound—how it still sounds... like madness.

CAPT. WALTON (*as FRANKENSTEIN'S young brother, ERNEST*) Welcome home Victor... I wish it didn't have to be this way... but it's good to see you... Father said—

FRANKENSTEIN Ernest... There's something I have to tell you—

CAPT. WALTON (*as ERNEST*) It can wait... My god, you look awful... have you slept? You should rest—

FRANKENSTEIN NO! No more rest. There's no time... no time...

CAPT. WALTON (*as ERNEST*) You should see father... he's not well. Later perhaps. But at least talk to Elizabeth, she misses you... and blames herself—

FRANKENSTEIN I know who killed him...

CAPT. WALTON (*as ERNEST*) You've heard the news? (*Beat.*) Who could believe that Justine, could be capable of such—

FRANKENSTEIN Justine?

CAPT. WALTON (*as ERNEST*) Justine Moritz... Elizabeth's friend—

FRANKENSTEIN She's accused? But they're wrong... no one believes it... do they?

CAPT. WALTON (*as ERNEST*) No one did at first, but the evidence is—I thought you knew... the trial is this afternoon—

> Blackout.

ACT 1 SCENE 11

THE CREATURE As I stared at my victim... I felt sorry for what I had done... and angry with you for giving me these emotions—

FRANKENSTEIN I went to see Elizabeth...

THE CREATURE He was your Father's son... your brother... but what was he to me?

FRANKENSTEIN But she wouldn't speak to me...

THE CREATURE I knew that you would feel this loss…

FRANKENSTEIN She couldn't even look at me…

THE CREATURE And for the first time I felt powerful.

FRANKENSTEIN She felt responsible…

THE CREATURE You are all so fragile…

FRANKENSTEIN The necklace she let William wear…

THE CREATURE I saw something around his neck glittering in the sunlight and I took it…

FRANKENSTEIN I was responsible but I didn't know what to say…

THE CREATURE It was the most beautiful thing I had ever seen…

FRANKENSTEIN Justine was her close friend… and I knew she was innocent…

THE CREATURE Then I opened it… and saw the face inside…

FRANKENSTEIN I would have confessed everything… but then I saw the look in her eyes…

THE CREATURE Those eyes… staring up at me… I felt peace…

FRANKENSTEIN So peaceful.

THE CREATURE But when I saw that it was only an image… and that I would never be this close to such a creature…

FRANKENSTEIN She'd think I was a raving madman—

THE CREATURE My rage returned and I left the body there for the crows.

FRANKENSTEIN I said nothing…

THE CREATURE I found a barn nearby that looked empty and went inside to hide…

FRANKENSTEIN The trial was over before it began.

THE CREATURE A woman was there sleeping on the straw. She was even more beautiful than the portrait I carried…

FRANKENSTEIN The facts were against her. She had been out the whole night of the murder—

THE CREATURE I bent over her, and whispered in her ear. "I would give my life… for your love."

FRANKENSTEIN She had been seen close to where the body was—

THE CREATURE But then I thought that she could never love me… or even look at me—

FRANKENSTEIN And the stolen necklace was found in her pocket—

THE CREATURE I put the locket in a fold of her dress—

FRANKENSTEIN She said she had been searching for the boy and had rested in a barn—

THE CREATURE It was a gift… it was all I had to give her.

FRANKENSTEIN But she could not explain how the necklace came to be there…

THE CREATURE She began to wake up… and I fled.

FRANKENSTEIN The ballots were cast… they were all black.

THE CREATURE I didn't mean for her to be blamed for my crime—

FRANKENSTEIN She died on the scaffold—

THE CREATURE Later when I understood what had happened—

FRANKENSTEIN Because of my creation—

THE CREATURE Something inside me felt revenged—

FRANKENSTEIN I told no one my tale—

THE CREATURE If I couldn't posses such beauty—

FRANKENSTEIN Not even Elizabeth—

THE CREATURE Then I wanted to destroy it—

FRANKENSTEIN Sleep fled from me and I wandered like an evil spirit—

THE CREATURE This was not what I had intended—

FRANKENSTEIN I began my work with benevolent intentions—

THE CREATURE I started off in this world clean and pure—

FRANKENSTEIN I wanted to be useful to my fellow men.

THE CREATURE But hatred turned me into the miserable creature before you.

FRANKENSTEIN Now, I am just a hollow shell of my former self, Walton… learn from me… don't throw your own life away.

CAPT. WALTON It's not my intention.

FRANKENSTEIN Do you have a home to return to?

CAPT. WALTON Yes… So, then you went after this… creature?

FRANKENSTEIN Yes.

ACT 1 SCENE 12

FRANKENSTEIN I left home in search of the thing and after months, I caught up with it on Mount Blanc. I was nearly at the summit when I saw the figure of a man coming towards me at superhuman speed. It jumped over the crevices in the ice and vaulted from boulder to boulder. I raised my rifle, it was almost upon me, I took aim, but then it stopped and spoke—

THE CREATURE Greetings… Frankenstein.

FRANKENSTEIN I almost dropped my gun… I couldn't believe it.

THE CREATURE I've waited my whole life to meet you.

FRANKENSTEIN How dare you approach me?

THE CREATURE I expected this welcome… All men hate me… even you—

FRANKENSTEIN You know who I am?

THE CREATURE Yes, I know you. We are bound together by chains that can only be broken by death.

FRANKENSTEIN If it would bring back the ones you've killed… I would gladly join you there—

THE CREATURE You want to kill me?

FRANKENSTEIN You're a mistake that I made… one that I will undo—

THE CREATURE How dare you. You treat my life like it's something you could just take back.

FRANKENSTEIN I created you… I can destroy you… You're a monster!

THE CREATURE That you made! If you do your duty towards me… I will do mine towards you and the rest of mankind.

FRANKENSTEIN You have to pay for your crimes…

THE CREATURE Father, please…

FRANKENSTEIN Don't call me that!

THE CREATURE What would you have me call you? Lord? Creator? God?

FRANKENSTEIN You and I are enemies—

THE CREATURE Not by my choice. Please listen to me… I will not harm you.

FRANKENSTEIN What do you have to say?

THE CREATURE If you will grant me one request... I will leave you in peace.

FRANKENSTEIN If I refuse?

THE CREATURE Do you... love your family?

FRANKENSTEIN Is that a threat?

THE CREATURE Would you miss them if they were... Gone?

FRANKENSTEIN I'll shoot you right now—

THE CREATURE Be calm. Remember that I am your creation. My life may only be pain and suffering but I will defend it.

FRANKENSTEIN You're a murderer—

THE CREATURE You accuse me of murder and yet you would, with a clear conscience put me to death. I ask you not to spare me... just hear my tale... and then if you are not satisfied... you can destroy the work of your hands—

FRANKENSTEIN Very well... I'll hear you...

THE CREATURE It's too cold for you here. Follow me.

FRANKENSTEIN (*to WALTON.*) It led the way across the ice and I followed. We entered a small hut where the creature must have been residing... I sat down next to an open fire and it began its tale...

THE CREATURE "It is with considerable difficulty that I remember my creation ... all the events of that period are confused in my mind."

   Blackout.

Intermission.

ACT II SCENE 1

FRANKENSTEIN It spoke... The thing spoke to me like a man... My god, it had even read Milton. As it told me the story of its brief existence... I just sat there and listened like a prisoner, until it finally finished—

THE CREATURE And that is my history... I wandered towards these mountains consumed by a passion which only you can satisfy. I have one request. I am alone, and miserable. I need a... companion.

FRANKENSTEIN Its words had a strange effect upon me. I felt that I should try to console it. But when I saw that filthy mass... moving and talking, my heart sickened and I felt horrified at what I had done.

THE CREATURE Humans will not associate with me, but one as... deformed as I am would not deny me. I want a mate. You will create her. She must be the same species. Let her be as hideous as myself. Our lives may not be happy, but they will be harmless, and free from the misery that I feel now.

FRANKENSTEIN I thought that even though I could not sympathize with the creature... I had no right to withhold the only happiness which was still in my power to bestow.

THE CREATURE Consent, and you will never see us again. We will go to the jungles of the new world and live in secret. My food is not like that of mankind. I don't destroy life to glut my appetite. My bride must be the same. We'll make our bed of leaves... we will live in the wilds... in total freedom. Far from the things of man—

FRANKENSTEIN His power was not omitted in my calculation... a beast that could survive these elements, hiding from pursuit among the inaccessible mountain peaks and moving with incredible speed.

THE CREATURE We'll grow old together and eventually die. Think of that. I'll feel the affections of another sensitive being, and become a part of creation... from which I am now excluded. My life will flow quietly away, and in my dying moments... I will not curse my maker.

FRANKENSTEIN I will consent to your... demand, on your solemn oath to quit this country and every other place in the neighborhood of mankind, forever... as soon as I deliver a female who will follow you into exile.

THE CREATURE I swear, by the sun, by the dark night, and by the fire that burns in my heart, that if you do this, you will never see us again.

FRANKENSTEIN Very well.

THE CREATURE There is your journal... You may need it to refresh your memory. Now go, and begin your labors. I'll be watching your progress. Don't worry... when you're ready, I'll appear.

He exits.

Blackout.

ACT II SCENE 2

CAPT. WALTON September sixth. Frankenstein's health is worse... but now I fear for his sanity. Since the death of the ship's surgeon I have been at his side every moment that I could spare. His story is... unbelievable. If it weren't for his continued survival and insistence on its truth... I wouldn't believe it myself.

FRANKENSTEIN I returned home, but I could not work there. I feared discovery but not as much as I feared the creature's vengeance on my family if I failed... and I had changed. I was no longer the eager student who was able to overcome his disgust at such a task. Besides, my health was now much restored and my spirits were high. I had no desire to cut myself off from the ones I loved. Elizabeth and I grew close. My father saw this change—

CAPT. WALTON (*as FRANKENSTEIN'S FATHER*) My son, I confess that I have always looked forward to your marriage with Elizabeth as the beginning of your domestic comfort and the stay of my declining years... Tell me whether you would object to an immediate wedding? Unfortunately, recent events have... but that is all past. You are young, but I suppose that an early marriage would not interfere with any plans that you have made?

FRANKENSTEIN The idea of an immediate union with Elizabeth filled me with both joy and despair. I was bound by a solemn promise, which I had not yet fulfilled, and dared not break. I had to make the monster depart with his mate, before I allowed myself any peace. I did not want to engage in my loathsome task in my family's house.

I expressed a wish to travel first... concealing the true reasons for this request. I would be gone a month... no more. I had my journal... the blueprint was clear. I only had to assemble the parts. But sensing my anxiety, my Father, without consulting me, took the precaution of asking Clerval to join me. There was no legitimate excuse that I could give to prevent him. It was understood that my wedding with Elizabeth would take place immediately after my return. Packing my chemical instruments, and the... raw materials I had collected into a trunk, I decided to finish my task in some remote outpost. We departed... but once we were on our way, I told Clerval that I needed to be alone to conduct some "research." He consented, and a date was set for our reunion. I went to a remote island to begin my work. The creature followed me, I could feel it. I knew that it would show itself once I was finished... so that it could receive its companion. I toiled day and night in order to complete my work. It was a filthy process. During my first experiment, an enthusiastic frenzy had blinded me to the horror of it all, but now that I went to it in cold blood, my heart sickened at the sight of it.

Blackout.

ACT II SCENE 3

CAPT. WALTON **September seventh.** The weather and the ice still prohibit our escape. My guest grows weaker every day. The only moments he seems alive are when he is relating his unbelievable story. (*To him.*) Are you saying you created a… mate, for this thing?

FRANKENSTEIN I'm ashamed to say that I did… I stood in my laboratory on the last night of my exile. I was to meet Clerval in the town the next day and then to return home. The thing was finished, only a spark was needed to bring it to life… I paused to rest before I brought my work to its conclusion… and I began to consider my actions. I had already created a monster that had killed my own brother and I was about to release another such creature on the world. This thing might become ten thousand times more destructive than its mate, and delight in murder. My first creation had sworn to quit civilization forever but this one had not. It might refuse to honor a contract made before its own creation. They might even hate each other. My creature despised its own deformity, wouldn't it hate those same faults in female form? They might turn away from each other in disgust. Even if they did leave Europe to inhabit the jungles of the new world, one of their desires would be children. A race of monsters would be propagated upon the earth. I had been moved by the creatures emotions and eloquence and struck senseless by his threats, but now, for the first time, the gravity of my promise dawned on me… Future generations would hate me. I decided that I should at least… sterilize it. But my heart stopped, when I looked up and saw the monster at the window.

THE CREATURE She was beautiful… I smiled, for the first time in months.

FRANKENSTEIN An evil grin wrinkled its lips.

THE CREATURE She was like me, but not like me…

FRANKENSTEIN It stood there gazing at me… it must have known how close I was…

THE CREATURE Only the spark was needed—

FRANKENSTEIN I saw its face clearly—

THE CREATURE And we would be united forever—

FRANKENSTEIN There was malice and treachery in those eyes—

THE CREATURE I had waited for so long—

FRANKENSTEIN It had followed me into my exile and now it had come to gloat and to claim its prize—

THE CREATURE I watched her eyes, closely… expecting to see them flicker—

FRANKENSTEIN I stood there on the point of throwing the lever that would bring it to life—

THE CREATURE Then I saw you staring at me—

FRANKENSTEIN I knew what I had to do… but my hands trembled—

THE CREATURE Your eyes were calculating and cold—

FRANKENSTEIN I tore the thing on the table to pieces—

THE CREATURE You ripped her apart with your bare hands—

FRANKENSTEIN The creature saw me destroy the thing it depended on for its future happiness and leaped into the room—

THE CREATURE Why have you done this?

FRANKENSTEIN I will not be the instrument of any future destruction—

THE CREATURE You… killed her—

FRANKENSTEIN That thing was never alive.

THE CREATURE You've destroyed my hope.

FRANKENSTEIN I destroyed my work.

THE CREATURE Remember what I told you—

FRANKENSTEIN Then kill me, if you can—

THE CREATURE No… that would be merciful. My god, you think you're miserable now?

FRANKENSTEIN You can't force me to finish this… abomination—

THE CREATURE I'll make you so wretched that the light of day will be hateful to you.

FRANKENSTEIN Your threats can't make me commit another atrocity—

THE CREATURE Will each man find a wife, and each beast a mate, while I remain alone?

FRANKENSTEIN I will not create a companion for you—

THE CREATURE Are you to be happy while I grovel at your feet?

FRANKENSTEIN Come a step closer and you'll share the same fate as that thing on the table—

THE CREATURE You are my creator, but I am no longer your creature… others can learn what you know.

FRANKENSTEIN I'll burn my journal… nothing will remain—

THE CREATURE You can't destroy what you don't posses.

Grabbing the journal from him.

FRANKENSTEIN Return that—

THE CREATURE I may die, but first you will regret the injuries that you have inflicted.

FRANKENSTEIN I will hunt you to the ends of the Earth—

THE CREATURE No need, I will be with you on your wedding night. Farewell, Father.

FRANKENSTEIN I grabbed an axe off the wall… but the creature jumped out of the window and in an instant I lost sight of it…

CAPT. WALTON When was this?

FRANKENSTEIN Two years ago—

CAPT. WALTON And that's when you began chasing this… creature?

FRANKENSTEIN No. I should have pursued it… but I hesitated…

ACT II SCENE 4

FRANKENSTEIN Before I departed, there was a task to perform. The remains of the thing I had destroyed were scattered all over the lab. I didn't want to leave anything behind. I placed it into a basket with a number of stones and went aboard a little boat. I sailed out a few miles from shore and threw it all into the sea. I listened to the gurgling sound as it sunk, and then sailed away from the spot. Suddenly, clouds hid the moon and the wind rose… the waves became very rough… It was dawn when I finally reached the coast. I saw a small town and entered the harbor… (*To CONSTABLE.*) You there… could you tell me the name of this town?

CAPT. WALTON (*as CONSTABLE*) You'll know that soon enough. Come sir, you must follow me to the magistrate… to give an account of yourself.

FRANKENSTEIN Why should I give an account of myself?

CAPT. WALTON (*as CONSTABLE*)) A gentleman was found murdered here last night. All strangers and foreigners are to be questioned… If you have nothing to hide… You'll be set free… Now come with me.

FRANKENSTEIN They took me to the morgue to identify the body. When they removed the cover… I saw the lifeless corpse of Henry Clerval stretched out before me. I became hysterical.

THE CREATURE I found him coming from the town to see you…

FRANKENSTEIN I don't remember much more about those days.

THE CREATURE I just wanted to speak to him… to tell HIM your terrible secret…

FRANKENSTEIN I blamed myself for his death.

THE CREATURE But he tried to run away... so, I stopped him.

FRANKENSTEIN My ravings, as I afterwards heard, were frightful.

THE CREATURE I have to admit... murder was on my mind—

FRANKENSTEIN Fortunately a local fisherman had seen me far out at sea at the time of the murder.

THE CREATURE Like father like son.

FRANKENSTEIN So, when I regained my senses everything I had said was put down to grief over my friend's death and I was released.

THE CREATURE Do you think the screams of your friend were music to my ears?

FRANKENSTEIN The only thing that kept me alive was a desire to return to my family and Elizabeth... to protect them from harm.

THE CREATURE I could destroy... but that didn't satisfy me. I still craved the things I couldn't have.

FRANKENSTEIN I took passage on board a vessel bound for home.

THE CREATURE And once again you left me all alone.

   Blackout.

ACT II SCENE 5

FRANKENSTEIN On my arrival, Elizabeth met me and it was as if we had never been apart. She was radiant and overjoyed to see me. The preparations had been made for our wedding. It was agreed that immediately after the ceremony we would travel to Lake Como and spend our first days of happiness there. I told her I loved her but that I had a secret that I could not reveal to anyone. I promised to tell her everything the next day... but for the moment I could not bring myself to reveal the details of Clerval's death... or my involvement.

THE CREATURE I wanted friendship... but I was spurned—

FRANKENSTEIN After the ceremony was performed a large party assembled at my father's, but Elizabeth and I began our journey that day.

THE CREATURE I wanted love... but I was denied—

FRANKENSTEIN I took every precaution to defend myself in case the creature should openly attack me. I carried pistols and daggers with me—

THE CREATURE I wanted to live like a man—

FRANKENSTEIN My hunting rifle was never out of reach.

THE CREATURE But I was forced to become an animal—

FRANKENSTEIN It was already evening when we landed. We walked on the shore for a little while… Those were the happiest moments of my life. I had been calm during the day, but as soon as night began to obscure the shapes of things… a thousand fears arose in my mind. Every sound terrified me. We entered the villa and as she had promised, Elizabeth retired for the night. I paced the house watching for any sign of the creature.

THE CREATURE I followed you every step of the way—

FRANKENSTEIN I pledged that I would sell my life dearly. The mistake I had made would be corrected. One or both of us would be dead before dawn—

THE CREATURE I was condemned to death the day I was born… was this justice?

FRANKENSTEIN It was nearly midnight when Elizabeth came down… I told her that I would come to bed soon after I made one more check of the doors and windows. She left me with a kiss. I stuck to my lonely vigil, uncertain if the demon had actually followed me.

THE CREATURE Am I a demon? When all mankind sinned against me?

FRANKENSTEIN I found no trace of it, and I had decided that something must have happened to prevent its appearance when—

THE CREATURE I only wanted to speak to her…

FRANKENSTEIN I heard a scream.

THE CREATURE To tell her what you couldn't bring yourself to admit—

FRANKENSTEIN It came from Elizabeth's room—

THE CREATURE That I was your creation…

FRANKENSTEIN I froze.

THE CREATURE Your son.

FRANKENSTEIN The whole truth rushed into my mind—

THE CREATURE She screamed as soon as she saw me—

FRANKENSTEIN I ran upstairs—

THE CREATURE She fainted… before I could say anything—

FRANKENSTEIN My heart was pounding when I found the door locked—

THE CREATURE When I grabbed her… it was just to pick her up—

FRANKENSTEIN I forced the lock—

THE CREATURE I was going to put her on the bed and leave—

FRANKENSTEIN I threw the door open—

THE CREATURE The look on your face changed my mind—

FRANKENSTEIN If I had only been faster—

THE CREATURE It was quick…

FRANKENSTEIN I could have saved her!

THE CREATURE Painless—

FRANKENSTEIN I heard a snap—

THE CREATURE She didn't suffer—

FRANKENSTEIN I fired both pistols at the monster as it jumped out of the window—

THE CREATURE I clung to a tree outside and watched—

FRANKENSTEIN She was thrown across the bed, the mark of the fiend on her neck. There was nothing I could do—

THE CREATURE A quiet death… It's more than you and I can hope for.

FRANKENSTEIN I looked up and I saw it outside, grinning at me—

THE CREATURE It was then that evil, became my good—

FRANKENSTEIN I tried to reload, but it ran as fast as lightning and plunged into the lake.

Blackout.

ACT II SCENE 6

CAPT. WALTON September eighth. We are still surrounded by mountains of ice and in imminent danger of being crushed. The cold is excessive, and many of my unfortunate crew have already found a watery grave in this scene of desolation. I can't help but feel responsible. Frankenstein has declined in health. He will not eat or sleep and a feverish fire glimmers in his eyes whenever he talks about his "quest" but when he stops… he rapidly sinks again into apparent lifelessness. I have encountered many forms of death since I first put to sea. Until today, I would have said that dying of a broken heart was just a romantic notion… now, I'm not so certain.

THE CREATURE It is true that I am a monster.

FRANKENSTEIN I was in a cloud of horror.

THE CREATURE I have murdered the young and the innocent—

FRANKENSTEIN The death of William, the execution of Justine, the murder of Clerval—

THE CREATURE I have strangled the helpless as they slept—

FRANKENSTEIN And now my wife—

THE CREATURE And grasped to death the throats of those who never injured me or any living thing—

FRANKENSTEIN At that moment was my family still safe from the fiend? I returned home with all possible speed.

THE CREATURE I have pursued my creator to utter ruin—

FRANKENSTEIN When I reached my home my father and brother still lived... but my father sank under the tidings that I bore.

THE CREATURE I have condemned him to misery—

FRANKENSTEIN He could not live with the tragedy that accumulated around him—

THE CREATURE My heart was fashioned to respond to love and sympathy—

FRANKENSTEIN His heart broke—

THE CREATURE I was wrenched by misery to vice and hatred—

FRANKENSTEIN He died in my arms—

THE CREATURE My soul endured the violence of the change with such torture... that you cannot possibly imagine.

FRANKENSTEIN One night I entered the cemetery where my family, Clerval and Elizabeth rested. I imagined their souls hovering over me. Accusing me. But everything was silent. I wept.

THE CREATURE I am satisfied.

FRANKENSTEIN I knelt on the grass and swore to pursue the demon who had caused this misery until either it... or I should perish. And then... I heard its voice—

THE CREATURE You have determined to live, and I am satisfied. Follow me, if you dare—

FRANKENSTEIN It was then, that my quest began, which will only come to an end when we are both destroyed. I have crossed a vast portion of the earth, and have endured intense hardships. Many times I have stretched my frozen body out upon the icy plain and prayed for death. But revenge has kept me alive... (*Coughs.*) Promise me Walton, that if anything should happen to me... you would continue my quest... swear to me... SWEAR you will kill this monster if you ever see it.

CAPT. WALTON I swear. (*Pause.*) I thought at least one of us was insane and I didn't believe that either of us would be getting out of the Arctic alive. So, of course I swore... I couldn't tell him the truth. That I was no longer interested in seeking a northern route by sea... That we had only enough food to last until the winter and the chances were that we would all die of the cold first.

   To FRANKENSTEIN again.

You need to eat... to keep your strength up. If it's still out there—

FRANKENSTEIN If? Walton, I hope to God that you take this threat seriously—

CAPT. WALTON A watch is posted on deck... there has been no sign of him—

FRANKENSTEIN It! Don't let it fool you... it may look like a man but it is a demon... sent to destroy all those that I come into contact with... and I am afraid that this includes you now my dear Captain.

CAPT. WALTON Then by all means continue... I'd like to know why I've been condemned to death—

FRANKENSTEIN Very well... I followed its trail for months. Sometimes peasants, scared by a horrid apparition, told me which way it had gone... and sometimes it even left messages for me to find, fearing that if I lost all trace of it I would despair and die.

CAPT. WALTON Messages?

FRANKENSTEIN I don't know how... but it had learned to write. It would leave inscriptions on animal skins or carved into the ice and snow. The last one read—

THE CREATURE Prepare yourself, wrap these furs around you and provide enough food. We shall soon begin a journey where your sufferings will satisfy my everlasting hatred.

FRANKENSTEIN I spent the last of my fortune on a sled and dogs. I followed it north until I saw the ocean in the distance. I gained on it, so much so that, when I reached the ocean, the creature was only one day's journey ahead. With new courage, I pressed on, and arrived at a village on the seashore. I asked the inhabitants about it and learned that a monster had arrived during the night. It put the occupants of a cottage to flight and had carried off their store of winter food by placing it on a dogsled. It then pursued its journey across the ice in a direction that led to no land. They said that it would be destroyed by the breaking up of the ice or frozen by the eternal cold and that I was mad to follow it. (*Laughs.*) I had to agree with them!

Blackout.

ACT II SCENE 7

CAPT. WALTON September ninth. Dear Margaret, Victor has been quiet all morning and I fear to disturb him… but his eyes are only half closed… he's conversing with ghosts. I have tried to record as accurately as possible his unbelievable story and it has had a strange affect on my mind. I cannot tell what is real and what is illusion anymore… My dear, when I left you… I thought only of my expedition and the adventures that awaited… I have come so far, only to become ice-bound… I wish now more than anything to see my home again and to hold you in my arms.

FRANKENSTEIN I departed from land across the inequalities of the frozen ocean. I viewed the expanse before me with anguish. But then my eye caught a dark speck in the distance… another sled… and the figure of the thing I sought—

THE CREATURE I led and he followed across a nightmare in white—

FRANKENSTEIN I was almost within reach of my foe when—

THE CREATURE When the angel reaches too high—

FRANKENSTEIN My hopes were suddenly shattered—

THE CREATURE He falls and becomes a malignant devil—

FRANKENSTEIN The wind rose, the sea roared and with the mighty shock of an earthquake, the ice split and cracked all around me—

THE CREATURE Even the enemy of God had companions in his desolation—

FRANKENSTEIN A tumultuous sea rolled between us and I lost all trace of it.

THE CREATURE I am alone.

FRANKENSTEIN I am alone.

FRANKENSTEIN I was left drifting on a scattered piece of ice which was slowly shrinking. Many hours passed and I was prepared for a hideous death. Most of my dogs had already frozen and I was about to sink when I saw your ship riding at anchor.

Blackout.

ACT II SCENE 8

CAPT. WALTON September tenth. The crew is terribly afraid. Not of the elements or even of the monster that haunts all of our dreams... they are afraid that if a passage does open up, that I will try and continue my voyage and lead them back into danger. I thought that we would probably never escape, but I promised them that if we could get clear of the ice I would instantly direct our course homeward. This evening the ice began to move. A roaring like thunder was heard at a distance as the islands split and cracked in every direction. We are in terrible danger, but since we can only remain still until morning, my attention is occupied by my unfortunate guest, whose illness has increased to such a degree that he is entirely confined to his bed. At dawn I could see that a passage south had become perfectly free. The crew called out—

FRANKENSTEIN Why are the men shouting—have they sighted it?

CAPT. WALTON They are cheering because they will be returning home soon.

FRANKENSTEIN (*Pause.*) Are you really going to return?

CAPT. WALTON Yes, I cannot lead them unwillingly into danger... please come with us.

FRANKENSTEIN I cannot leave my adversary alive.

CAPT. WALTON I must go back... you said yourself—

FRANKENSTEIN Then do so, but I will not—

CAPT. WALTON Please understand—

FRANKENSTEIN You may give up your quest... but I dare not... at least furnish me with a boat—

> *He tries to stand but can't.*

I'm afraid that the strength I relied on is gone. I will soon die and my enemy, may still be alive. You must kill it Walton... It killed my friends, my family and my wife. It must be destroyed... Please do not think that I still feel that burning need for revenge that I once expressed... but I do feel justified in desiring the death of that monster. The task was mine, but I have failed. I ask you to undertake my unfinished work... it must end with me my friend... you swore to me—

CAPT. WALTON He held my hand... and then he closed his eyes forever.

> *Blackout.*

ACT II SCENE 9

CAPT. WALTON September eleventh. It is over. We are returning home. The crew is much heartened by the prospect, as for myself, I have lost all hopes of glory and... I have lost my friend. Frankenstein is dead. I will not despair... but I will try to chronicle these bitter circumstances while I sail towards home and you.

THE CREATURE That is also my victim, in his murder my crimes are consummated and the miserable series of my being is wound to its close!

CAPT. WALTON There was a voice coming from the cabin where the remains of my ill-fated friend lay.

THE CREATURE Oh, Frankenstein, what does it matter now that I ask you to pardon me?

CAPT. WALTON I entered the room... I cannot find words to describe the creature hanging over him.

THE CREATURE Your son who irretrievably destroyed you by destroying all that you loved?

CAPT. WALTON It was gigantic and distorted. Its face was concealed by long locks of ragged hair and one huge arm was extended, its color and texture was like that of a mummy.

To the creature.

My god—

THE CREATURE Stay back! I want no more blood on my hands—

CAPT. WALTON You're the creature—

THE CREATURE Yes, you think you know me? I heard him telling you my story. I clung to the porthole outside and listened.

CAPT. WALTON Then it's true—

THE CREATURE It was only half true.

CAPT. WALTON What do you mean?

THE CREATURE Men lie.

CAPT. WALTON Why have you come?

THE CREATURE Not for revenge... I came to beg for his forgiveness and to bid farewell to my creator—

CAPT. WALTON Forgiveness?

THE CREATURE But now, he is cold.... He cannot answer me.

CAPT. WALTON You are the sole cause of his misery. If you had felt remorse before, he would still be alive. You've been deprived of your revenge… and now you repent? But he has gone where you can't follow. He is free from you forever.

THE CREATURE Do you dream, Captain? Do you think that I am dead to agony and remorse? He didn't suffer in the consummation of the deed. He felt nothing. Not a portion of the anguish that I felt during its execution. You may have knowledge of my crimes and his misfortunes but he never knew what I went through. He never claimed me as his own. He never even gave me a name. As far as he was concerned, I was an abortion.

CAPT. WALTON I swore… to kill you…

THE CREATURE If that is what you must do… then I will not stop you. I will not be the instrument of any future horrors.

CAPT. WALTON Do you… wish to die?

THE CREATURE Do you? (*Pause.*) Why are you here Captain? You must have a home… a family… all the comforts of men? And yet you leave them behind to seek a new path… across this frozen hell… on a fool's errand.

CAPT. WALTON What do you know of such things?

THE CREATURE I've been there.

CAPT. WALTON North?

THE CREATURE There is no "northern passage." There is nothing out there but a wasteland… and your death if you continue on this course.

CAPT. WALTON We are returning home now… What will you do?

THE CREATURE Don't be afraid… No man's death is needed to consummate the story of my life… but it does require my own. On my own terms. When I die, I am satisfied that hatred will be my only legacy. Once my mind was soothed with dreams of virtue. Once I falsely hoped to meet people who would pardon my outward form and love me for the excellent qualities which I was capable of expressing. In my exile I was nourished with the high thoughts of honor and devotion. But now my crimes have degraded me beneath the lowest animal. No guilt, no malignity, no misery can compare. When I reflect on the frightful catalogue of my sins, I can't believe that I am the same creature whose thoughts were once filled with sublime, transcendent visions of beauty. He is dead who called me into being… When I am gone the very remembrance of us both will vanish. I shall no longer see the sun or stars, or feel the wind play on my cheeks. My senses will pass away and in this condition… I must find happiness. Some years ago, when I felt the warmth of summer, and heard the rustling of the leaves and the songs of the birds, and these were all new to me, then I would have wept to die. Now, it is my only consolation. I will leave your ship, and seek the most northern point of your world… and I will consume to ashes his journal and this miserable frame. Nothing will remain to light the way for any curious wretch who would create another like me.

The light of my funeral pyre will fade away and my ashes will be swept into the sea by the winds. My spirit will sleep in peace… or if it thinks… it will not think thus. Farewell, Captain.

CAPT. WALTON Before I could say anything, it—(*Correcting himself.*) He… jumped out of the cabin-window onto an ice-raft which lay close by, and was soon borne away by the waves and lost in the darkness and distance.

Slow fade to black.

End of play.

TENDERS IN THE FOG

A PATERNAL TRIPTYCH
(IN FOUR-PART DISSONANCE)

BY

TREVOR ALLEN

Tenders in the Fog

Shanachie, or traditional Irish storyteller, tells the tale of the Bailey Banshee and the ghost ship, *Trinity*. As the audience meets the crew of the doomed ship (three generations of fishermen) the Shanachie becomes a shape-shifting Banshee, taking on different guises in a siren-like attempt to lure the men into the sea. The story is a haunting and fugue-like exploration of the lives of three men and their relationships to each other and the sea as well as a possible explanation of their sudden disappearance.

Production Information

Originally commissioned and developed by PlayGround / Jim Kleinmann.

World Premiere: San Jose Stage Company, 2005

Executive Director:	Cathleen King
Director:	Kent Nicholson
Artistic Director, San Jose Stage Company:	Randall King
Artistic Director, PlayGround:	Jim Kleinmann

Cast

The Shanachie/Banshee	Jessa Brie
James "Papa" Bailey Senior	Paul Myrvold
James "Da" Bailey Junior	Randall King
James "Jimmy" Bailey III	Nick Sholley

TENDERS IN THE FOG

CHARACTERS

JAMES "PAPA" BAILEY SR.: *Man, 75 An old Irish crab fisherman from San Francisco. Captain and owner of the Trinity.*

JAMES "DA" BAILEY JR.: *Man, 55 A Navy submarine veteran, retired, back on board the Trinity to help his father.*

JAMES "JIMMY" BAILEY III.: *Man, 25 A Marine Biology major (Scripps college dropout) and Greenpeace activist, back on board the Trinity to help his grandfather and himself.*

THE SHANACHIE & THE BANSHEE: *Woman, An ageless "storyteller" she doubles as The Banshee/Selkie/Merrow from Celtic mythology, part shape-shifter and part Siren. The living embodiment of the sea herself. She also becomes KAITLIN, EVELYN and DIANA, the dead wives of Papa and Da and the dead fiancée of Jimmy.*

Time:

November, 1987

Place:

Aboard a crab fishing boat off the coast of San Francisco

SHANACHIE INTRODUCTION

A cloaked figure of an old woman appears from the darkness as if stepping closer to an open fire. Her face is in shadow under a cowl.

THE SHANACHIE Hello and welcome to you. I'll be your "Shanachie," your storyteller, for this evening. And you know the old saying. "*Bíonn dhá insint ar scéal agus dhá leagan déag ar amhrán.*" loosely translated for the uninitiated, "There are two versions to every story and twelve arrangements to a song." I'm here to tell you the story of the good ship Trinity and her crew. Lost at sea. In the fog. Shall I begin it? Well, that all that's in it. (*She laughs.*) There was a crab fishing boat with a three man crew. They went out and they were never seen again. And that's all that's known for sure. Now there are many versions of what may have happened and this may seem a tall tale to tell, but that's my business. The three men aboard her were each named James Bailey. The Bailey clan, a lost family to be sure. And this is the story they tell, those that tell tall tales, of the Bailey Banshee and the ghost-ship Trinity. First the facts. She had 50 crab pots loaded aboard her when she sailed, at the start of the crab season. The air was cool and it was foggy, like it is tonight…

Stepping back out of the circle of firelight she seems to fade from sight as if she were a ghost herself.

The fog: radio.

There is the sound of a big bang and then static. Through the crackle a voice can be heard in the darkness as a thick fog seeps onto the stage and over the first few rows of the audience. A radio announcer's voice can be heard.

RADIO VOICE (*voice-over*) National Weather Service bulletin, San Francisco. Point Arena to Point Piedras Blancas and out sixty nautical miles including the San Francisco and Monterey Bays.

Current surface conditions, small swells with an extremely dense fog bank, zero visibility.

This just in, there is a small craft advisory for hazardous seas and a high-surf forecast overnight.

The sound of static and then silence.

PRELUDE: "GHOST SHIP REMIX"

The sound of wind blowing across the sea. A large "ship" appears through the fog, her bow pointed toward the audience. She swivels broadside to the front of the stage.

The notes of Beethoven's "ghost trio" the largo assai ed espressivo passage wafts over the following scene.

Images are projected onto the curtain of fog surrounding the ship.

1) A male dungeness crab (cancer magister) big enough to eclipse the boat.

2) A steel crab pot big enough to enclose the boat.

3) The painting, Le Chateau des Pyrenees by René Magritte. (A castle in the air, atop a giant boulder hanging suspended in the sky above the waves of the sea).

The images fade.

Then silence as if time has stopped.

The three Bailey men appear in their own pools of light. PAPA silhouetted by the bow lights, DA in the stern next to a portable lantern and JIMMY illuminated by lights inside the wheel house. They speak as if to the sea herself. A mixture of hope and loss.

JIMMY What happened to the crew of the *Mary Celeste*?

DA They just disappeared.

PAPA All gone, full fathoms down.

JIMMY Into the void.

DA The unknown.

PAPA The darkness.

JIMMY The unknown.

DA The darkness.

PAPA The void.

JIMMY The darkness.

DA The void.

PAPA The unknown.

> *All three in unison.*

The void. The unknown. The darkness.

> *Blackout.*

> *Fugue 1.1: Allegro "The Vicious Cycle And Variations"*

> *PAPA sits in the wheelhouse behind the steering wheel. DA is behind him, pulling on a block and tackle rig. The rope goes over the port side where JIMMY stands hauling up an unseen crab pot from over the side of the boat.*

PAPA You feel that… the calm. Like time just… stopped? Keep an eye out for the Banshee, boys. She's out there, I heard her cry—

DA Papa, we should head back in. There's a storm comin' (*No response.*) You hear me? (*No response.*) Fine don't listen to me. (*No response.*) Old fool.

JIMMY Da, please leave him alone… let's just finish this. Get the rest of the pots in and get back to shore before…

PAPA She's tricky, she might come in the form of a Selke a "seal-woman" or a Merrow or somethin' worse.

DA He's as mad as a sack of newts.

JIMMY True. But still…

> *Hauling on the rope.*

He was a better father than you were—

DA Here we go again—

> *Hauling on the rope. They continue their motions over and over again speaking to the air as if each one is only partly aware of the others' existence. Time has stopped.*

PAPA Thick fog.

JIMMY You were always gone—

PAPA No stars.

DA It was the cold war—

PAPA Compass on the blink again.

JIMMY You never spoke to me—

DA Well, I was in the "Silent Service"—

PAPA We could just be going round and around out here.

JIMMY You want to talk about "silent service"?

DA Now it all comes around again—

PAPA I feel like I've been here before.

JIMMY She was always the quiet one—

DA Like the circling of sharks—

PAPA Buoy on the port boys!!!

JIMMY When you were around—

DA Every time a bell sounds or an alarm goes off —

JIMMY She worshiped you—

PAPA Look lively!

DA I still jump—

JIMMY Of course she never said anything to you—

PAPA I knew it would come back to this…

DA Always on red alert—

JIMMY When you were home… she was just glad to have you there—

PAPA The three of us out on the boat again—

DA Never a moment's rest—

JIMMY That's why she didn't tell you—

PAPA Just like the good old days.

DA The tests—

JIMMY She didn't want you to worry.

PAPA Bailey and sons.

DA The crisis—

JIMMY She wasn't even going to tell you—

DA The fear—

PAPA A way of life—

JIMMY I made her send that wire—

DA Thinking I'd never see my family again—

PAPA Father… to son… to grandson—

JIMMY The only reply she got was the official one from the Navy—

DA I miss your mother more than you will ever know—

PAPA A circle of life—

JIMMY You were out on patrol —

DA I missed her every time I went out—

PAPA Crab fishing—

JIMMY They said you'd be back in port in a month—

DA But it was my duty!

PAPA A way of life—

JIMMY Duty? What do you know about that? We were your family—

DA She knew why I had to go—

PAPA The hard way—

JIMMY Six months a year out at sea?

DA She understood…

PAPA A sustainable system.

JIMMY You couldn't hear her crying in the night—

DA But… she didn't tell me what the doctors found.

PAPA Some of them are killed.

JIMMY When the pain was the worst…

DA By the time I came home…

PAPA Some are thrown back.

JIMMY You came home to an empty house.

DA How could I have known?

PAPA Some escape.

JIMMY That was never a home.

DA The base personnel couldn't have taken care of you.

PAPA Not exactly perfect.

JIMMY I wanted to be with you.

PAPA Not really meant to be.

DA And you didn't want to stay there—

JIMMY And then you left me here… with him.

PAPA Planned inefficiency.

DA Kept you out of trouble.

JIMMY This was all I knew thanks to you.

PAPA Keeps the stock… stable.

DA You were better off with family.

PAPA Avoids over-fishing.

JIMMY Instead of taking a desk job.

PAPA Just take what you need.

JIMMY And raising me yourself.

DA They said you were afraid of her ghost or some such shit.

PAPA The sea… be good to her—

DA All those shrinks made my head spin around.

JIMMY I was raised on this boat.

PAPA She'll be good to you.

DA At least you learned a trade.

JIMMY But I never wanted to be a fisherman… either.

> *The sound of the waves beating against the hull of the small boat and the call of a foghorn in the distance as the three men continue turning the wheel, hauling the ropes and going through their motions… locked in a perpetual cycle.*

SHANACHIE BAILEY HISTORY 1

> *The cloaked figure of the woman reappears from the darkness, as if stepping closer to an open fire. Her face is in shadow under a cowl.*

THE SHANACHIE The Baileys? Well a family history would take all night, so I'll just give you a taste. A toccata if you will. Aye, this goes back a long ways. To the old country. Ireland. Where the history comes from. Seven generations of Bailey's at sea. Irish born and Celtic bred. They all spoke in the one true tongue of the green land. But long before the revolution and the troubles, they were taken from their homes and forced to fight in foreign wars. Gone away to Wales and England. (*Pause.*) Where was I? Ah, yes. The Bailey Banshee. Once upon a time… for so the tale goes… long ago in a time… well, too long ago to tell… A certain James Bailey was accused of treason… to the crown of England. Defacing public property, it was. A bridge of Her Majesty's subjects. Her Royal Majesty, god save us from her, Victoria Regina, feminine ending, you see. From the Normans, you know. Well our lad, one James Aloysius Bailey wrote something treasonous against the Queen on the side of a stone bridge in Sturminster Newton, Dorset England. He carved it with a dirk he'd forged himself… being an apprentice blacksmith as he was… though his father and his father's father and his father's father's father (*Clears throat.*) were all fishermen or sheepherders. They all stuck with what they knew. From the old country, you see. For as we all know and were taught from the cradle to the grave. "The old ways will never leave you hungry." But… not him. Not their greatest ancestor. And not in that foreign land. Not quite Oxbridge was this Mr. James A. Bailey. Vagrant. Outcast. Loner. Speaker of little English. The Queen's English. Opinionated and outspoken, our young lad of eighteen. A rebel without a nation. No place to call home. Just like his descendant, the Captain of the *Trinity*…

> *Stepping back out of the circle of firelight into the fog she quickly fades from sight as if she were a wraith.*

SEVENTY-FIVE YEARS OLD

A pool of light appears around PAPA who stands in the bow of the ship looking up at the moon, barely visible through the curtain of fog. The moonlight plays on his face revealing the ravages of time and weather. He speaks out to the audience as if talking to the sea, but with a paternal familiarity.

PAPA My name is James Bailey, Senior and no matter what any man says… I am not sixty-five years old. I am seventy-five years old. But they think I've gone around the bend. Well, maybe. Yes, I may be an old man but at least I know exactly how old I am. I've been on this ocean, both man and boy some seventy years. I came to it when my Da brought us here. The whole clan. I couldn't have been any more than five. Never did see the inside of a school house or crack a book. For I was the oldest boy and a fisherman's son to boot… and to strap… and to bootstrap. Character building. Working before the dawn. Hard work for months on end. 'Till the crab season was over. But no rest then. Always somethin' to catch. Always somethin' to heave up out of the blue and onto the deck, to put coins in your pocket and stew in your belly and warm homemade bread on the hearth when you get back to shore. If you do. Glad to be alive. But I could never really sleep sound on land. Too still. Too calm. Too many distractions. And then there were the women. All those beautiful women. Got in a little trouble once. So I did the family thing. But she died... but the child lived. So I had myself a son. No more like me than an oyster. And my son had a son. Who came back to live with me. Like the shadow of my own father, rest his soul. The youngest of seven brothers. The strongest of them all too. But the sea gives and the sea takes. And nothing is stronger than the sea. Not time, nor tides nor the turning of the moon. This sea knows how long it is I've been upon her and she will know me long after I've gone. What I was. And what I took. And she will take me back unto herself like she took my father and his father and so on down the line. But now the times have changed and my son and my son's son will never understand. They want to take me out one last time. They say it's over... that I'm over... over sixty-five. They figure its retiring time for me. Well, I'll be damned if I am. And none of them can prove it. My birth certificate was issued in another country and all my records were lost in a glorious fire. No. I am not celebrating any more birthdays. And I am not quitting. I won't give up my boat and I won't sleep on dirt. I can't find rest there. Not ever.

Fog rolls in over the boat obscuring the bow as the set shifts around and darkness envelops him.

BANSHEE/KAITLIN 1 The BANSHEE stands in the fog speaking to PAPA in the voice of KAITLIN, his dead wife.

BANSHEE *(as KAITLIN)* Hello James, I've been a long time in the arms of the sea. The mist rolling around me and now, I've found you. The breeze seems to stop around your boat, can you hear me in this calm? There was a time when I wouldn't go near the water and now it's all I have left. Once I thought the world would end and whirl and wing its way around again and someday you'd come back to me. But now I'm gone and the day will come when you will step off your boat and into the wild, wild sea. James, come back to me.

The fog swirls around her and she vanishes as if into the sea.

Fugue 1.2 Allegro "The Vicious Cycle And Variations"

PAPA sits in the wheelhouse behind the steering wheel. DA is behind him, pulling on a block and tackle rig. The rope goes over the port side where JIMMY stands hauling up an unseen crab pot from over the side of the boat.

They continue their motions over and over again speaking to the air as if each one is only partly aware of the others' existence. Time has stopped.

PAPA Pay attention to what you're doing boys.

DA When you were old enough you could have signed up like me.

JIMMY I didn't join the Navy because you wanted me to.

PAPA You get lazy you'll lose a finger.

DA But you had to go off to school, didn't you!

JIMMY Yeah, I wanted to become a Marine Biologist.

DA On my dime!

PAPA Like fathers like sons.

JIMMY I just wanted to learn to talk to dolphins.

PAPA Never listen to me do you?

JIMMY Study the sea. The life out there.

DA Wanted to listen to fish farting!

PAPA Down the line.

DA Never cared about tradition.

JIMMY College was the only way out of this life.

PAPA The buoy.

DA Always had to do your own thing.

JIMMY You always resented me for that.

PAPA The pot.

DA I paid for it though, didn't I?

JIMMY But you finally got your way, didn't you?

PAPA Haul 'em up.

DA I always had to work for everything I got.

JIMMY So did I but... There was just too much heady stuff. Math.

PAPA Open the cage.

DA You were too lazy, never studied!

JIMMY Diana tried to help me... But by the time I past the statistics to the higher stuff—

PAPA Scoop 'em out.

DA Thought I didn't understand.

JIMMY It was so far beyond me I couldn't keep up.

DA So what if I didn't?

PAPA Re-bait the trap.

JIMMY And when she drown… I just lost who I was.

DA It was all those drugs you took.

JIMMY I had a mind meltdown on acid.

PAPA Toss 'em overboard.

JIMMY There was no way to resolve my discrepancies.

DA You can't blame that on me.

PAPA Go in to sleep and then come back out.

JIMMY I became a "terminal singularity."

DA That was your own fault.

PAPA Repeat.

JIMMY I gave up school because I just wasn't smart enough, okay!

DA At least you have this to fall back on—

PAPA The buoy. The pot.

JIMMY All I know is this… crabbing.

DA Now I can't do the one thing that mattered to me anymore.

PAPA Haul 'em up. Open the cage. Scoop 'em out.

JIMMY Hunting in the sea.

DA Early retirement, cashiered out at my age… a cold warrior.

PAPA We only catch the males, you see.

DA You could have followed in my footsteps you know?

JIMMY But I still wanted to make a difference.

PAPA We let the females go.

DA You could have made a good sailor.

JIMMY Give something back.

PAPA Gotta make more little ones.

DA But no… my only son puts out to sea with those pinkos.

JIMMY Greenpeace.

PAPA The next generation.

JIMMY Stop the whalers.

DA Total bullshit.

PAPA Keep up the population.

JIMMY Then the anti-nuke stuff.

DA I suppose that was aimed at me.

JIMMY That really pissed you off, didn't it?

PAPA Round and round we go.

DA When I heard what you and your friends did at that protest.

JIMMY That "direct action" down in Tahiti during the nuclear testing.

PAPA I think we've been here before…

DA I just thought… that'll teach him.

JIMMY The time I spent in a French prison.

DA Let's see him get out of that by himself—and you did!

PAPA Buoy on the port boys!

JIMMY You wouldn't even return my phone calls.

DA But it didn't do any good did it?

JIMMY Well, I'm back here now and there's nothing you can do about it.

> *The sound of the waves beating against the hull of the small boat and the call of a foghorn in the distance as the three men continue turning the wheel, hauling the ropes and going through their motions… locked in a perpetual cycle.*

SHANACHIE BAILEY HISTORY 2

> *The cloaked figure of the woman reappears from the darkness, as if stepping closer to an open fire. She smiles and resumes her tale as if she had just paused for a sip of something.*

SHANCHIE So, on one St. Stephen's day… an old pagan holiday, you see… celebrated on the day after your modern Christmas. Had to do with being after the Winter Solstice. They'd nail a wren up on stick and the young boys would parade it around town. Fire festivals, don't you know? And tricks to be played on the unwary. An excuse for shenanigans is what I call it. Our little Bailey lad… on the advice of his closest friends—though with friends like that you don't need the devil. Our young Master James A. Bailey found himself hanging by his ankles over the Queen's Bridge. Aye. He did. No denying it. Guilty as black sin, he was. It is true to say that he did what they said he did. He even said so himself. Fool that he was… being honest. James Aloysius Bailey hung backwards over the side of the stone bridge with a little help from his fellow conspirators… and proceeded to carve in Gaelic runes. "Down with the Monarchy!!!" Three exclamation marks. Punctuation was new to him, you see. And as he hung there upside down admiring his handiwork he happened to glance up—or rather, down… at a movement he saw in the water below the ice. He thought he could see the face of a beautiful woman… with long flowing hair smiling down at him… or rather, up at him. The blood was rushing to his head and pounding in his ears so he did not hear the calls when they came and his eyes were fixed on the face of the woman in the water so he did not see the policeman on the far shore. But his good "friends" on seeing the constable running across the bridge towards them… let go their grip and down this Bailey ancestor fell into the river and through the ice knocking himself nearly unconscious until he floated into the arms of the most beautiful "woman" he had ever seen who was somehow swimming under the ice and breathing, if you'll believe me. Well, this "Banshee" or "Selkie" or "Merrow", for she goes by many names… this water spirit saved him from drowning and upon exacting a promise from him on the point of death to be her love, she brought him to the bank and left him there. But then the constable fished him out and dragged him sputtering into custody. When asked politely, Mr. Bailey would not say what he wrote on the side of the bridge. Nor would he give the names and addresses of his accomplices. The ones who had dropped him to his almost-certain death. He said nothing. Lips tight as a drum. Such a silence has not been heard since the first one. Before the fall. Or big bang if you prefer. Oh, our boy didn't keep quiet out of any loyalty, but because he was concussed and besides the poor lad knew very little English… So he didn't even know what the Bobbys were saying to him, or yelling at him when he was being questioned. He just nodded and smiled for hours on end as they beat him again and again and then his head lolled a little to the left on the side where the guards had been questioning him particularly vigorously. No, our James Bailey never said a word. Because you see, he was thinking about what the Banshee had told him. That "time was on his side…" unlike another successor of his, the current first mate of the *Trinity*…

Stepping back out of the circle of firelight she seems to fade from sight.

FIFTY-FIVE YEARS OLD

DA stands at the stern of the boat looking over the railing as he mends a crab pot with a pair of pliers. He speaks to the audience, as if talking to the sea.

DA My name is James Bailey, Junior. I turned fifty-five years old, last week. So technically, I'm fifty-five years… and seven days old. That's six hundred and sixty months (660) plus seven days, two thousand eight hundred and sixty-one weeks (2,861), twenty thousand and twenty-seven days (20,027), four hundred eighty thousand six hundred and forty-eight hours (480,648), Twenty-eight million, eight hundred thirty-eight thousand, eight hundred and eighty minutes (28,838,880) and by the time I finish saying this… add another minute, for a grand total of one billion, seven hundred thirty million, three hundred thirty-two thousand, eight hundred and sixty seconds (1,730,332,860) Jesus. That's a lot of seconds. But they go *(snaps his fingers)* just like that. I feel like just a couple of minutes ago I was out on patrol, a few hours ago I was burying my dead wife and just the other day we had a son together. Hell, I could have sworn it was just last week I was marrying her and it feels like just a month before that I met her and we fell completely in love and I asked her to wait for me when I went out on my first submarine.

Turns to look towards JIMMY.

And God, it seems like it's only been a year since I was his age. Standing up there and looking down on my old man and hating everything he believed in…. just because he did… and I didn't. (*He laughs.*) But that's just how it all feels in here.

He taps his head.

But I know that I'm fifty-five and he's twenty-five and there's not a damn thing I can do about it. Now I know that he won't listen to me any more than I listened to him. Besides, now that I'm back on this damn boat… I don't really know anymore… not any more now, than I did when I was his age and I let the seconds slip through my fingers… and into the sea.

Fog rolls in over the boat obscuring the stern as the set shifts around and darkness envelops him.

BANSHEE/EVELYN 1 The BANSHEE stands in the fog speaking to DA in the voice of EVELYN, his dead wife.

BANSHEE (*as EVELYN*) Hello Jim, I'm still here waiting for you. This seems familiar. But you know, waiting was not the worst. It was the not knowing if you were ever coming back from your latest patrol. There were nights here that I could have sworn I heard you breathe your last under the ice. And I'd see your boat go down like the Scorpion. I would never get to say goodbye again. Except maybe on a Sunday standing beside your empty coffin wondering who will help me bring the flag home? They hand it to me cornered and creased and I am swallowed by well wishers. All in black and they sweep me along to an unexpected ending. Under the long tree-lined path filled with white stones and the rows and rows of crosses of all those lost at sea. The wild, wild sea. Come back to me Jim, come back to me.

The fog swirls around her and she vanishes as if into the sea.

Fugue 1.3 Allegro "The Vicious Cycle And Variations"

PAPA sits in the wheelhouse behind the steering wheel. DA is behind him, pulling on a block and tackle rig. The rope goes over the port side where JIMMY stands hauling up an unseen crab pot from over the side of the boat.

They continue their motions over and over again speaking to the air as if each one is only partly aware of the others' existence. Time has stopped.

PAPA Look lively, lads.

DA You are always taking the old man's side.

JIMMY He said he was going to give me this tub.

PAPA I knew it would come back to this.

DA You know what he's like with money.

JIMMY I know he owes.

PAPA The three of us out on the boat again.

DA I was doing the right thing… for him.

JIMMY I even know how much he owes.

PAPA Just like in the good old days.

JIMMY But instead of just letting him go under—

DA For his own good.

PAPA A way of life.

JIMMY I'm going to help him.

DA We had a deal—

PAPA Father to son to grandson.

DA One last outing and then we'd sell this barge.

JIMMY And myself.

PAPA Be good to her.

DA And now you're giving him this false hope.

JIMMY I'm thinking of going North—

PAPA She'll be good to you.

DA Making more promises—

JIMMY Do the Alaskan crab season—

DA That you won't keep.

JIMMY Make some good money for a couple of weeks work—

PAPA Pay attention to what you're doing!

DA I've been up there in those waters—

JIMMY Come back and pay off the bank—

PAPA You get lazy you could lose your life.

DA We'll never see you again.

JIMMY Then settle down in some little town up the coast.

PAPA Never listen to me do you?

DA It's all a pipe dream...

JIMMY And when he wants to retire he can.

PAPA Like fathers like sons.

DA Smoke rings—

JIMMY And I'll take the boat.

PAPA Down the line.

DA Circles in the sky—

JIMMY We don't need you—

DA Going round and round—

PAPA The buoy.

DA But you never get anywhere.

JIMMY I never did.

PAPA The pot.

JIMMY Now, I'm back where I started.

PAPA Haul 'em up.

DA I feel like we've been here before.

JIMMY And I want my life back you S.O.B.

PAPA Open the cage.

DA Why are you blaming me for this?

JIMMY It's all your fault.

PAPA Scoop 'em out.

DA Because... I left you?

PAPA Re-bait.

JIMMY You were always gone.

DA It was the cold war.

PAPA Toss the small ones overboard.

JIMMY You never spoke to me—

DA I was in the "Silent Service."

PAPA Go in to rest, come back out.

JIMMY You want to talk about "silent service"?

DA Now it all comes around again…

PAPA And repeat.

JIMMY She was always the quiet one…

DA Like the circling of sharks.

PAPA (*Beat.*) You feel that… the calm. Like time just… stopped?

> *The sound of the waves beating against the hull of the small boat and the call of a foghorn in the distance as the three men continue turning the wheel, hauling the ropes and going through their motions… locked in a perpetual cycle.*

SHANACHIE BAILEY HISTORY 3

> *The cloaked figure of the woman reappears from the darkness, as if stepping closer to an open fire. She smiles and resumes her tale as if she had just paused to catch her breath.*

THE SHANACHIE So, without his cooperation, the court would have to go through the trouble of figuring out what this Bailey boy had carved on the side of the bridge. Now had it been "God save the Queen" written in a bit of collegial high spirits, then knowing eyes would have winked or looked the other way… but as it was an unknown… and an Irish one at that. Well, one of the local ex-patriot boys… a rogue and a scholar… who had a facility for languages… translated it for the Magistrate. The verdict was guilty. Treasonous. His crime was punishable by death… or deportation… to a penal colony… in Australia… New South Wales. They went easy on him. Since they thought he was an idiot. They sent him off down under… never to return. And when he recovered his wits, he never looked back. But something mysterious happened to the convict ship and he alone was cast adrift and found himself down in Queensland. Then it was over to New Zealand. Fellow fishermen and sheep farmers. Stick with what you know, eh? But then the island wasn't big enough. So then it was off to Tahiti. As if something was chasing him the whole way. The island hopping of the Bailey boy is legendary. That is... it is the stuff of legends. Not tales to be trusted. Still... there are more "green-eyed-half-bred-fair-skinned-sons" in Polynesia than many would care to admit. But then the wind shifted. And he headed further East. Setting sail again over to the Kingdom of Hawaii. The palace in the sand. There was good fishing off Oahu. But then the Kingdom became a Queendom and then it was annexed by the Yankees. And why not? It was their "manifest destiny" you see. And then he heard the call of "westward-ho, the wagons." So it was over to America with wife and sons in tow. California. San Francisco. Those Golden Gates with gold in the hills... and there it was, the Golden State stretching out beyond into the wide green valleys... Eureka, he had found it! A safe harbor. Not to mention good sheep country and wheat to be shipped back to Portsmith and Dublin. A chance to put back out to the sea. And go home again... the long way round. But he stayed behind in the Golden-land because there was also fishing in the San Fran-don't-call-it-FRISCO Bay... stick to what you know, eh? And then there was Angel Island. And living in the Mission District and the pubs and the fights and the tramping out to sea. Living in the Bear Flag Republic by the bay. And trying to make an honest living fishing and feeding lots and lots of kids. And the oldest boy, he has to help feed the family. Meat on the table. Once more out to sea. Singing the shanties and ditties from far off old Eire. Echoes from the past. The Banshee's call, a half forgotten memory. And that brings us to the latest incarnation of the Bailey sons...

Stepping back out of the circle of firelight she seems to fade from sight.

TWENTY-FIVE

JIMMY stands in the wheel house, behind the wheel, which he steers throughout his monologue. He speaks out to the audience as if to the sea, as if she cared to hear what he had to say.

JIMMY My name is James Bailey... the third. And I hate my name. I am twenty-five, god-damn years old. And I'm a fourth generation "Irish American." Which means... next to nothing, apparently. It also means that I just finished college and that means that I am in debt. Well actually, I dropped out. Scripps. Oceanography. Too much book-shit not enough blue-time. I actually couldn't get a long-term field project at sea. No one would take me on. They said I was "unstable" which is ironic because I've got rock solid sea-legs. Ever since I was a kid. I could climb a mast before I could climb a tree. I could only get to sleep with the sea rocking me gently through the night. Up on deck with just the sky over me. This is home. I've seen long days before the sun came up. Hauling and loading, baiting and re-baiting the same pots year after year. I even went north to Alaska. Couldn't get out on a factory trawler but I did some cannery work. I know I could do it now though. Make more money in three months out there on an Arctic factory crabber than I could make all year jerking "java" for trust-fund cases down in San Diego. My dad's Navy, really old school. Subs… nukes. Really scary cold-war-shit. He's retired. Pensioned out. Now he golfs and fishes. I guess he doesn't know what to do on land since his wife, my mom… She had just started chemotherapy and he was out on patrol when she… I was there by her hospital bed at the end… The last thing I heard her ask the doctors was if her hair would grow out in time before he got back. He found out at sea. But then he stayed out for another two and a half months. When he got back he was like a stranger. I mean, I never saw him cry. Not once. Ever. Yeah, I know he can, I've heard him. When he came back home after she… passed away. I knew every sound that old navy housing unit made in the wind, in those long nights. And I could hear him crying in her room. That's how I always thought of it, as "her" room. Not "theirs." He wasn't there long enough during the year to make it his. Not surprisingly, he went back out to sea and I went to live with my Grandfather, the crab fisherman. I guess I grew up with him. It was like I had two fathers. An old one that I knew, as well as I know this boat, and a younger one who would drop in to check up on me from time to time. He'd lecture me and tell me I should join up and that he could put in a good word for me. We spoke little. The only thing we all had in common was our names, each other and the sea.

> *Fog rolls in over the boat obscuring the wheel house as the light fades to a long slow blackout. Foghorn in the distance. The cry of a seagull.*

> *BANSHEE/DIANA 1 The BANSHEE stands in the fog speaking to JIMMY in the voice of DIANA, his dead fiancee.*

BANSHEE (*as DIANA*) Jimmy, I can hardly remember the feel of the sand and the surf and the life of the student I once was with you. And our time on Oahu. The beach and the stars and the biology. Ever the optimist I went into the water with my eyes open. But that wave that took me was unstoppable. When I lost sight of you there on the beach. I wept that you would be alone. What is the life expectancy of a fantasy? The best part is what is not said. But I have found a way for us to be together again. Come with me Jimmy… back out into the wild, wild sea. Come back to me, Jimmy.

> *The fog swirls around her and she vanishes as if into the sea.*

PAPA AND THE BANSHEE

PAPA sits in the wheelhouse behind the steering wheel. DA is behind him, pulling on a block and tackle rig. The rope goes over the port side where JIMMY stands hauling up an unseen crab pot from over the side of the boat.

PAPA Look, out there. (*Pointing over the rail.*) There she is. I told you, didn't I?

JIMMY Where?

PAPA There, can you not see her?

DA I don't see anything—

PAPA Out there. Jimmy can you see her?

JIMMY Papa, all I see is a seal—

PAPA She's come back from the grave.

DA Great! He's seeing mirages now.

JIMMY Papa?

PAPA She's calling to me on the waves.

DA He's hearing things too!

JIMMY Grandpa?

PAPA She's singin' to me… it's beautiful.

DA He's gone right over the edge this time.

PAPA Be patient, I'll be with you soon enough—

JIMMY Who are you talking to?

PAPA (*To JIMMY.*) It's your Grandma. (*Pointing at DA.*) And your mother. My wife. She's come to bring me home.

DA Papa, listen to me, she's dead.

PAPA Kaitlin?

JIMMY That can't really be her out there.

PAPA Darling, is that you?

BANSHEE/KAITLIN Jamie, it's really me. I've come to tell you your time has come. The waiting is over. All is forgiven. Come back to me.

PAPA (*Crossing to the rail.*) It's been so long… ever since the boy was born.

SELKIE You can come back home with me. Now.

JIMMY Jesus he's going to—

DA Oh, God.

BANSHEE/KAITLIN Come to me.

PAPA (*He starts to climb over.*) It's been so long.

JIMMY Stop him!

DA Papa she's been dead for fifty-five years!

> *JIMMY leaps at PAPA, pulling him back onto the boat. They collapse onto the deck. DA stops and stares over the side at the BANSHEE, as if seeing her for the first time. He stands motionless as she disappears.*

JIMMY Papa, look at me. Can you see me?

PAPA (*As if waking from a dream.*) Jimmy?

JIMMY Are you all right?

PAPA Yes, I'm fine now. Get off of me.

> *They stand.*

DA What… was that?

PAPA (*Shaking his head.*) Oh, nothin'. Just a banshee, tryin' to lure me to a watery grave. But then, you don't believe in that sort of thing, now do ya?

> *PAPA smiles and begins to laugh. DA and JIMMY turn and stare at each other. Blackout.*

STORM WARNING RADIO (VOICE-OVER)

> *There is the sound of a big bang and then static. Through the crackle a voice can be heard in the darkness as a thick fog seeps onto the stage and over the first few rows of the audience. A radio announcer's voice can be heard.*

RADIO VOICE National Weather Service bulletin, San Francisco.

Point Arena to Point Piedras Blancas and out sixty nautical miles including the San Francisco Bay and Monterey Bay.

Northwest winds expected twenty to thirty knots. Waves six to twelve feet. Wind swell increasing ten to fifteen feet at fourteen seconds. Heavy showers overnight.

High seas will continue to increase as the low pressure system moves over the region and the storm surge is predicted to rise above twenty feet by tomorrow morning.

> *Blackout.*

INTRODUCTION TO THE SECOND FUGUE

The cloaked figure of the woman reappears from the darkness, as if stepping closer to an open fire.

THE SHANACHIE Three seamen. A crabber, a submariner and an agitator… or do they prefer to be called activists these days? "Greenpeacers"? I know, you can't even call them "Hippies" nowadays… but this was back in the "Year of our Lord" nineteen hundred and eighty-seven… our boys are hard at work out at sea. The Crab Derby is going strong. Crab stocks are dropping fast due to corporate competition. There is a quota to be met… to pay off a debt. The forecast for rough seas was disregarded and the Bailey boys went out… one last time and… were lost at sea. Three generations gone. The last of the Bailey's lost in the fog. But, what happened? The storm? A rogue wave maybe? Could be. But there are some that say it was the curse of the Bailey Banshee brought over from the old country.

She removes her cloak shedding its weight and her age into the fog as it swirls around her feet.

THE CURSE OF THE BAILEY BANSHEE

The SHANACHIE has shed her cloak and become the BANSHEE. She stands in the fog addressing the audience.

BANSHEE I fell in love with a mortal man once… a long time ago… Jimmy Bailey, from over the sea. He fell into my arms and he kissed me and I saved his life and he pledged to be mine forever and ever. But they came and they took him from me and he was sent away across the sea… so, I followed him, and I saved him again but he soon forgot all about me. He married and he had a son who married and had a son who married and had a son. And now I have waited long enough. He belongs to me… and now he will come back to me, and live with me forever… in the sea.

The fog swirls around her and she vanishes as if into the sea.

Fugue: 2.1 Largo "Tabula Rasa Triptych"

The three men stand on the deck of the ship. PAPA is looking at something in the distance. DA is watching him. JIMMY is speaking into the ship's radio.

PAPA There! You heard something didn't you?

DA No, of course not. You think I'm crazy, like you?

JIMMY (*Into radio.*) Mayday! Mayday!

PAPA You're right, we're nothing alike—

DA Ha! You hated your father for coming here. For bringing you to this country—

PAPA Aye, I couldn't stand the S.O.B.—What of that?

DA Well, we've got that in common.

JIMMY Great, you both hate your fathers! And right now I hate both of you. That so called "engine" ate itself and since I want to get off this boat alive—just shut up while I try and raise someone!

PAPA He's got your temper.

DA And your stubbornness.

JIMMY (*Into radio.*) Mayday! Mayday!

> *The lights shift and the men are each isolated in their own spots as before. They stand and speak to the air as if from the deck of a distant ship each one only partly aware of the others. Time has stopped.*

PAPA (*Standing at the bow of the boat looking forward.*) The Sea… A way of life.

DA A fisherman's son.

JIMMY I'm five years old in bed at night.

PAPA My life.

DA No life for me.

JIMMY In a new costal town,

PAPA Our life.

DA A life at sea.

JIMMY Just another nomadic navy brat.

PAPA Generations of fishermen from the old country.

DA Seasick and sick of fish and the stink of it.

JIMMY I pick up the walky-talky from my night stand.

PAPA Then the old man packs us all up and here we are.

DA I hated the wide openness of it all.

JIMMY By my night light.

PAPA A fresh start.

DA The first time I saw the sea…

JIMMY I speak in whispers to the night.

PAPA No village this.

DA I thought there was no end to it.

JIMMY I only have the one walky-talky, you see.

PAPA A city.

DA And I knew it had a memory because time has found a home there.

JIMMY I'm hoping that someday somebody will answer me from out there on the wide sea.

PAPA A new world.

DA Moving back and forth restlessly for what seemed like an eternity.

JIMMY I slip into dreams still speaking softly with the red "send" button held down.

PAPA A new coast.

DA That day when I was about five or six and you took me down to Ocean Beach.

JIMMY A huge mast rises out of the center of my bed and takes the sheets with it on up into the sky.

PAPA The ocean is even on the wrong side.

DA I was sitting on the sand in the sun where you'd left me.

JIMMY And the bed-ship rolls into the darkness of the night.

PAPA A wharf.

DA Building a line of castles along the shore.

JIMMY The ocean is calm all around me.

PAPA A fishing fleet.

DA Watching the waves creep slowly up the beach.

JIMMY With the occasional white cap or—

PAPA Jobs to be had.

DA With long tentative fingers of foam.

JIMMY St. Elmo's frozen fire in rippling slow motion.

PAPA A booming business.

DA Feeling their way up the strand.

JIMMY The surface of the sea a blank slate all around me.

PAPA The old man sank everything into his first tub.

DA And into the moat I had dug in front of my fortress.

JIMMY I am alone on the deck of this new ship...

PAPA Some say he was lost at sea.

DA For just this reason.

JIMMY Just a mattress on promotion sailing across an open ocean.

PAPA The uncles whispered about running off with the cash and getting caught and killed.

DA And an old man walking along the beach said "You're just prolonging the inevitable kid."

JIMMY My pajamas are blown in the breeze.

PAPA Some even said he owed that old Chinese "gentleman" a lot of money.

DA I looked up at him and his halo of white hair like those paintings of the saints.

JIMMY The sea salt sprays over me.

PAPA And the tong threw him overboard and sank his boat.

DA He says "The waves will win in the end."

JIMMY The stars roll overhead into a cloudless night.

PAPA All I know is that we were a family of fishermen and I was the oldest boy... when the sea calls you answer it.

DA I said "I know... But then... I'll just build another one. It's only a game."

JIMMY I watch the waves crest beneath the foot of my four poster bed.

PAPA So I went to sea... even though I didn't want to.

DA "Ain't that the truth!" The old man says and then he laughed out long and hard.

JIMMY And where the wind blows my sheet/sails...

PAPA I don't like fish.

DA "Keep digging kid... you've got your work cut out for you."

JIMMY I will follow.

PAPA I don't even like crabs.

DA And then he sighed and smiled and walked off down the beach.

Fog rolls in over the boat obscuring it as the set shifts around.

CRAB DERBY

The cloaked figure of the woman reappears from the darkness, as if stepping closer to an open fire. She smiles and resumes her tale as if nothing has happened.

THE SHANACHIE *"Níl sa saol ach gaoth agus toit."* In life there is only wind and smoke. A father, a son and a grandson. Gone. Three souls lost to the sea. The little boat was found floundering off the coast… after the storm somewhere south of Point Bonita. A dozen pots left on board. The seas were rough that November. The first month of the season. The mad crab-dash. Rain or shine. They go out to ensure they catch their limit early. A Dungeness Crab derby. Insanely overloaded small boats… ready to be tendered for parts… make that one last sprint… in rough seas. Storm tossed for three days and nights… a small boat in a big, big sea. They risk it all. They risk everything they have… or everything they don't have. On one first season's catch. Otherwise you find yourself in January seas wading though a pot full of females that you have to throw back… only a handful of males above the legal size. Back breaking work. Take a full season to catch the limit. Make back your license fee… replace a few of your fifty pots. Maybe even buy a few more. Pay your crew… not much because they're family and you can. Not much left over for maintenance. Not much in reserve. Your heart lies in Atlantis's halls. Full fathoms down. Davey Jones and all. No wonder then that such a life has been known to drive men mad.

The fog swirls around her and she vanishes as if into the sea.

MOONSHINE

PAPA is in the bow. He is looking up at the moon barely visible through the curtain of fog surrounding the ship. He speaks to the night sky as if it can hear and acts as if it cares.

PAPA Out I come every night to talk to you… but you never answer me do you? I worked my whole life for you. Never faltered. Never failed. Kept my… what is it now? Faith? Kept it safe. Aye that's true enough. Holdin' onto it so tight that the crucifix cut into my hands. Believin' in ya when there was nothin' else to be done. Knowin' you was looking out for me and my lads. Spent a lifetime talking up to you. Thought I almost heard you answer back a few times when I was out here alone. Just me and you and the crabs. You up there lookin' down on all there is. And now where are you? Still silent. Just watchin'. Waitin' for the right moment to speak up? Must be nice to be ineffable. I think I'd like to try it sometime—

There is the sound of far off thunder and the flash of distant lightning.

Up there tonight, are ya? Was that you clearin' your throat? Well, well. That's a surprise. I don't mean no disrespect, you see. I was just tryin' to get your attention. I think I'm in a bit of a trap myself, if you see what I mean. My boy and my boy's boy. More like the son I never had if you take my meaning. Raised him up right I did. His father should be proud. But they won't get off the boat. They won't let me alone. I need to go out there on my own. What to do? "Do what must be done." But, what must be done?

> *There is the sound of far off thunder and the flash of distant lightning.*

Oh, aye. And you'll look after them when I'm gone then? Good. That's good. That'll make it easier when the time comes. (*He looks up.*) Ah, here comes the darkness. (*He smiles.*)

> *Blackout.*

> *BANSHEE/KAITLIN 2 The BANSHEE stands in the fog speaking to PAPA in the voice of KAITLIN, his dead wife.*

BANSHEE (*as KAITLIN*) James, can you hear me? You were out at sea when the storm came. The storm came into our bedroom and it washed over me. It washed the life right out of me. There was so much pain when my time came. I gulped for air like a fish on the sand but my lungs were full of wet and I couldn't breathe. I was drowning in my bed. Calling to you. Clawing at the air. Trying to tear it into pieces and stuff as much of it as I could into my mouth. Gasping for my last breath. I saw the midwife take our child... our son... I heard him cry. But then the darkness came and I was gone. James, come back to me.

> *The fog swirls around her and she vanishes as if into the sea.*

> *Fugue: 2.2 Largo "Tabula Rasa Triptych"*

> *The three men stand and speak to the air as if from the deck of a distant ship each one only partly aware of the others. Time has stopped.*

PAPA Crabs! Oh sure, they taste fine once you cook 'em up.

JIMMY A tropical breeze all around me now.

DA No school, thanks to you.

JIMMY There are giant ukulele's lashed together like outriggers.

PAPA But the little scuttling things remind me of spiders.

DA No college.

JIMMY A red white and blue colored canvas stretched between them.

DA No way out.

PAPA But after a while you get used to it like anything.

DA I enlisted when I was old enough and got on that "skunk-boat."

JIMMY A huge catamaran slicing through the water off the port side.

PAPA Just bring in the cages.

DA Being down below.

JIMMY One ukulele-pontoon up out of the water and the "Williwaws" blowin' strong offshore.

PAPA Haul 'em in and dump 'em out.

DA Under it all.

JIMMY The canvass barely visible in the darkness.

PAPA Start fresh with new bait.

DA Cut off.

JIMMY It's red white and blue… A union jack? A Hawaiian national flag? No… just one patch of blue in the upper left corner.

PAPA And over they go.

DA Isolated in cramped quarters for six months at a time suited me just fine.

JIMMY I can't quite make out the stars but the red and white stripes are quite visible. Barber pole bright.

PAPA A livelihood, if nothing else.

DA Some of the men couldn't take it.

JIMMY There goes "Old Glory" the American dream off into the night.

PAPA Years of back breaking work.

DA That was the life.

JIMMY As Aloha Oy! is heard in the air like an echo of lost rights.

PAPA And when I finally get my own boat…

DA A fat missile boat.

JIMMY As if sung by the old queen of the islands herself.

PAPA Who wouldn't follow in his father's footsteps?

DA Out of Oahu.

JIMMY The keening sound of it coming from her palace.

PAPA Me only begotten son. Seasick was it? Or just sick of the sea.

DA The crisis… now, that's how I should have bought it.

JIMMY That's the trouble with living in paradise—

PAPA Oh no, he goes to sea alright, to get away from me.

DA But then the wife.

JIMMY Everybody always wants your little piece more than you do.

PAPA In one of them black bellied behemoths.

DA The mistake.

JIMMY And they will stop at nothing to take it from you.

PAPA Silent service indeed.

DA The kid.

JIMMY The islands are fogged-in and the coast's not clear.

PAPA Underwater killers.

DA Shore duty.

JIMMY And the cold wraps around my bed, but I have no cold weather gear.

PAPA Brought us all to the bloody brink, didn't you?

DA Going "island happy."

JIMMY I take the quilt from the foot of the bed and I wrap it all around me as the fog closes in off the coast of "Cali–"

PAPA And for what?

DA The transfer.

JIMMY There is a foghorn howling in the bay and I pass under the bridge.

PAPA If you had stayed here, with me on this boat.

DA Mare Island.

JIMMY International orange? It doesn't look golden to me.

PAPA Just think of what we could have done together.

DA Her death.

JIMMY Floating through the water between the high cliffs.

PAPA Bailey and Sons.

DA And back home to be a caretaker for you.

JIMMY Between you two, the Scylla and the Charybdis…

> *Fog rolls in over the boat obscuring the stern as the set shifts around.*

THE DEATHS OF LITTLE MEN

The cloaked figure of the woman reappears from the darkness, as if stepping closer to an open fire. She smiles and resumes her tale as if nothing has happened.

THE SHANACHIE *"Imeacht gan teacht ort,"* goes the old curse. May you leave without returning. Well it seems they did. Crabbing. A loosing proposition if ever there was one. A hell of a way to make a living. And then only one big buyer when you get back to port. Ocean Choice Seafoood... or "no-choice" as they're known around here. The big boys... with the big boats. Lots and lots of pots. Big crews... work round the clock to bring 'em in quick. Many "unfortunate fatalities." They use that phrase a lot when talkin' bout the fleet now. They never say... a lot of good men died... for next to nothing. If you ask me and I know you didn't. The model is all wrong. The little family fishermen pay the price. They are truly a dying breed. The family who fishes together... well that was the way it used to be. They go on. Because they have to. They go out... because they have no choice. They went out overloaded in a storm and they were never seen again. No bodies were ever found. And the boat... a ghost ship adrift off the coast in the fog for days and nights. But where were the men? What happened to them? Three men... out on a boat. A family. The end of an era. No. It was no surprise to anyone in the fleet. Another casualty to an imperfect... but sustainable system. Who mourns the deaths of little men?

The fog swirls around her and she vanishes as if into the sea.

GHOSTS UNDER THE ICE

DA stands at the stern of the boat looking forward over the rail speaking to the audience as if to the sea.

DA I knew one day the sea would take me. I always expected it to be during the war. Past crush depth. Full fathoms down. A communal coffin like the *Thresher*. Or washed overboard in a squall. Or even something trivial like body surfing off the North Shore. I thought I'd get a burial at sea. Up and over the rail. The flag remaining dry above me and my body sliding into the wide open ocean. My voice silenced, forever. Just another name lost at sea. I was once under the polar ice cap, out on patrol. We were going to punch through the ice to take some readings. And the sonar-man let me listen in on the passive sonar. If you've never heard it... the cracking up of the ice-pack sounds like... ghosts. Talking to each other. Under the ice. And I remember thinking at the time "that would be a hell of a way to go." Trapped under the ice and your "soul" if you want to call it that would just bounce around under there like an echo. Forever. And now I know. Those were just echoes of all the other souls lost at sea calling to each other over the vast distances… and what I was hearing was their voices… bouncing off the ice cap. Amplified somehow. And now I'm one of them aren't I? You took me down didn't you? When I least expected it. So, how come… I'm still here? On this boat. With them. In the fog. When will it end? When I fall asleep this time? Or when I wake will it start all over again? God, I hate the unknown.

Fog rolls in over the boat obscuring the stern as the set shifts around.

BANSHEE/EVELYN 2 The BANSHEE stands in the fog speaking to DA in the voice of EVELYN, his dead wife.

BANSHEE (*as EVELYN*) Jim can you hear me? It wasn't so bad. Losing little pieces of my mind one at a time, that was my biggest fear. So to die suddenly—was a kind of relief. Very little pain thanks to the nice young doctors and their nice little pills and the liquid drip. The opium in the night. The dreams I had there toward the end were wonderful. And little Jimmy holding my hand. And I'd see you there in the dark. Under the sea. I thought I could feel you moving through the ocean. Under the waves. Under the ice. I would smile and you would wave. But then, there were those last days and that long last night. My hair was all gone. My hands too feeble to ring for the nurse down the hall. Jimmy asleep in his bed. The silence when it finally came. The ending, so soft and still, I wondered if I had missed something… but when I turned to look back. All was darkness. Jim, I miss you, please… come back to me.

The fog swirls around her and she vanishes as if into the sea.

Fugue: 2.3 Largo "Tabula Rasa Triptych"

The three men stand and speak to the air as if from the deck of a distant ship each one only partly aware of the others. Time has stopped.

JIMMY My bed-ship sails through the Golden Gate and there is Alcatraz right in front of me. "The rock," a milestone on the trail of tears and the native's rights taken away, again.

PAPA I can't go back, don't you see that?

DA This rust bucket should have been sold for parts or scuttled for the insurance years ago.

JIMMY And the non-native's right of passage over there on Angel Island… an abode of tears.

PAPA There's nothing left for me now.

DA You could have started over too!

JIMMY These islands have a dark and brooding presence in the fog.

PAPA I just wanted to sail beyond the sunset... once more.

DA Scrape the table clean and just throw the dishes away.

JIMMY Or is that just their memories there?

PAPA God... I sometimes wonder if there's anybody up there...

DA A clean sweep.

JIMMY The bed lifts from the water at my command.

PAPA Or is it nothing...

DA But not you.

JIMMY And I fly over the tall ships with their sails all stored and battened down below.

PAPA For a minute there I lost myself...

DA Had to go out one last time.

JIMMY I sweep on into the night through the fog into the city of lights.

PAPA What was I going to say?

DA And I just had to go with you.

JIMMY And back to my room in this new seaport town.

PAPA Something? Nothing.

DA There aren't any cutters out this far and we're not in the sea lanes.

JIMMY And I wake in the morning still clutching the walky-talky in my hand.

PAPA Nothing comes of nothing... just an old man's mutterings.

DA The way we're taking on water we'll be lucky if they find our oil slick.

JIMMY Up again and off to a new school and a new life, starting all over again.

PAPA Time slips away under the door and through the streets and over the dunes into the sea.

DA And is lost forever in the waves and beneath the blue of the deepest darkest days.

JIMMY Beneath the sky.

PAPA What this calls for is...

DA A fresh start...

JIMMY A new beginning…

PAPA It's a very delicate time to be sure.

DA Nothing is sure.

JIMMY The fog rolls in and nothing can be seen.

PAPA A clean slate.

DA Just three men on a boat…

> *All three in unison.*

Tenders, in the fog.

> *The sound of the waves beating against the hull of the small boat and the call of a foghorn in the distance.*
>
> *You can't subpoena the dead.*
>
> *The cloaked figure of the woman reappears from the darkness, as if stepping closer to an open fire. She smiles and resumes her tale as if nothing has happened.*

THE SHANACHIE "*Bíonn súil le muir ach ní bhíonn súil le tír.*" There is hope from the sea, but there is no hope from the land. These proud men reduced to selling live crabs off the back of their boats for some extra cash. Or steamin' them in tubs right there on the dock. The first catch of the season. The sweet meat. Just molted. Just mated. Boiled down to just the right color of red. The real lively ones kick off a leg or two in the pot. A defence mechanism. To escape a predator. Like a lizard detaching a tail. Only they have to pull them off with their own oversized claws. They feel the water heating up, you know? Think of that. Boiled alive. Not a nice way to go. Better to "live-pack 'em" right there. Get it over with. Slice 'em in two with a clever and a mallet. Quicker than slow boiling. Poor buggers. But, ah they do taste nice. With a little lemon in a crab-butter 'n garlic sauce… or just roasted over an open fire on the beach. Toasting the setting sun. And another day in this world of scuttling life. (*Beat.*) So, where was I? Oh yes, the *Trinity* and her crew. Destroyed by "market forces" the bottom line and ledger books… souls lost on the wild seas… for cash. For crabs. "Fresh caught and flash frozen for freshness." No. No surprises why they died. We may never know how, but we do know why they went out. Perhaps they weren't wearing life jackets. Whose fault was it? Well, you can't subpoena the dead, you know? They just disappeared. Never to be found again. All gone full fathoms down.

> *The fog swirls around her and she vanishes as if into the sea.*

WHALE SONG

JIMMY sits in the wheel house.

JIMMY There was a time when the oceans sang with cetacean songs. The whales communicated over vast distances. A language. A culture all their own. Another life under the sea. Beautiful beyond words. But now all the world's oceans hum with the sounds of ships' engines. Screwing their way through the water. Sonar pings. Long range, deep radio pulses. Auto-electronic beacons and buoys. The jangle of the constant noise must be unbearable. But the whales continue to sing. I mean, what else can they do? They sing all the louder to be heard above the noise. Their warm hearts slip through the cold dark waters. The cry of one to another… through the long nights. Even if their songs can't be heard over such large areas anymore…. they still sing to each other. And sometimes you can hear them calling to you. Across the void.

Fog rolls in over the boat obscuring the wheel house as the set shifts around.

BANSHEE/DIANA 2 The BANSHEE stands in the fog speaking to JIMMY in the voice of DIANA, his dead fiancee.

BANSHEE/DIANA Jimmy, can you hear me? I can still feel us surfing… slicing through the water across the face of that wave, together. Smiling all the way. Then I turned to you and saw you smile back at me… but when I turned back it had closed out. Down I went and up went my board and around my neck went the cord and over and over under the pounding surf and looking up and seeing nothing but blue so far above me and the distance from me to you and the hot sand so far away and I was calling to you and the trail of bubbles out of the corner of my mouth leading up into the bright blue light and feeling it all slip away into darkness. Jimmy, I miss you so much… come to me.

The fog swirls around her and she vanishes as if into the sea.

DA AND THE SELKIE

PAPA sits in the wheelhouse behind the steering wheel. DA is behind him, pulling on a block and tackle rig. The rope goes over the port side where JIMMY stands hauling up an unseen crab pot from over the side of the boat.

DA You hear that… that singing?

PAPA Here we go again.

DA Your mother used to—

JIMMY Da, what are you talking about?

DA I know that voice.

JIMMY Ma's been gone since—

DA I don't care—there you see her?

BANSHEE/EVELYN Jim, dear. Yes, it's really me. I've been waiting for you. Now you've come home to me. Remember the times we'd have? After you came back from a tour? Like having a honeymoon all over again. Well I'm here now. Come to me, Jim. I'm waiting.

DA She's out there… waiting for me.

JIMMY That's a dolphin!

PAPA It's a Selkie out to find a mate. Don't listen to her, son.

DA Evelyn, I'm coming—

> *He starts to climb over the side.*

JIMMY Da, No!

PAPA You go over that railing and you are no son of mine.

JIMMY Stop.

> *Slapping him.*

Look at me. Think about where you are.

DA What—

> *Snapping out of it.*

Jesus, Why… I… would have.

PAPA Drown like the fool you are. And your head would have been found in some cod's mouth like that poor fellow down under.

DA Jimmy?

PAPA That's right, your "worthless" boy just saved your life.

> *JIMMY is standing at the railing, looking over it. He sees the BANSHEE, just as she disappears.*

JIMMY Did… did you see that?

PAPA What did you see?

JIMMY Nothing… just a trick of the light.

> *DA and PAPA stare at each other.*
>
> *Blackout.*

FATA MORGANA

There is the sound of a big bang and then static. Through the crackle a radio announcer's voice can be heard.

RADIO VOICE (*voice-over*) National Weather Service bulletin, San Francisco. Point Arena to Point Piedras Blancas and out sixty nautical miles including the San Francisco and Monterey Bays.

Current surface conditions, small swells with an extremely dense fog bank, zero visibility.

The sound of static and then silence.

The cloaked figure of the woman reappears from the darkness, as if stepping closer to an open fire. She smiles and resumes her tale as if nothing has happened.

THE SHANACHIE "*Chomh sean leis an cheo agus níos sine faoi dhó.*" As old as the mist and older by two. The spirit of the sea. Only the fog knows what really happened. Rolling around the cages and the men who brought them in. Their thoughts and dreams, hopes and prayers. Their stories... their souls. Mixed with salt and sea vapor. The cages remain empty but the fog has a memory. (*Beat.*) The last clear radio transmission from the *Trinity* was just two words... "fata morgana." The name of a rare mirage caused by the presence of vertically adjacent layers of surface temperature density gradients that produce a complex mirage, characterized by a fanciful distortion of images on the horizon. Fata Morgana... also known as "Morgan le Fay," a fairy enchantress skilled in the art of changing her shape. She was said to have lived in a marvelous castle under the sea and she could make this castle appear in the air, causing seamen who mistook it for a safe harbor to be lured to their deaths. Fata Morganas may also be the cause of legends about phantom ships that sail the sky. Reports of the ghost ship the *Flying Dutchman* may well have been the reflection of some distant vessel looming over the horizon. Or... the old tales could all be true... There really could be shape shifting sirens in the sea cursing men and luring them to their deaths. And as the old saying goes... "*Ní cleas é go ndéantar trí huaire é.*" It isn't a trick until it's done three times.

The fog swirls around her and she becomes the BANSHEE once again.

BANSHEE/KAITLIN 3 The BANSHEE stands in the fog speaking to PAPA in the voice of KAITLIN, his dead wife.

BANSHEE (*as KAITLIN*) James, this is the last time I'll call to you... I can come to you no more. Your work is done and it is time for you to rest. You can leave all your troubles behind. Just step over the side and come to me and we'll be together forever. Come to me James...

The lights change to reveal the men on the ship.

FUGUE: 3.1 PRESTO "THE ACTION"

Darkness. The sound of wind blowing across the ship. The sound of a single gunshot echoes then there is silence as if time has stopped. The three Bailey men appear in their own pools of light. PAPA silhouetted by the bow lights, DA has been shot and is in the stern next to a portable lantern and JIMMY illuminated by lights inside the wheel house as he speaks into the ship's radio.

PAPA (*Standing at the bow of the boat looking out.*) I sometimes wonder if there's anybody up there.

DA (*Lying down astern, bleeding, he has been shot.*) Oh…

JIMMY (*On the boat's radio.*) Mayday, Mayday!

DA My…

PAPA Then I think…

DA God…

PAPA I'm too old for this.

JIMMY (*Into the radio.*) This is the fishing trawler *Trinity*…

PAPA I didn't want you two here, you know?

DA Son of a bitch.

JIMMY (*radio*) We are in trouble. We have an injured man aboard. Engine's dead and adrift. Taking on water—

PAPA It was your own fault.

DA Give the position—

PAPA I didn't ask for you to be here.

JIMMY (*radio*) We're somewhere southwest of Point Bonita—

DA Oh, it hurts like hell—

PAPA You shouldn't have got in the way—

JIMMY (*radio*) Can anybody hear me? Over.

PAPA Told you two—I wanted to go out alone!

JIMMY (*radio*) Am I getting through? Over.

DA You crazy son of a bitch!

PAPA You wouldn't let me.

DA So you shot the radio—

JIMMY I don't know if this is even getting through…

DA Shot me—

JIMMY You shouldn't have grabbed for the gun—

PAPA Never listen to me do ya?

DA I can't feel my feet anymore!

PAPA It was an accident damn it! I was tryin' to shoot the Banshee… out there in the sea.

DA I need some water—

JIMMY None left—

PAPA You should have got off in San Francisco like I told you.

JIMMY A stray shot hit the water supply.

DA Great. No food. No water—

PAPA Oh well. (*Drinking from a bottle.*) Cheers boys, here's to your health.

DA So, what's he drinking?

JIMMY Papa? What are you drinking?

PAPA Forty year old Scotch…

DA It was open on deck during the storm.

PAPA Saving it for a rainy day…

JIMMY Oh, shit!

DA Stop him! It's mostly salt water—

PAPA (*He laughs.*) It's too late now!

JIMMY Papa don't, that's not alcohol… it's seawater—

PAPA Water of life. Always wanted to know what this tasted like.

> The sound of the waves beating against the hull of the small boat and the call of a distant foghorn.

> BANSHEE/EVELYN 3 The BANSHEE stands in the fog speaking to DA in the voice of EVELYN, his dead wife.

BANSHEE (*as EVELYN*) Jim, I know you can hear me. This is the last time I can call to you. You've done your duty, your time has come. You'll never have to be alone again. We'll swim through the blue water together forever. You and me just like it used to be when we were young. Just reach out to me… come and take my hand. Jim, come to me…

> The lights change to reveal the men on the ship.

FUGUE: 3.2 PRESTO "THE ACTION"

The sound of wind blowing across the ship. A gunshot is heard.
Then silence as if time has stopped. The three Bailey men appear
in their own pools of light. PAPA silhouetted by the bow lights, DA
has been shot and is in the stern next to a portable lantern and
JIMMY illuminated by lights inside the wheel house as he speaks
into the ship's radio.

DA If HE wants to kill himself, let him.

JIMMY There are quicker ways to do it.

PAPA How? You threw the gun overboard, boy.

DA It's a good thing he did or I'd have blown your head off!

JIMMY You want to kill him, why not just push him over the side?

DA I would, if I could reach him.

PAPA Bastard. You're not my son—

JIMMY (*Back on the radio.*) Mayday! Mayday! (*static*) Jesus!

DA Christ, a nice family outing—ha!

   Laughs.

PAPA This was never a "nice family"—

JIMMY Would you two just shut up!

PAPA How could it be?

DA Shut up Papa—

PAPA That's no way to talk to your elders, boy

DA We've got to get back to shore—

JIMMY Papa I'm trying to raise somebody on the radio—

PAPA Kaitlin, do you hear this? If I ever talked to my old man that way...

   Takes a long swig from the bottle.

DA Oh great—

JIMMY I can't tell if we're sending...

DA He's gone...

PAPA My old man—

DA (*He starts undoing his bandage.*) Ah!

JIMMY What are you doing?

DA I've got to loosen this tourniquet

PAPA Now there was a crab man!

JIMMY Don't do that—

PAPA Captain Red they'd call him, red as a cooked crab—

DA The bleeding's stopped—

PAPA Captain "Bloody" Bailey!

DA Papa shut up, you know great-grandpa wasn't a captain—

JIMMY Keep it tight Dad—

PAPA So what if he didn't own his own boat?

JIMMY Or it'll start again—

DA Look college boy—

PAPA Cap'n Bloody.

DA I don't want to lose my leg—

JIMMY Fine then, bleed to death.

DA For the last time Papa, he just worked on that old tub—

JIMMY While you're at it—

PAPA Man can't help it if he's poor.

JIMMY Why don't you take a few shots of grandpa's seawater scotch!

DA Don't you remember?

PAPA Of course I remember—

JIMMY And just get it over with.

PAPA I remember everything—

DA Ah, Jesus that hurts.

PAPA It's like a curse—

DA Don't talk to me about the past, old man—

PAPA (*Offers the bottle to JIMMY.*) Want some, boy?

JIMMY It's poison, Papa, put it down.

PAPA Nah, it's a little salty… but it's smooth.

DA It'll make you crazy!

PAPA I told you I don't want you here!

JIMMY Papa, please put the bottle down.

DA You drunk bastard!

PAPA You never did listen to me.

JIMMY (*radio*) Please respond, is there anybody out there at all?

> *The sound of the waves beating against the hull of the small boat and the call of a distant foghorn.*

> *BANSHEE/DIANA 3 The BANSHEE stands in the fog speaking to JIMMY in the voice of DIANA, his dead fiancee.*

BANSHEE (*as DIANA*) Jimmy, this is your last chance… after this, there is no going back. I can't explain how… but I've been sent back to you… and if you want to come with me you can. Now. We'll ride the waves again and swim in seas so blue… it's like falling into the sky. Those warm tropical waters where the fish are painted all the colors you've ever seen in your dreams. Jimmy, just dive in and come to me.

> *The lights change to reveal the men on the ship.*

JIMMY AND THE MERROW

> *PAPA sits in the wheelhouse behind the steering wheel. DA is behind him, pulling on a block and tackle rig. The rope goes over the port side where JIMMY stands hauling up an unseen crab pot from over the side of the boat.*

JIMMY There's that sound again.

PAPA What sound, boy?

JIMMY Like singing… or a woman… crying.

DA Are you hearing voices too?

JIMMY There, don't you see her?

PAPA "Her," is it?

DA We've been on this boat too long.

JIMMY God, look at her fly through the water.

DA Who, Jimmy? All I see is a fin.

JIMMY My fiance, she's come back to find me.

DA It's just a shark… following us for scraps.

PAPA Thanks to all the chum you threw up over the side.

JIMMY But it can't be, you drown. I saw you.

BANSHEE/DIANA It's really me Jimmy. I've come back to you. Come surfing on the waves with me like we used to.

JIMMY Diana's out there—

PAPA That's just your common variety merrow out there—

DA There's no such thing as mermaids or selkies or banshees!

PAPA Tell her that.

JIMMY (*Crossing to the railing.*) No, that's really her…

DA Stay where you are.

JIMMY My fiancée, alive again—

DA Stop! That's an order!

PAPA Listen to your father, boy. You go over that side. You're never comin' back. You hear me?

DA (*Reaches over and grabs him.*) Look at me.

JIMMY (*As if waking from a dream.*) Da?

> He looks back over the side.

No. She's still there—

> PAPA grabs the rifle from inside the wheelhouse and crosses to the railing.

PAPA Not for long—

JIMMY No!

DA Don't shoot!

> PAPA brings it up to his shoulder trying to take aim at the BANSHEE. DA reaches out to take the gun from PAPA as JIMMY lunges towards him. JIMMY crashes into DA knocking him into PAPA who falls backwards against the wheel house. There is the sound of several gunshots as the stage goes to black. The sounds of the sea and the cry of a distant gull. Then silence as if time has stopped.

> Blackout.

FUGUE: 3.3 PRESTO "THE ACTION"

The sound of wind blowing across the ship. A gunshot is heard. Then silence as if time has stopped. The three Bailey men appear in their own pools of light. PAPA silhouetted by the bow lights, DA has been shot, is in the stern next to a portable lantern and JIMMY illuminated by lights inside the wheel house as he speaks into the ship's radio.

PAPA I told you to get off my BOAT!!!

DA How? I can't even swim like this you old S.O.B.!

JIMMY (*radio*) This is the fishing trawler *Trinity*. Over.

PAPA You never were a good sailor.

JIMMY (*radio*) We are adrift and in need of help. Come back.

DA We need to get back to shore—

PAPA I can't go back, you know that…

JIMMY (*radio*) S.O.S. (*Beat.*) Is anybody out there?

DA We've got to go back—

PAPA I've got nothin' to go back to.

JIMMY (*radio*) We are adrift and in need of help—

PAPA I sold the trailer… and everything in it.

JIMMY (*radio*) This is the fishing trawler, *Trinity*—

PAPA I been livin' on this old tub.

JIMMY (*radio*) We are adrift and in need of help—

PAPA They want to tender my boat… for spare parts.

JIMMY (*radio*) Can anybody hear me?

DA Ah, it's goin' dark…

PAPA Over my dead body!

DA I can't see…

JIMMY Hang in there, Da!

DA God Damn!

PAPA I'm not goin' to prison either, it was an accident!

JIMMY Nobody said anything about sendin' you to prison.

PAPA Kaitlin knows… she saw everything… from out there.

DA Great he's hallucinating now.

PAPA I told you I'm not goin' to an old folks home—

JIMMY Da, you're not gonna leave me alone with him are you?

DA Kid, I can't hold on much longer—

JIMMY Oh, Jesus, Da!

PAPA Out past the breakers…

JIMMY Da, keep talking…

PAPA Past the fog, oh, we're—

DA Really cold—

PAPA Sailing beyond the sunset boys—

DA I can't feel my feet—

PAPA And nothing can stop us now.

JIMMY Help is on the way...

DA My eyes are gone...

JIMMY Just hold on.

PAPA To the sea!

> *He finishes the bottle.*

JIMMY (*radio*) Mayday, Mayday!

PAPA And I looked...

JIMMY (*radio*) This is the fishing trawler *Trinity*—

PAPA And I saw a beast—

JIMMY Papa?

PAPA Rising out of the sea—

DA Son—

PAPA And it looked—

JIMMY Nothing's getting through—

PAPA A lot like me.

DA Don't let me down—

JIMMY Dad? Stay awake—

DA Keep calling—

PAPA I just want to sail...

DA Gotta get help...

PAPA Beyond the sunset...

JIMMY Look at the fog...

DA Keep talking...

PAPA Forever...

JIMMY It's so dark...

DA I can't...

He blacks out.

PAPA And ever...

JIMMY (*radio*) This is the *Trinity*...

PAPA Amen.

JIMMY (*radio*) Can anyone hear me?

> *The sound of static.*

Can anyone hear me, at all?

> *The sound of static.*

Look at that...

> *Still into radio.*

Fata Morgana...

> *He drops the radio.*

> *The sound of the waves beating against the hull of the small boat and the call of a distant foghorn. PAPA's light goes dark and then DA's light goes out. JIMMY's light goes out as we hear the static of the radio swell to a crescendo.*

> *Blackout.*

CODA: THE CURSE OF THE BAILEY BANSHEE

> *The cloaked figure of the woman reappears from the darkness, as if stepping closer to the burning embers of a burnt out fire. She smiles and finishes her tale.*

SHANACHIE "*Ar dheis Dé go raibh a anam.*" May they rest in peace. Well now, there's an end to the mystery, for that's how these things came to be, as sure as I am a truthful Shanachie. It's said you can kill an albatross and still have a long life and die in your bed. And you may hear a banshee wailing in the night and live to see the dawn. But if you try and harm her in any way... then your fate is sealed. For the tale goes that after they tried to shoot the banshee... A voice in the fog said:

> *As the BANSHEE.*

"I have followed generations of Baileys out to sea... and tonight it ends with you three. Hear your fate for it is sealed, you will toil hard 'till doomsday comes. But you shall never more set foot on dry land."

> *As the SHANACHIE.*

And with that she put a curse upon them. They were doomed to roam the sea forever. And for every crab pot they pulled up... another would take its place. But when the sun rose every morning all the cages aboard the ghost ship would disappear and the three men would start all over again… with no knowledge of what had gone before. Repeating their actions forever and ever. Feeling hunger and thirst but finding no rest. Deathless for all eternity. And what of the Banshee? It is said that her heart was broken that day and now she wanders the world telling the tale of the curse of the Bailey Banshee and the Ghost Ship *Trinity*. But then, *"Bíonn dhá insint ar scéal agus dhá leagan déag ar amhrán."* "There are at least two versions to every story and twelve arrangements to a song."

She pulls her cowl back to reveal her face and then she smiles.

Blackout.

End of play.

CHAIN REACTIONS

BY

TREVOR ALLEN

Chain Reactions

Three interwoven fugue-like stories are held together by a young physicist who is a mother-to-be. The piece is an experiment with theatrical form and structure, which is influenced by musical composition as well as quantum theory. It combines Einstein, the atomic bombing of Nagasaki and the view through a goldfish bowl in an exploration of the nature of reality, morality and the consequences of our actions. This thought-provoking piece won Best of the San Francisco Fringe Festival in 2000, where it was staged inside the Morrison Planetarium in Golden Gate Park.

Production Information

Festival Premiere at San Francisco Fringe Festival: September 2000 at the Morrison Planetarium in Golden Gate Park, San Francisco, CA.

Producer:	Karen McKevitt
Director:	Trevor Allen

Cast: Helen Slayton Hughes, Ellen Koivisto, Paul Gerrior and Kieron Edwards

World Premiere: April 2002 Combined Artform Entertainment at the Next Stage SF.

Director:	Rob Melrose
Producers:	Matthew Quinn and Bertha Rodriguez

Cast

Physicist	Melanie Sliwka
Kara	Elizabeth Bullard
Prof. Keith	David Sinaiko
The Bookman	William Boynton
Albert	Dan Wilson
Leo	Kurt Gundersen
The Flyer	Paul Gerrior
Little Girl	Rachel Rehmet
Woman	Dawn Walters
Man	John Sugden
Bachelor	James Craft

CHAIN REACTIONS

CHARACTERS

PHYSICIST: F, a pregnant physicist giving a lecture to her first-year students.

KARA: F, a woman sitting at a bar tells a story about her husband, PROF. KEITH.

PROF. KEITH: M, a creative writing professor talking to his student, the BACHELOR.

THE BOOKMAN: M, an ex-student turned street vendor selling a book to KARA.

ALBERT: M, Albert Einstein circa 1939.

LEO: M, Leo Szilard circa 1939.

THE FLYER: M, grandfather of PHYSICIST, present day.

LITTLE GIRL: F, a young Japanese girl, timeless.

WOMAN: F, a middle-aged woman in bed at night, the wife of MAN.

BACHELOR: M, a young man who just found out that his girlfriend, PHYSICIST, is accidentally pregnant.

MAN: M, a middle-aged man in a coma after an automobile accident, WOMAN's husband.

OPENING FUGUE

All characters are in various positions and separate realities. The dialogue is overlapping, repeating three times and building to a crescendo.

PHYSICIST We are all connected, you know

THE BOOKMAN Come on, I know you can see me!

ALBERT We look for the infinite in nature…

LEO You won't regret this…

WOMAN You ever notice… a pattern?

KARA Thoughts fought for control of my mouth.

THE FLYER I think that was our greatest thrill.

MAN Falling is a kind of relief.

PROF. KEITH I'm interested in the spaces… between the lines.

LITTLE GIRL We lived on the other side of the hills.

BACHELOR Is there any room left for the fish?

PHYSICIST What am I? Why do I exist?

Blackout.

SHARD 1

The PHYSICIST is behind a podium as if speaking to a class of undergraduates.

PHYSICIST Welcome to physics made simple. (*She laughs.*) I'll try and connect the dots for you. We are all connected, you know at the quantum level and we are all interconnected by our relationships to each other and to our individual perceptions of reality… through a recognition of these patterns of interconnections. This relational matrix implies mutual dependence… mutual coexistence, which also implies the interconnected—and inseparable existence of complementary realities.

Blackout.

SHARD 2

THE BOOKMAN is standing on a blanket with books and trinkets spread out in front of him hawking his wares to passers-by on the street.

THE BOOKMAN Book, lady? Wanna buy a book? Lady? How 'bout a nickel? Walk past, yeah just walk past. Knowledge? Anybody wanna buy a book? Ah! You looked—Gotta dime, dude? How bout a novel? Yeah, yeah walk past…It's cold, 'n late 'n dark and I'm sleepin' in the park… how 'bout a blanket, buddy? Spare change? Come on, I know you can see me! Cash? Come on man anybody got some? Yeah you! I'll give you a book for a buck. People, don't care whether or not… I am, who I am. Was that Descartes that said that, or Popeye? Spare some change in all this wind and rain? The wind and rain will fall and blow. Democracy is for the used, hypocrisy is for the few, the few, the fused, the fusion… yeah, I refuse, I refuse to do a scene and not be heard. To be seen and not be heard from like—You know? This ability to suck air and form it into meaning to spew a rain of words collapsing the soul down to just zeros and ones. So, can you spare some change my man? Yes you… Come on down Mr. Brown and buy yourself another story. One with a happy ending. Stroll up, stroll up I've got what you need… paperbacks trinkets and amulets a sidewalk full of possibilities. Pay a small fee, and set your soul free. Buy a book, a shirt, a ring. Stop your guilty gawking.

If you pay me… thank you—I'll stop talking… for now. Hey Lady, don't forget your book.

Blackout.

SYNCHRONICITY FUGUE 1

KARA sits on a bar stool, THE BOOKMAN is on his patch, PROF. KEITH is at a table with coffee and the PHYSICIST is at the podium.

KARA "IBID SYNCHRONICITY," he says.

PHYSICIST Welcome to physics made simple. (*Laughs.*)

PROF. KEITH Hey, I'm talking to you…

THE BOOKMAN Book, lady?

PHYSICIST I'll try and connect the dots for you.

THE BOOKMAN Wanna buy a book?

PHYSICIST We are all connected, you know?

THE BOOKMAN Lady?

KARA "RETROSPECTIVE OF THE SECOND," he says—

PHYSICIST At the quantum level—

PROF. KEITH You know who you are. Don't you?

KARA "GETTING WORD OF THE NEW," he says—

PHYSICIST And we are all interconnected—

KARA "WRITTEN IN INK… BORROWED FROM MY WIFE."

PHYSICIST By our relationships.

PROF. KEITH Look, I don't care about the lines…

THE BOOKMAN How 'bout a nickel?

KARA And then, he called that a poem. (*Laughs.*)

PROF. KEITH I'm interested in the spaces…

KARA Between you and me—

PHYSICIST To each other and—

PROF. KEITH Between the lines.

THE BOOKMAN Walk past, yeah just walk past.

KARA I thought he was kidding…

PHYSICIST To our individual perceptions of reality…

PROF. KEITH I don't give a damn about the form—

KARA So I just looked at him…

PHYSICIST Through a recognition of—

THE BOOKMAN Knowledge? Anybody wanna buy a book? Ah! You looked—

KARA Right through him… as if I hadn't heard—

PHYSICIST These patterns of interconnections.

PROF. KEITH It's all about communicating…

KARA My head buzzed.

PHYSICIST This relational matrix implies mutual dependence—

THE BOOKMAN Gotta dime, dude? How bout a novel? Yeah, yeah walk past…

KARA I was a fly on the wall of—

PHYSICIST Mutual coexistence.

PROF. KEITH There are no mistakes, you know—

KARA My own mind, trying to get out—

PHYSICIST Which also implies—

THE BOOKMAN It's cold, 'n late 'n dark and I'm sleepin' in the park…

KARA Through the wrong half—

PHYSICIST The interconnected—

PROF. KEITH I just want to open the vistas—

KARA Of a half-opened window.

PHYSICIST And inseparable existence of—

THE BOOKMAN How 'bout a blanket, buddy?

PHYSICIST Complementary realities.

KARA I blinked… he was still there.

PROF. KEITH The theatre of the eyes, ears and the mind!

KARA The moment that I should have said something… passed.

PHYSICIST Mutual coexistence is…

KARA —like a gallstone.

THE BOOKMAN Spare change? Come on, I know you can see me!

PHYSICIST It's not a static state, but it is.

PROF. KEITH Moving outside these little black boxes!

KARA So, I start to say "You are so..."

PHYSICIST Based upon—

THE BOOKMAN Cash! Come on man, anybody got some?

KARA He was just smiling...

THE BOOKMAN Yeah you!

PHYSICIST An ongoing dynamic.

THE BOOKMAN I'll give you a book for a buck.

PROF. KEITH Those safe, black and white rational thoughts...

KARA Smiling at me and the thoughts fought—

PHYSICIST Between these mutually coexisting—

THE BOOKMAN People... Don't care—

KARA For control of—

PHYSICIST Realities. (*Beat.*) It's very simple. (*Smile.*)

   Blackout.

SHARD 3 (A DUET)

ALBERT EINSTEIN and LEO SZILARD at a desk with a letter and a pen circa 1939.

ALBERT You know I don't like this. I'm a pacifist, Leo... this feels wrong, somehow.

LEO Albert it is not a thing to like, only to do. This is not something I ask lightly. We don't want your help.

ALBERT What do you want from me?

LEO You only need to lend us your name.

ALBERT Do you think this will have any affect? That it will shorten the war? That it will save lives?

LEO You know that they have a head start... they will build it. If they succeed, then there will be no more safe places.

ALBERT I know what is happening In Europe... in our Homeland. But don't forget... I am a man without a nation. Don't try to appeal to my patriotism.

LEO The president can keep a secret. How many people know that he can't walk without crutches? It's just a letter. It's only research. It's your duty to warn them. It will never be used by our side. Not on civilians.

Not on children. Can you say the same about them? You know what they are capable of.

ALBERT I will dictate it, yes? Then I will sign it… but I want nothing more to do with it.

LEO All of us are decided. There will be a test and scientists from around the world will come to see what we have done.

ALBERT We are like children in the dark. We see a candle. We reach out to it… and it burns us. This is not a fire that can be put out once it has been ignited. What you and Fermi are proposing would be like bringing a star to earth. Setting the sun upon the ground. You know what would happen to a city so close to the sun. To the people… to the children.

LEO They will lay down their arms. The fighting will end. There will never be another war. I promise you.

ALBERT We look for the infinite in nature… Only two things are infinite… the universe and human stupidity… and I'm not sure about the former.

LEO Just sign it—

ALBERT Yes, I'll sign it.

LEO You won't regret this… as long as you live.

> *Blackout.*

CHAIN REACTION FUGUE 1

> *ALBERT and LEO are at the desk with the letter, THE FLYER is looking at the sky and the LITTLE GIRL is folding a paper crane.*

LITTLE GIRL There was a flash—

ALBERT We are like children in the dark—

LEO Just sign it—

THE FLYER I took my granddaughter to see—

LITTLE GIRL A shockwave.

ALBERT We see a candle—

LEO You won't regret this—

THE FLYER Her first baseball game—

LITTLE GIRL A rush of air—

ALBERT We reach out to it and it burns us—

LEO As long as you live.

THE FLYER The stadium was packed—

LITTLE GIRL The valley below us glowed—

ALBERT This is not a fire that can be put out—

LEO Albert it is not a thing to like, only to do—

THE FLYER A record crowd—

LITTLE GIRL Paper cranes and paper walls—

ALBERT Once it has been ignited—

LEO This is not something I ask lightly.

THE FLYER Seventy thousand is what they said—

LITTLE GIRL Caught fire and burned.

ALBERT What you and Fermi are proposing...

LEO We don't want your help.

THE FLYER Over the loudspeaker—

LITTLE GIRL Like butterflies in the breeze—

ALBERT Would be like bringing a star to earth—

LEO You only need to lend us your name—

THE FLYER The ball dropped out of the sky—

LITTLE GIRL The ash was everywhere—

ALBERT Setting the sun upon the ground—

LEO You know that they have a head start—

THE FLYER She caught it... while I cried.

LITTLE GIRL The ash was poison—

>   *Blackout.*

SHARD 4

> *WOMAN is in her bed at night. She stares up at her ceiling and out her window at a stoplight.*

WOMAN Green. Yellow. Red. Green. Yellow. Red. You ever notice... a pattern? And identify it, for the first time? A stoplight... right? Green. Yellow. Red. Go. Speed up. Stop. You don't even have to look. You just know... the pattern. Making a mistake is easy... like falling off a wagon. Lying in bed... looking up at the ceiling... It looks like the surface of the moon. I wish you were here with me. I see... light reflected through that window. The seasons must change up there too. Red... green...

yellow. The pattern repeats… at intervals. Yellow, red, green. Close your eyes… it's still there. Like a mistake you can't undo. Light through your eyelids, a shading. Colors filtered through them like stained glass… membranes and veins. Green, yellow, red. The clock runs down in the corner. Signaling outside in that blackness. That "Urban Beacon" is giving orders. Eyes open… and the pattern repeats in another order. Scarlet emerald and gold. I've made mistakes. Spinning on this ball of rock, floating on my back, I think of all those polar opposites. Sun and moon. Light and dark. Yin and Yang and now… You and me… I dream of a world without signals.

   Blackout.

MISTAKEN VARIATIONS FUGUE 1

WOMAN is in her bed, MAN is in a coma in a hospital bed beside her, BACHELOR is looking into a fishbowl, PHYSICIST is at the podium.

WOMAN Green—

MAN Memory of an island and you.

PHYSICIST Think of the smallest things you can—

BACHELOR Little rocks on the bottom.

WOMAN Yellow—

MAN Fish, in a tank on my desk—floating.

PHYSICIST A baby's fist, holding—

BACHELOR Plastic coral, for color.

WOMAN Red—

MAN Shirt and white socks, the same load.

PHYSICIST A grain of sand. A cell?

BACHELOR Foil along back for privacy.

WOMAN Green—

MAN Mown grass and cuttings—rotting.

PHYSICIST A molecule?

BACHELOR Air filter, and pump… bubbles.

WOMAN Yellow—

MAN Post-it-note, with a manifesto on it.

PHYSICIST An atom?

BACHELOR A treasure chest.

WOMAN Red—

MAN Break lights ahead—stopping.

PHYSICIST Electrons?

BACHELOR Diver with air-hose.

WOMAN You ever notice... a pattern?

MAN These days are getting shorter—

PHYSICIST In their orbits.

BACHELOR Propeller on the bottom.

WOMAN And identify it, for the first time?

MAN You remember that first time?

PHYSICIST Spinning around their nucleus—

BACHELOR Tiny anchor chain.

WOMAN A stoplight... right?

MAN Eyes wide and the whole world new.

PHYSICIST Made up of protons.

BACHELOR No swimming sign.

WOMAN Green—

MAN Willow, on the edge of that lake.

PHYSICIST Made up of quarks.

BACHELOR No fishing sign.

WOMAN Yellow—

MAN This pen-light, examining my pupils.

PHYSICIST Leptons, and gluons and so on.

BACHELOR No diving sign.

WOMAN Red—

MAN My eyes are still bloodshot, dilated.

PHYSICIST There's where identity breaks down...

BACHELOR No kidding... it's so small.

WOMAN Go—

MAN Have you seen me?

BACHELOR I mean—

WOMAN Speed up—

MAN Do you still know me?

BACHELOR Is there any room left for the fish?

WOMAN Stop.

MAN Would you ever?

Blackout.

SHARD 5

The PHYSICIST is behind a podium as if speaking to a class of undergraduates.

PHYSICIST Mutual coexistence is… It's not a static state, but it is based upon-an ongoing dynamic between these mutually coexisting realities. (*Beat.*) It's very simple. Lean two sticks against each other. The resulting relational structure… It appears static, but that static structure is based upon the ongoing dynamic of each stick pushing against the other. Space and time are inseparable because space-time exists as a dynamic structure. It's obvious that the space aspect is primarily a manifestation of the universal relational structure and the time aspect is primarily a function of the universal dynamic of that relational structure.

Blackout.

SHARD 6

KARA is sitting on a bar stool drinking and talking to a friend about her husband PROF. KEITH.

KARA IBID SYNCHRONICITY," he says "RETROSPECTIVE OF THE SECOND," he says "GETTING WORD OF THE NEW," he says "WRITTEN IN INK I BORROWED FROM MY WIFE." And then, he called that a poem. (*Laughs.*) Between you and me, I thought he was kidding…so I just looked at him… right through him as if I hadn't heard. My head buzzed. I was a fly on the wall of my own mind, trying to get out—through the wrong half of a half-opened window. I blinked… he was still there. The moment that I should have said something… passed—like a gallstone. So I start to say, "You are so…" he was just smiling… smiling at me and the thoughts fought for control of my mouth, forming the words too slowly "So…" what? Obtuse, but in a good way? Brave? Nah, he'd kill me… Cryptic, and it's a shame… that nobody cares enough to find the key? You're so… Misunderstood, especially by me? Just then that voice came back and said, "so, cool." He blinked… but then his smile faded a little. I smiled because, my artistic integrity was still in tact… and because I wasn't going to hurt his feelings. He said "Cool?!?" I froze… all the levels of meaning cut through me… a thought surfaced, I grabbed at it like a drowning woman, hoping it would be a buoy and not an anchor. So then I said, "To be able to mean so much…" "While actually writing so little." Two more smiles. One was his… the obligatory grin now plastered on my face belonged in a fun house. I felt stuck behind it… like he couldn't see the real me. Like a moth in an entomologist's collection. Peering out from behind this glassy non-expression, that last refuge of the cornered Left leaning, right thinking PC talkin' gal. I concentrated on my breathing. "It's language poetry." He said… I said, "Really…???" but my upward inflection got cut off by the rest of that sentence, and thoughts ricocheted around my mind like… "'Language?' What, as opposed to 'cement' poetry? or the poetics of meaning?" He says, "I'm a language poet." And then it hit me. He's being real. So, I kissed him and we went to bed. I bought him a used thesaurus for his birthday.

Blackout.

SYNCHRONICITY FUGUE 2

KARA sits on a bar stool, THE BOOKMAN is on his patch, PROF. KEITH is at a table with coffee and the PHYSICIST is at the podium.

PHYSICIST It's very simple.

PROF. KEITH We all think we know, but we don't.

KARA My mouth, forming the words too slowly—

PHYSICIST Lean two sticks against each other.

THE BOOKMAN Whether… or not…

KARA So, what? Obtuse, but in a good way?

PHYSICIST The resulting relational structure…

PROF. KEITH Synchronicity, is not for weak minds… it's—

KARA Brave? Nah, he'd kill me…

PHYSICIST It appears static,

THE BOOKMAN I am, who I am? Was that Descartes that said that, or Popeye?

KARA Cryptic, and it's a shame…

PHYSICIST But that static structure is—

PROF. KEITH Like a baby's grip on your reality—

KARA That nobody cares enough to find the key?

PHYSICIST Based upon the ongoing dynamic—

THE BOOKMAN Spare some change in all this wind and rain?

KARA You're so… Misunderstood, especially by me?

PHYSICIST Of each stick pushing—

PROF. KEITH Plato, Aristotle… they're all geeks!

KARA Just then that voice came back—

PHYSICIST Against the other.

THE BOOKMAN The wind and rain will fall and blow.

KARA And said, "so, cool."

PHYSICIST Space and time are—

PROF. KEITH Self-referential?

KARA He blinked… but then—

PROF. KEITH Everything is self-referential, to me.

KARA His smile faded a little.

PHYSICIST Inseparable because space-time—

THE BOOKMAN Democracy is for the used—

KARA I smiled because, my artistic integrity—

PHYSICIST Exists as a dynamic structure.

PROF. KEITH Or else what have you got?

KARA Was still intact… and because—

PHYSICIST It's obvious that—

THE BOOKMAN Hypocrisy is for the few—

KARA I wasn't going to hurt his feelings.

PHYSICIST The space aspect is primarily—

PROF. KEITH Don't ask questions…

KARA He said "Cool?!?" I froze…

PHYSICIST A manifestation of—

THE BOOKMAN The few, the fused, the fusion…yeah, I refuse—

KARA All the levels of meaning cut through me—

PHYSICIST The universal relational structure—

PROF. KEITH You already know the answers to.

KARA A thought surfaced—

PHYSICIST And the time aspect—

THE BOOKMAN I refuse to do a scene and not be heard—

KARA I grabbed at it like a drowning woman—

PHYSICIST Is primarily a function of—

PROF. KEITH It's all process, you know...

KARA Hoping it would be a buoy and not—

PHYSICIST The universal dynamic.

THE BOOKMAN To be seen and not be heard from... like—

KARA An anchor—

PHYSICIST Of that relational structure—

THE BOOKMAN You know?

Blackout.

SHARD 7

THE FLYER is outside, looking up at the sky while talking about Nagasaki.

THE FLYER I heard our Captain say "do it now." When the clouds opened up over the target... the city was pretty as a picture. We made our run. Dropped our load. I think that was our greatest thrill. But, I wasn't thrilled. I was terrified. If a scrawny kid could do this to an entire city... what could the rest of the world do to us? Fat Man, Bock's Car and me. Bombs away baby. Because the blast was deflected by the surrounding mountains the casualties were not as high as we would have liked. We had hoped for half a million—We only got about seventy thou—That didn't seem like much then. Later of course, I felt different. I took my granddaughter to see her first baseball game. The stadium was packed. A record crowd. Seventy thousand is what they said over the loudspeaker. The ball dropped out of the sky. She caught it... while I cried.

Blackout.

CHAIN REACTION FUGUE 2

ALBERT and LEO are at the desk with the letter, THE FLYER is looking at the sky and the LITTLE GIRL is folding a paper crane.

ALBERT You know what would happen—

LEO They will build it.

THE FLYER I heard our Captain say "do it now"—

LITTLE GIRL Children's shadows—

ALBERT To a city so close to the sun—

LEO If they succeed then there will be—

THE FLYER When the clouds opened up over the target—

LITTLE GIRL Burnt into the paint—

ALBERT To the people… to the children—

LEO No more safe places—

THE FLYER The city was pretty as a picture—

LITTLE GIRL On the sides of the school house.

ALBERT We look for the infinite in nature—

LEO The president can keep a secret—

THE FLYER We made our run—

LITTLE GIRL I woke—

ALBERT "Only two things are infinite—"

LEO How many people know that he—

THE FLYER Dropped our load—

LITTLE GIRL And the world had gone dark.

ALBERT The universe and human stupidity—

LEO Can't walk without crutches?

THE FLYER I think that was our greatest thrill.

LITTLE GIRL We had heard—

ALBERT And I'm not sure about the former."

LEO It's just a letter—

THE FLYER But I wasn't thrilled. I was terrified—

LITTLE GIRL About that other city—

ALBERT Yes, I'll sign it.

LEO It's only research—

THE FLYER If a scrawny kid could do this—

LITTLE GIRL They dropped—

ALBERT You know I don't like this—

LEO It's your duty to warn them—

THE FLYER To an entire city—

LITTLE GIRL Leafs?

ALBERT I'm a pacifist, Leo—

LEO It will never be used by our side.

THE FLYER What could the rest of the world do to us?

LITTLE GIRL Words fail.

Blackout.

SHARD 8

MAN is in a hospital bed. He is comatose from a car accident. We hear his thoughts.

MAN Memory of an island and you. Fish in a tank on my desk— floating. Shirt and white socks, the same load. Mown grass and cuttings... rotting. Post-it-note with a manifesto on it. Break lights ahead... stopping. These days are getting shorter. You remember that first time? Eyes wide and the whole world new. Willow on the edge of that lake. This pen-light, examining my pupils. My eyes are still bloodshot, dilated. Have you seen me? Do you still know me? Would you ever? Falling is a kind of relief. At least it's a forward momentum. This hospital bed feels like a raft. I'm glad there are no mirrors in here. My flying dreams have stopped. Do you know that I'm still... dreaming? What does that mean to you? God, this feeble kind of exile is tedious. Outside the trees change clothes. This wheel keeps on turning... while this machine is still in me. Pumping away, circulating. Breathing with my lungs... Life... Beating with my heart. Fluids... keeping me alive, still. Whose mistake was it? Whose fault? Asking, "Can you identify the body?" I wish they would open my eyes so I could see... the light again. They want me to blink... but this meat is not me. I can't move it. I might as well be a brain in a jar. I can't tell how long it's been. Time has no meaning. The coming and going of years, or is it minutes? I can't tell now. Why am I here? I think I'm still here... so I must be... are you out there? I can still see your face... you know. I'll only stay as long as that's true...

Blackout.

MISTAKEN VARIATIONS FUGUE 2

WOMAN is in her bed, MAN is in a coma in a hospital bed beside her, BACHELOR is looking into a fishbowl, PHYSICIST is at the podium.

BACHELOR Look, this is nuts…

WOMAN You don't even have to look—

PHYSICIST At the smallest level… because—

BACHELOR She knows it was a mistake…

WOMAN You just know… the pattern.

PHYSICIST We were mistaken… there is nothing.

MAN Falling is a kind of relief—

BACHELOR Right? Maybe I should get a dog.

WOMAN Making a mistake is easy—

MAN At least it's a forward momentum…

WOMAN Like falling off a wagon.

PHYSICIST There are no things… nothing solid.

BACHELOR A little black Lab puppy?

WOMAN Lying in bed—

MAN This hospital bed feels like a raft.

BACHELOR Chasing sticks and balls on the beach—

PHYSICIST No little "sticks and balls," just waves.

BACHELOR He'll have floppy ears and cute eyes—

WOMAN Looking up at the ceiling…

MAN I'm glad there are no mirrors in here.

BACHELOR With feet too big for his body.

PHYSICIST Measure the motion, plot the position.

MAN My flying dreams have stopped—

BACHELOR Howling at the moon—

WOMAN It looks like the surface of the moon.

MAN Do you know that I'm still…

BACHELOR Pissing on the bed… so what?

WOMAN I wish you were here. With me. I see…

PHYSICIST Patterns emerge... interconnections.

MAN Dreaming... what does that mean to you?

BACHELOR Unconditional love, it's worth it—

WOMAN Light, reflected through that window—

MAN God, this feeble kind of exile is tedious—

BACHELOR Isn't it?

PHYSICIST The chaos dissolves into order.

BACHELOR Maybe a cat?

WOMAN The seasons must change up there, too.

MAN Outside the trees change clothes—

BACHELOR They're self-cleaning.

PHYSICIST Probability coalesces into a point.

BACHELOR I'll call him Shrodinger.

WOMAN Red... green... yellow.

MAN This wheel keeps on turning—

BACHELOR Coming and going... in and out—

PHYSICIST Reality comes into focus.

BACHELOR Nah, too moody.

WOMAN The pattern repeats... at intervals—

MAN While this machine is still in me.

PHYSICIST Interference patterns intersect.

BACHELOR A turtle, a pig, maybe a parrot?

WOMAN Yellow, red, green.

MAN Pumping away, circulating—

PHYSICIST To define a shadow... an outline.

BACHELOR I just can't identify with fatherhood.

WOMAN Close your eyes... it's still there—

MAN Breathing with my lungs—

WOMAN Like a mistake you can't undo.

PHYSICIST A glimpse at the true nature of—

MAN Life...

BACHELOR Does she really want one?

PHYSICIST The water... in which we all swim.

BACHELOR And can I support us?

WOMAN Light, through your eyelids, a shading—

MAN Beating with my heart.

BACHELOR The three of us on this salary?

WOMAN Colors, filtered through them like—

MAN Fluids... keeping me alive, still—

BACHELOR She says...

WOMAN Stained glass... membranes and veins.

MAN Whose mistake was it? Whose fault?

BACHELOR "It doesn't matter."

PHYSICIST Matter is merely our minds way of—

MAN Asking, "Can you identify the body?"

PHYSICIST Making sense of our perceptions.

BACHELOR What's wrong with them?

WOMAN Green, yellow, red—

MAN I wish they would open my eyes.

BACHELOR They grow up—

WOMAN The clock runs down in the corner.

MAN So I could see... the light again—

BACHELOR And turn into.... Teenagers...

PHYSICIST Time is an illusion caused by—

BACHELOR Shit. That means—

PHYSICIST The passage of matter through space.

BACHELOR I'm turning into my father.

WOMAN Signaling outside in that blackness—

MAN They want me to blink... but—

BACHELOR I won't. "Make a good one."

WOMAN That "Urban Beacon" is giving orders.

MAN This meat is not me, I can't move it.

PHYSICIST So, everything... is made of nothing—

BACHELOR She didn't really say that did she?

Blackout.

SHARD 9

The PHYSICIST is behind a podium as if speaking to a class of undergraduates.

PHYSICIST This dynamic structure of the 4th Dimension can be non-mathematically modeled in terms of what we will describe as a relational matrix of coexisting realities, pseudo-similar, quasi-independent from each other… and yet they're fundamentally bound together at the quantum level. So that what we all perceive as completely independent points of view and totally separate sometimes diametrically opposed perceptions of this reality are… in a real way the same. The same old sights become new when seen through different eyes from another's perspective. Put simply… we are all dreaming each other's dreams. We're just dancing to the music of the spheres.

Blackout.

SHARD 10

PROF. KEITH is drinking coffee at a cafe and talking to one of his writing students.

PROF. KEITH Hey, I'm talking to you… You know who you are, don't you? Look, I don't care about the lines… I'm interested in the spaces… between the lines. I don't give a damn about the form—It's all about communicating… There are no mistakes, you know? I just want to open the vistas… The theatre of the eyes, ears and the mind. Moving outside these little black boxes! Those safe, black and white rational thoughts… we all think we know, but we don't. Synchronicity, is not for weak minds. It's like a baby's grip on your reality. Plato, Aristotle… they're all geeks. Self-referential? Everything is self-referential, to me. Or else what have you got? Don't ask questions you already know the answers to. It's all process, you know. You know? You think you're finished. But you're not—by a long shot in the dark. This mind printing technique… I don't know… it's just a howl… in the wilderness. It's just mental pornography anyway. It's all about the evocation of form. Not the structure of thought. Come to a "why" in the road, take it! Frosty was right, don't look back. I lost my copy of the book of life and I don't want another one. Just sayin'… you should see the world from at least four sides. I know it all sounds crazy. But, what's ugly and dumb today… could be Picasso tomorrow.

Blackout.

SYNCHRONICITY FUGUE 3

KARA sits on a bar stool, THE BOOKMAN is on his patch, PROF. KEITH is at a table with coffee and the PHYSICIST is at the podium.

PROF. KEITH You think you're finished… But you're not—

KARA So then I said, "To be able to mean so much…"

PHYSICIST This dynamic structure—

PROF. KEITH By a long shot in the dark—

THE BOOKMAN This ability to suck air and form it into meaning—

KARA "While actually writing so little."

PHYSICIST Of the 4th Dimension.

KARA Two more smiles—

PHYSICIST Can be non-mathematically modeled—

THE BOOKMAN To spew a rain of words—

KARA One was his… the obligatory grin now plastered—

PHYSICIST In terms of what we will describe as—

PROF. KEITH This mind printing… technique—

KARA On my face belonged in a fun house.

PHYSICIST A relational matrix of—

THE BOOKMAN Collapsing the soul down—

KARA I felt stuck behind it… like he couldn't see the real me. Like—

PHYSICIST Coexisting realities.

PROF. KEITH I don't know… it's just a howl in the wilderness—

KARA A moth in an entomologist's collection—

PHYSICIST Pseudo-similar, quasi-independent—

THE BOOKMAN To just zeros and ones—

KARA Peering out—

PHYSICIST From each other… and yet—

PROF. KEITH It's—just mental pornography anyway.

KARA From behind this glassy non-expression—

PHYSICIST They're fundamentally bound together.

THE BOOKMAN So can you spare some change my Man?

KARA That last refuge of the cornered—

PHYSICIST At the quantum level—

PROF. KEITH It's all about the evocation of form—

THE BOOKMAN Yes you—

KARA Left leaning, right thinking "PC" talkin' gal.

PHYSICIST So that what we all perceive—

THE BOOKMAN Come on down Mr. Brown—

KARA I concentrated on my breathing—

PHYSICIST As completely independent points of view—

PROF. KEITH Not the structure of thought—

THE BOOKMAN And buy yourself another story.

KARA "It's language poetry." He said…

PHYSICIST And totally separate—

THE BOOKMAN One with a happy ending—

KARA I said, "Really…???" but—

PHYSICIST Sometimes diametrically opposed—

PROF. KEITH Come to a 'why' in the road, …take it—

THE BOOKMAN Stroll up, stroll up—

KARA My upward inflection got cut off by—

PHYSICIST Perceptions of this reality.

THE BOOKMAN I've got what you need… paperbacks?

KARA The rest of that sentence… and thoughts—

PHYSICIST Are… in a real way, the same.

PROF. KEITH Frosty was right, don't look back…

THE BOOKMAN Trinkets and amulets—

KARA Ricocheted around my mind like… "Language?"

PHYSICIST The same old sights become new—

THE BOOKMAN A sidewalk full of possibilities—

KARA What, as opposed to 'cement' poetry?

PHYSICIST When seen through different eyes—

PROF. KEITH I lost my copy of the book of life—

THE BOOKMAN Pay a small fee, and set your soul free—

KARA Or the poetics of meaning?

PHYSICIST From another's perspective—

PROF. KEITH And I don't want another one.

THE BOOKMAN Buy a book, a shirt, a ring—

KARA He says, "I'm a language poet." And then it hit me. He's being real.

PHYSICIST Put simply… we are all—

PROF. KEITH Just sayin'… you should see the world from at least four sides.

THE BOOKMAN Stop your guilty gawking—

KARA So, I kissed him and we went to bed—

PHYSICIST Dreaming each others dreams.

PROF. KEITH I know it all sounds crazy, but—

THE BOOKMAN If you pay me… (*Sound of money.*) thank you, I'll stop talking… for now.

PHYSICIST We're just dancing to the music of the spheres.

KARA I bought him a used thesaurus for his birthday.

PROF. KEITH What's ugly and dumb today—

THE BOOKMAN Hey Lady, don't forget your book.

PROF. KEITH Could be Picasso tomorrow…

Blackout.

SHARD 11

The LITTLE GIRL is sitting on the ground, folding a paper crane.

LITTLE GIRL We had heard about that other city. They dropped… leafs? Words fail. How do you say? Leaflets. Telling us that if we would not surrender… they would unleash "a rain of ruin the like of which has never been seen on earth." We lived on the other side of the hills. So… we lived through it. There was a flash. A shockwave. A rush of air. The valley below us glowed. Paper cranes and paper walls caught fire and burned like butterflies in the breeze. The ash was everywhere. The ash was poison. Children's shadows burnt into the paint on the sides of the school house. I woke… and the world had gone dark.

Blackout.

CHAIN REACTION FUGUE 3

ALBERT and LEO are at the desk with the letter, THE FLYER is
looking at the sky and the LITTLE GIRL is folding a paper crane.

ALBERT This feels wrong somehow—

LEO Not on civilians—

THE FLYER Fat Man—

LITTLE GIRL How do you say?

ALBERT What do you want from me?

LEO Not on children—

THE FLYER Bock's Car—

LITTLE GIRL Leaflets—

ALBERT Do you think this will have any affect?

LEO Can you say the same about them?

THE FLYER And me—

LITTLE GIRL Telling us—

ALBERT That it will shorten the war?

LEO You know what they are capable of—

THE FLYER Bombs away baby!

LITTLE GIRL That if we would not surrender—

ALBERT That it will save lives?

LEO All of us are decided—

THE FLYER Because the blast was deflected—

LITTLE GIRL They would unleash "a rain of ruin—"

ALBERT I know what is happening—

LEO There will be a test—

THE FLYER By the surrounding mountains—

LITTLE GIRL The like of which has never been seen—

ALBERT In Europe… in our Homeland—

LEO And scientists from around—

THE FLYER The casualties were not as high—

LITTLE GIRL On earth—

ALBERT But don't forget. I am a man without a nation—

LEO The world will come to see what we have done—

THE FLYER As we would have liked.

LITTLE GIRL We lived—

ALBERT Don't try to appeal to my patriotism—

LEO They will lay down their arms—

THE FLYER We had hoped for half a million—

LITTLE GIRL On the other side of the hills—

ALBERT I will dictate it, yes?

LEO The fighting will end—

THE FLYER We only got about seventy thou—

LITTLE GIRL So—

ALBERT Then I will sign it—

LEO There will never be another war—

THE FLYER That didn't seem like much then—

LITTLE GIRL We lived through it—

ALBERT But I want nothing more to do with it—

LEO I promise you—

THE FLYER Later of course, I felt different.

    Blackout.

SHARD 12

The BACHELOR is staring into a fishbowl. He has just found out his girlfriend is pregnant, by accident.

BACHELOR Little rocks on the bottom. Plastic coral, for color. Foil along back for privacy. Air filter, and pump... bubbles. A treasure chest. Diver with air-hose. Propeller on the bottom. Tiny anchor chain. No swimming sign. No fishing sign. No diving sign. No kidding... it's so small. I mean—Is there any room left for the fish? Look, this is nuts... She knows it was a mistake... Right? Maybe I should get a dog. A little black Lab puppy. Chasing sticks and balls on the beach. He'll have... floppy ears and cute eyes... with feet too big for his body. Howling at the moon... pissing on the bed... so what? Unconditional love, it's worth it... Isn't it? Maybe a cat? They're self-cleaning. I'll call him Shrodinger. Coming and going in and out... Nah, too moody. A turtle, a pig, maybe a parrot? I just can't identify with fatherhood. Does she really want one? And can I support us? The three of us on this salary? She says... "It

doesn't matter" What's wrong with them? They grow up and turn into...
Teenagers... Shit—that means... I'm turning into my father. I won't.
"Make a good one." She didn't really say that did she? She knows how
I feel... I mean we talked. It's too soon. I don't know if I'm ready. I like
the "idea" of new life. Maybe I should start out small with like, a fish in
a bowl... or maybe two? I've got nine months. God! That's a long time...
But, my inner child still wants out.

   Blackout.

MISTAKEN VARIATIONS FUGUE 3

*WOMAN is in her bed, MAN is in a coma in a hospital bed beside
her, BACHELOR is looking into a fishbowl, PHYSICIST is at the
podium.*

WOMAN Eyes open... and the pattern repeats.

MAN I might as well be a brain in a jar—

WOMAN In another order—

PHYSICIST Nothing but patterns and waves.

BACHELOR She knows—

WOMAN Scarlet emerald and gold.

MAN I can't tell how long it's been—

BACHELOR How I feel...

WOMAN I've made mistakes...

PHYSICIST And nothing exists, but this relationship—

BACHELOR I mean we talked.

WOMAN Spinning on this ball of rock—

PHYSICIST Between reality and our perceptions—

MAN Time has no meaning.

BACHELOR It's too soon.

WOMAN Floating on my back I think of—

PHYSICIST A perception of patterns, in this chaos.

MAN The coming and going of years—

BACHELOR I don't know if I'm ready.

WOMAN All those polar opposites.

PHYSICIST 15 billion years ago carbon formed—

MAN Or is it minutes? I can't tell now.

BACHELOR I like the idea of new life—

WOMAN Sun and moon.

PHYSICIST And it asked itself these questions—

MAN Why am I here?

BACHELOR Maybe I should start out small with—

WOMAN Light and dark—

PHYSICIST What am I? Why do I exist?

MAN I think I'm still here—

BACHELOR Like, a fish in a bowl. Or maybe two?

WOMAN Yin and Yang and—

PHYSICIST We are just now beginning—

MAN So I must be…

BACHELOR I've got nine months—

WOMAN Now—

PHYSICIST To find a answers to these questions.

MAN Are you out there?

BACHELOR God! That's a long time.

WOMAN You and me—

PHYSICIST In these patterns that we can detect.

MAN I can still see your face… you know.

BACHELOR But, my inner child still wants out.

WOMAN I dream of a world without signals.

MAN I'll only stay, as long as that's true.

> *Blackout.*

FINAL SHARD

Standing at the podium. The PHYSICIST is still giving a lecture to her class, but she has now come out from behind the podium and is very obviously pregnant. She smiles.

PHYSICIST Think of the smallest things you can. A baby's fist, holding… a grain of sand. A cell? A molecule? An atom? Electrons? In their orbits. Spinning around their nucleus… Made up of protons. Made up of quarks. Leptons, and gluons and so on. There's where identity breaks down… At the smallest level. Because we were mistaken… there is… nothing. There are no things… nothing solid. No little sticks and balls, just waves. Measure the motion, plot the position. Patterns emerge… interconnections. The chaos dissolves into order. Probability coalesces into a point. Reality comes into focus. Interference patterns intersect. To define a shadow… an outline. A glimpse at the true nature of the water in which we all swim. Matter is merely our minds way of making sense of our perceptions. Time is an illusion caused by the passage of matter through space. So, everything… is made of nothing. Nothing but patterns and waves and nothing exists, but this relationship between reality and our perceptions. A perception of patterns, in this chaos. Fifteen billion years ago Carbon formed… and it asked itself these questions "What am I? Why do I exist?" We are just now beginning to find answers to these questions, in these patterns that we can detect.

Blackout.

CLOSING FUGUE

All characters are in various positions and separate realities. The dialogue is overlapping, repeating 3 times and building to a crescendo.

PHYSICIST We're just dancing to the music of the spheres.

THE BOOKMAN This ability to suck air and form it into meaning.

ALBERT We are like children in the dark.

LEO All of us are decided.

WOMAN I dream of a world without signals.

KARA It's language poetry.

THE FLYER Later of course, I felt different.

MAN I'll only stay, as long as that's true…

PROF. KEITH It's just mental pornography anyway.

LITTLE GIRL I woke… and the world had gone dark.

BACHELOR But, my inner child still wants out.

PHYSICIST A perception of patterns, in this chaos.

Blackout.

End of play.

THE PLAYWRIGHT

Trevor Allen is an award winning San Francisco Bay Area based playwright. Productions include: *Lolita Roadtrip* (San Jose Stage Company). *The Creature* (Black Box Theatre Company, BACC award) *Tenders in the Fog* (San Jose Stage Company, Dean Goodman Award, Original Script), *Working for the Mouse!* (Impact Theatre, EXIT Theatre), *49 Miles* (Crowded Fire Theater), *Chain Reactions*, (Theatre of Yugen, CAFÉ and The Cutting Ball). He received a San Francisco Arts Commission grant for his play, *Zoo Logic*. He is a Bay Area Playwrights Festival alumni and his play, *One Stone* (Einstein) was developed through their "Incubator" and "In the Rough" programs. Two of his plays have received the San Francisco Fringe Festival's "Best Of" awards. His short play, *Mamlet*, won American Conservatory Theatre's "Mamet" contest. He received PlayGround's Emerging Playwright Award, Playwriting Fellowship and two Alumni full length play commissions for *Lolita Roadtrip* and *Golden Gate Fair*. He was a Playwright in Residence at the Djerassi Resident Artists Program. He was originally commissioned by San Jose Repertory Theatre to write *Valley of Sand*, a new play about Silicon Valley before that theatre company's untimely demise (which was not his fault). He is an active member of the Dramatist's Guild of America. He holds a BA in Theatre from UCLA and a MFA in Creative Writing from SFSU. At the time of this printing he lives with his wife Karen in the North Bay and writes plays. For more information, go to www.blackboxtheatre.com.

MORE PLAYS FROM EXIT PRESS

Woyzeck, Pelleas and Melisande, Ubu Roi: translated by Rob Melrose

"Rob Melrose is a kind of magician, and his theater, Cutting Ball, is one of the most exciting and integrity-filled enterprises going in the sometimes-shabby field of the American theater. These translations, lucid and sharp, are a beautiful testimony to the value of Rob's achievement." — Oskar Eustis

Three Plays by Mark Jackson

"Playwright/director Mark Jackson has made his name as a first-class theatrical provocateur. Gutsy showmanship, brainy literary instincts and laser-sharp satire mark his canon." — San Jose Mercury News This collection of plays by Mark Jackson includes three plays based on incredible historic events: *God's Plot*, *Mary Stuart*, and *Salomania*.

Songs of Hestia: Plays From the 2010 San Francisco Olympians Festival

Playwrights Nirmala Nataraj, Bennett Fisher, Stuart Eugene Bousel, Claire Rice, and Evelyn Jean Pine adapt some of Western culture's oldest stories, illuminating our present-day concerns with imagination, creativity, curiosity and passion.

The Chamber Plays of August Strindberg translated by Paul Walsh
The Ghost Sonata, The Pelican, The Black Glove, Storm, and *Burned House*. Yale professor Paul Walsh provides modern translations while keeping Strindberg's "curiosity and his strangeness as specific and opaque as they are in the Swedish."

EXIT Press is the publishing division of EXIT Theatre, a San Francisco theater company founded in 1983. EXIT Press is distributed by Small Press Distribution of Berkeley, California. www.exitpress.org

Made in the USA
San Bernardino, CA
08 November 2017